HOW TO BE A

teenage

MILLIONAIRE

HOW TO BE A

teenage

ART BEROFF & T.R. ADAMS

MILLIONAIRE

Entrepreneur Press

Entrepreneur Press
2445 McCabe Way, Irvine, CA 92614

Managing Editor: Marla Markman

Book Design: Sylvia H. Lee

Copy Editor: Peter Kooiman

Proofreader: Megan Reilly

Cover Design: Amy Moore

Indexer: Ken DellaPenta

Production Designers: Mia H. Ko, Marlene Natal

This publication is designed to provide accurate and authoritative
information in regard to the subject matter covered. It is sold with the
understanding that the publisher is not engaged in rendering legal, accounting
or other professional services. If legal advice or other expert assistance is
required, the services of a competent professional person should be sought.

Library of Congress Cataloging-in-Publication Data

Beroff, Art.

How to be a teenage millionare: start your own business, make your own
money, and run your own life/by Art Beroff & T. R. Adams.

p. cm.

Includes index.

ISBN: 1-891984-17-9

1. New business enterprises--Management. 2. Entrepreneurship.
3. Teenagers--Finance, Personal. 4. Millionaires. I. Adams, T.R. II. Title.

HD62.5.B484 2000

658.02'2'0835--dc21   00-055107

Printed in Canada

09 08 07 06 05 04 03   10 9 8 7 6 5 4

This book is dedicated to the memory of my grandfather, David Sternlicht, an immigrant who came to America with only hopes and dreams for a better future. He instilled in me a great enthusiasm for the opportunities that abound and a vision for success.

—*Art Beroff*

This one's for our parental units.
Thanks for being there!

—*T.R. Adams*

Acknowledgements

We could not have made this book what it is without the terrific assistance of the 17 teenage entrepreneurs who shared their stories, experiences and advice. You're all terrific. Thank you! We also received lots of assistance from the great people at youth business organizations all over the country—thank you, too. And, as always, a big thanks to Marla Markman, book editor/adventurer extraordinaire.

Table Of Contents

Words Of Wisdom

"**I** think you need to do something you really believe in, no matter what other people say. If you want to start your own business like I did, you shouldn't wait for someone to tell you it is a good idea. You have to believe in yourself and your ideas. You have to be willing to try things and make lots of mistakes. Don't look at what other people are doing and copy that, but instead, come up with your own plan."

—Michael Dell, founder
Dell Computer

"**Z**ig when everyone else zags. And never give up. If you get knocked down, just get back up and approach the situation in a different way."

—Daymond John, co-founder
FUBU The Collection

"**G**o into the field where your heart leads you. Listen to what the so-called experts tell you, but don't take it for gospel. You're the one who knows your business best. Sift through all the sand to find the gold. Don't go by the book. Do whatever it is you need to do. Trade with anyone you can, and spend your money on what really matters. Always keep a nest egg—things cost about two times as much as you expect and life and business is full of surprises. I always find I learn the most from other entrepreneurs. Trading stories, information, and contacts are invaluable. Be strong, don't give in, don't give up."

—Tish, co-founder
Manic Panic NYC

"**D**o what you love, and love what you do. Dare to be different, and never take no for an answer."

—Snooky, co-founder
Manic Panic NYC

Introduction

Congratulations! You've successfully completed the first step in becoming a teenage millionaire. You've picked up this book. You might be standing in the bookstore, thumbing through the pages and trying to decide if you should actually buy it. Maybe you're kicking back in your room with the book propped on your desk or bed. You might be at the beach or in the car—it doesn't matter.

The point is that by reading this book, you've put yourself into motion. You're about to become a teenage entrepreneur. You're about to start your own business. Make your own money. Run your own life. And also have a heck of a lot of fun.

◀ Making It Happen ▶

What exactly is an entrepreneur? It's a person who creates and runs his or her own business. Not the kid behind the counter at the local burger joint or the college student cleaning up popcorn at the movie theater or even that adult paid to sit behind a desk all day and push papers for "the company." Instead, an entrepreneur is the kid who sets up and runs her own business selling custom-made jewelry. The one who develops and operates a lawn-mowing service for his ultra-busy neighbors. Or the one who turns his talent for Web site design into a full-fledged business putting up sites for other companies.

Entrepreneurs don't work for somebody else. They go out and *make it happen*—create their own businesses, make their own money and run their own lives.

◄ The Driver's Seat ►

Being in charge is what makes being an entrepreneur cool. There's nothing else in life that lets *you* take the driver's seat in quite the same way. It's a rush!

It's also a big responsibility. Just like driving a car, where you go and how you get there is suddenly on your head and not your parents' or your teachers' or your friends'. But not to panic. That's what this book is for— to help you explore everything you need to know to become a teen success story and have fun while you're at it.

We've written the book to help you design the perfect business for you. You'll discover everything from how to start a simple neighborhood business like child care or landscaping to a sophisticated global business like an online store or a Web site design studio. We've talked with teens all over the country who have successful businesses of their own and share their insights with you.

So whether you're new to the world of business or an old hand who's already started a company, this book is for you. If some parts seem elementary, as Sherlock Holmes would say, they are. And if other sections seem more sophisticated, they are, too. That's because we've written the book to teach you to think like a true millionaire-in-the-making—to give you the tools to design a real business instead of a toy. By the time you've finished this book, you'll know more than a lot of adults do about being a successful entrepreneur.

◄ Designing The Perfect Biz ►

Here's what you'll find within these pages:

▸ **Eight chapters on everything** from how to think like an entrepreneur to designing the perfect business. Finding cash to get your new company up and running to whipping up an advertising storm. Building profits to building in time to be a regular kid.

▸ **Up-close-and-personal interviews** with 17 teenage entrepreneurs who really have made it happen.

▸ **Business Brainstormers:** do-it-yourself work sheets where you can start designing your own company. Go ahead—scribble on the pages!

▸ **A resource section jammed with places to go** for even more help, from organizations designed just for teen millionaires-in-the-making to Web sites to associations and assistance you may be able to find in your hometown.

▶ **A special bonus book** packed with 21 hot businesses for the 21st-century teen entrepreneur. If you haven't already invented your own company, choose from one of these! For each one you get:

- **The Inside Story:** what the business is about
- **Starring Talents:** the skills or interests you need to do the job
- **Necessities:** any supplies you'll need
- **Start-Up Costs:** the money you'll need to get up and running
- **Charge It:** what to charge your customers
- **Earn It:** what you can expect to earn
- **Advertising Blitz:** special advertising tips
- **What's Next:** how to get started

◀ Get Ready ▶

So what are you waiting for? If you're still standing in the bookstore, take this book to the register and then get it home. If you're already at home—or wherever—take a deep breath, get ready to have fun, and get reading.

Chapter One

Entrepreneur? $ure!

ou've decided to take the plunge, or at least to skim through this book and decide if the life of a teenage entrepreneur is for you. This is good. But don't do it only because your parents or your favorite aunt or a well-meaning teacher forced the book into your hands. Do it for yourself.

As an entrepreneur, you can:

▶ **Make money.** With your own business, you can earn enough cash to buy a car, the latest clothes, pizzas, movie tickets, CDs and more. You can tuck away funds for college and beyond. While other people your age are scrimping, you'll already have a tidy nest egg. Robert Sek started ID Enterprises when he was 17—four years later, he projects current annual earnings of $500,000. "I started this for two reasons," Robert says. "To gain experience and to make some money. And I've done both."

▶ **Learn to think like a millionaire.** Which means you'll be light years ahead of most people when you graduate to adulthood and join the business world. "Having your own company is a great learning experience and is really fun," says Elise Macmillan, 12, who started The Chocolate Farm, a gourmet chocolate company, at age 10. "It gives you a head start on your future."

▶ **Build confidence**—something Kiera Kramer, who started Parties Perfect at 15, was surprised to discover. "Before all this, I really had no confidence. I wasn't doing as good as I could in school—I had problems. The business and the business camp I attended made me so much more confident in myself, that I could actually do it." And, adds Kiera, now 17 and president of her student council as well as an entrepreneur, "It's the greatest feeling, being a boss at 15, 16 and 17."

▶ **Get into the university of your choice more easily.** College admissions boards tend to think that if you already have your own business, you're smart, ambitious and creative (which is true). And more and more often, they'll take somebody with these qualities over a kid with straight As but no "real world" experience.

▶ **Meet all sorts of fascinating people** who can help you with your new business, with other school or business projects you may develop now or later, and who just might become friends and associates for life. K-K Gregory, 16, who started the glove-design company Wristies at age 10, has appeared on the "Today" show as well as on "Oprah Winfrey" and "Donny & Marie." Kevin Colleran, 19, who started CyberMarketing Solutions, an e-marketing company, at age 12, has partied with Michael Jordan and Jerry Springer and spent New Year's Eve 2000 with the MTV crowd. Jason Ryan Dorsey started Golden Ladder Productions, an educational training company, at 18—three years later, he's conference-calling with President Clinton and Steve Case of America Online. And Jasmine Jordan, 16, started *Tools for Living* magazine at 12 and recently appeared on "The Montel Williams Show."

> "Having your own company is a great learning experience and is really fun. It gives you a head start on your future."

◀ Taking It To Heart ▶

Being an entrepreneur means taking control of your money-earning ability as well as the rest of your life. It means harnessing awesome powers.

Taking on some adult responsibilities. And having more fun than you might believe possible. But it's not easy.

"Starting your own business is a thousand times harder than you expected," says Sarah Levinson, who started Ripe cosmetics with her sister Anna five years ago when they were 14 and 17, respectively. Sarah and Anna's business now boasts sales of $200,000. "It's wonderful. Your heart's in it, and it's amazing."

Kiera Kramer, a Southold, New York, teen, agrees. "It just seemed like a lost dream at first," she says of her party-assist company. But when Kiera and her best friend, Jaclyn, started planning the business, it just took off. "Well, yeah, we were talking about it," Kiera recalls. "But I didn't know if it was going to happen. All of a sudden it was there, so real. Jaclyn and I work really well together and we just love doing it."

Moneymaking Choices

Why not fixate on becoming a corporate employee with a corner office (considered ultra-slick because it has a view of the outside world instead of a wall) and an expense account instead of being an entrepreneur? Good question.

For one thing, it's pretty tough to be a corporate whiz kid when you're still in high school. You generally have to go through the whole college/graduate school/get-a-job thing first. And you don't usually start at the top.

As a high school student, unless you're really lucky or have fabulous connections, your moneymaking choices are limited. You can:

▶ Get a job at a fast-food franchise.

▶ Work at a movie theater.

▶ Bag groceries.

▶ Work at the mall.

▶ Rely on your parents for an allowance.

▶ Baby-sit.

▶ Sell all your possessions at the flea market.

Now, none of these choices is necessarily a terrible one. But for the true entrepreneur, none is exactly perfect, either. Let's rewind and take a look at why:

Option	Pluses	Minuses
Fast-Foodie	•You get paid.	•You might not earn more than minimum wage. •You have to wear a goofy uniform. •You have to work the hours they assign. •Working with all that grease can lead to zits. •Standing on your feet for hours is a killer.
Movie Theater Maniac	•You get paid. •You get to see free movies.	•You might not earn more than minimum minimum wage. •You have to wear a goofy uniform. •You have to work the hours they assign. •Popping corn and making change can get extremely boring. •Standing on your feet for hours is a killer.
Grocery Bagger	•You get paid. •You can move up to checker and because it's a union job, checkers can make a lot of dough.	•You might not earn much more than minimum wage. •You have to wear a goofy uniform. •You have to work the hours they assign. •Standing on your feet for hours is a killer. •You mumble "paper or plastic?" in your sleep.
Mall Store Maniac	•You get paid. •You get discounts on the products.	•You might not earn much more than minimum wage. •You have to work the hours they assign. •Standing on your feet for hours is a killer.
Rely On Allowance	•You get paid.	•It's less than minimum wage. •Your parents control the purse strings.
Baby-sitter	Bonus! •This can be the seed of an entre-preneur business.	•It's less than minimum wage—unless you turn it into a business!
Worldly Possession Sales	Bonus! •This is another seedling entre-preneur business.	•You end up with no possessions—unless you turn it into a business!

◀ Control Issue ▶

You'll probably agree that—except for baby-sitting and flea market selling (more to come on these)—there are more minuses than pluses with these average teen moneymaking options. Which makes them not so hot. The amount of money you can earn is under somebody else's control—not yours. The amount of time you can work is under somebody else's control—not yours. The actual days and hours you work, whether it's on Saturdays when you'd rather be hiking in the hills or on Monday evenings when you'd like to be watching your favorite TV program, is under somebody else's control—not yours.

And on top of all that, the jobs usually open to kids are not all that much fun. Sure, it's cool to hang with your friends if they work in the same place. And it's nice to make your own money (even if it is a small amount). But let's face it, frying onion rings, scooping popcorn and slinging soda cans into grocery bags for hours on end do not qualify as glamour jobs. And they don't usually lead to much.

> **"I started making money for the pleasure of doing something that I liked and being paid for it. It's everybody's dream to do that."**

So what's a teen to do? More choices: You can: a) take one of the low-paying nonglam jobs because you're "just a kid" and be done with it; b) resign yourself to never having a dime, going to school in your older sister or brother's hand-me-downs, and not ever buying a single CD, movie ticket or candy bar in your whole teenage life; or c) take the entrepreneur's approach: Get creative and develop your own business.

Take Shawn Gollatz, a 19-year-old professional magician and balloon sculptor who's had his own business for three years, with sales of almost $20,000 in 1999. "It started out as a hobby," Shawn says. "And turned into a profession. I started making money for the pleasure of doing something that I liked and being paid for it. It's everybody's dream to do that."

◀ The Baby-sitting Biz ▶

Let's go back to our potential teen businesses. The first one is Baby-sitting! It may not strike you as particularly glamorous or lucrative—or even businesslike. But take a second look.

Baby-sitting is not a job where you go in, fill out an application, then (hopefully) get hired and go to work for somebody else. And it doesn't have to be just a way to earn spare change—not if you get creative and turn it into a business.

Instead of calling yourself a baby-sitter, call yourself a Child Care Specialist or Mom's Away Kid Fun Specialist, or whatever other intriguing title you can dream up. Instead of just *sitting*, design a special play program or Parents' Night Out slumber party, or take the kids on outings to museums, the movies or the park.

Tell parents the talents that make you more than a baby-sitter—maybe you're a kid-care expert because you have younger brothers or sisters or because you've taken a child-care course at the YMCA. Possibly you're a pro at cooking or computers or arts and crafts or some other activity you can turn into a business.

As your business grows, you can charge more money and even hire others to do the work while you recruit new clients. You can check out the specifics on a child-care business in the bonus section at the back of the book—the point is that it's a business instead of a job. And your schedule and potential earnings are entirely up to you.

◄ Possession Sales ►

What about selling all your possessions? At first glance, it doesn't sound promising—after you get rid of last year's algebra book and that ugly shirt Aunt Ethel sent, you're going to start missing things. Before long you'll be wearing rags and sleeping on the floor. Not much of a business, right?

Wrong! What you do is buy other people's possessions and sell them at the flea market. Instant business. Of course, you have to be selective about your products. You might buy and sell collectible toys like Barbies or Beanie Babies. Or funky vintage clothing. Or skateboards or roller blades. Or candles, like Amy Beaver, 18, who with her brother Keith, 16, runs a successful candle sales business at flea markets and crafts shows. But the point, again, is that you're running your own company, with a schedule you set and unlimited potential earnings. This is what makes you an entrepreneur.

> **Hot Tip**
>
> The best way to find out what being an entrepreneur is really like is to go to the source. Ask local business owners to share with you the pros and cons of being your own boss.

Catching On
To Cashing In

Evan Macmillan, 14, began netINVENT, a Web site design company, in 1999 when he was 13. "I thought the business would be a fun way of turning a hobby into a moneymaking opportunity," the Denver teen says.

Actually, Evan was an accomplished Web guru years earlier. He designed his first site for his soccer team while in the fifth grade. After preparing a project on John Steinbeck in seventh grade, Evan put up a site on the famous writer's life and work—which soon became the second most-visited Steinbeck site in the world. "After school, I was always answering e-mail from high school and college students about Steinbeck," Evan says. "Some of them even thought I was John Steinbeck!" (Who at that time had been dead for about 30 years.)

NetINVENT now boasts a dozen steady small businesses as clients. Evan doesn't do any advertising—instead his clients find him through word-of-mouth and from publicity he's garnered as webmaster for sister Elise's gourmet chocolate company, The Chocolate Farm (see the "Biz Whiz" sidebar on page 255).

But it's not all a piece of candy, er, cake. "It's a lot of hard work and a lot of effort making customers happy," Evan explains. Besides caring for his own company, Evan keeps The Chocolate Farm's financial records, tracks orders and plans business strategy.

"I've learned that one thing leads to another," he says. "Something catches, and you'll get somebody who likes you and remembers your name. That's how we've gotten where we are: People remembering our names and our products and coming back. If you keep working and you get a little lucky, something's bound to catch."

> "**Something** catches, and you'll get somebody who likes you and remembers your name. That's how we've gotten where we are: People remembering our names and our products and coming back. If you keep working and you get a little lucky, something's bound to catch."

Everything Old Is New Again

As an entrepreneur, you'll join a very exclusive club—people like Bill Gates, the man behind Microsoft; Debbie Fields, the original Mrs. Field's Cookies baker; Martha Stewart, the hostess with the mostest; and George Lucas, the master of the Jedis.

Being an entrepreneur is not new—innovative businesspeople have been around for centuries. Think car mogul Henry Ford and chocolate king Milton Hershey, to name just two. For a long time, though, entrepreneurs were considered eccentrics. Creative, sure, but too weird to make it in the "real" world of corporate business. If you worked for yourself, people figured it was because nobody else would hire you.

But in the last 10 years or so, being an entrepreneur has become new and exciting again. Entrepreneurship is the "in" thing. SOHOs (small office/home offices) are springing up all over the country, with enterprising entrepreneurs at the helm.

◀ Millionaire-In-The-Making ▶

These new entrepreneurs aren't just Baby Boomers (people from your parents' generation). Grandparents and Gen Xers (people in their 20s) are also into entrepreneurship—and are doing a good job at it. And, of course, there are teenagers. Teens make terrific entrepreneurs. They're creative, imaginative, original, and—except for those desperate few days before finals—optimistic. Which brings us back to you.

As a teen, you probably already have what it takes to be a millionaire-in-the-making. The fact that you're a young person gives you these distinct advantages:

▶ **Your brain is set on warp speed**—you can learn faster and more easily than adults. You can pick up entrepreneurship skills in a snap and keep them for a lifetime.

▶ **You can think "out of the box,"** which means creatively and unconventionally. Adults are often brainwashed by years of living and working in a corporate environment, so it can be hard for them to attack problems and challenges in new ways. As a teen, you don't have the same problem—not knowing that something "can't be done" gives you the freedom to go out there and do it successfully.

▶ **You have the freedom to take risks**—which can make your business mega-cool. Robert Sek, who started a successful dotcom company at age 17, says, "If I started a company, I wasn't doing it because I had to survive and feed my family. I was young, my parents were still supporting me and that allowed me to take greater risks."

▶ **You have a tremendous amount of energy on tap,** which is an incredibly valuable resource. Ask Robert, who's now a 21-year-old student at the University of Texas as well as starting another business and pursuing a professional speaking career. "One of the things that helped me now and in the past is the youthful energy I bring to new ventures, my excitement and the new and fresh ideas I have to offer."

▶ **You are the Next Generation.** Your ideas are hot, new and up-to-the-nanosecond. You are likely to have your fingers on the pulse of the country—or even the world.

Teen Entre-Personality

OK, you've got youth in your favor. But surely it takes more than just being a kid to be a business success. All entrepreneurs—whether they're 15 years old, 50, or even 90—share the same personality traits, from confidence to drive to creativity.

You may recognize these characteristics in yourself as we go through them in this section. You may possess them and not realize it. If you can't count all these elements as part of your personal personality package, don't worry. Most of them can be learned.

Pizza Powerhouse

Photo Courtesy: Domino's Pizza Inc.

In 1960, 19-year-old Tom Monaghan borrowed $500 and purchased a pizza store called DomiNick's. One year later, he bought out his partner, brother James, with a Volkswagen Beetle. Four years after that, Tom renamed his company Domino's Pizza.

And the rest is history—today Domino's is a pizza powerhouse, with sales in 1999 alone of more than $3.4 billion from 338 million pizzas. That's a lot of pepperoni!

◀ Vision ▶

One of the first things you need to be an entrepreneur is *vision*—not the ability to see your hand in front of your face but the ability to see something that doesn't yet exist: your future business. You have to be able to look with your inner eye—your imagination—and focus on a product or service you can sell to potential customers.

Tom Monaghan had a vision for pizza. Debbie Fields dreamed of chocolate chip cookies. (Who doesn't?) Bill Gates envisioned software. And George Lucas imagined an entire galaxy for his "Star Wars" sagas. Different entrepreneurs with different visions. But all these people saw beyond where they were at the moment to where they could go and what their companies could achieve.

How do you know if you have vision? By dreams you've already made come true. Maybe you wanted to play in a band—so you got a guitar, practiced, gathered together a group of friends, and started your own group. That's vision.

Maybe you decided to make gifts for everyone on your Christmas or Hanukkah list—so you bought T-shirts and fabric paint and went to work. And everybody was delighted with your custom clothing. That's vision.

Or maybe your church or school wanted to raise money for summer

beyond basic

Bill Gates was a geeky Harvard University freshman in 1973 when he developed the BASIC programming language for the first microcomputer. Beyond BASIC, Gates had a vision of a personal computer in every home and office—computers that anybody could run with simple software. He believed so firmly in that vision that two years later, in 1975, he left Harvard to concentrate on Microsoft, the fledgling software company he had already developed with friend Paul Allen.

Microsoft and Bill Gates are now household names, and once-geeky Gates is the company's chairman, chief executive officer (CEO), and the brains behind a multibillion-dollar company that employs more than 31,000 people in 60 countries.

Photo Courtesy: Microsoft Corp.

camp or new uniforms. So you and your friends chose a fund-raiser, a car wash-athon, made arrangements with a local business to use its parking lot for the day, pitched in to get soapy and soaked, and earned the necessary money. That's vision.

◄ Creativity ►

Creativity is another personality trait of the entrepreneur. Some people are obviously creative—the kids who take all the art classes and always think up new ways to design their clothes, jewelry or hair. If this is you, great! But there are lots of different kinds of creativity. There's the creative genius who designs Web sites, new software or new microprocessors. There's the person who's a whiz in the kitchen, whipping up foods in new and tasty combinations.

And there's the person who's not creative in any of these ways—can't paint, can't draw, can't do anything exceptional with a computer, and can't even boil water in the kitchen, but is a business genius, able to create a moneymaking operation out of a vision.

> Everybody has creativity—the main thing is to nurture it and keep it growing along with you, and to use it to your advantage.

Some people want to insist that they're not creative in any way, shape or form. But unless you're a major couch potato with no aim in life but vegging (in which case you probably wouldn't be reading this book), this is not true. Everybody has creativity—the main thing is to nurture it and keep it growing along with you, and to use it to your advantage.

If you've ever made something out of nothing or taken an object and transformed it into something different, you've been creative. Besides the obvious, like arts and crafts and writing stories, how about writing an essay? If you've done that, you've pulled together different elements to make something that came from your brain. That's creativity.

Maybe you like tinkering with cars, training dogs or decorating your room. All these activities are creativity in action.

◄ Adaptability ►

Adaptability is an important trait for the successful entrepreneur. It's the ability to go with the flow or roll with the punches. As you've probably already learned, life doesn't always work out precisely as planned—no matter how well you think things through, something comes along to challenge you. Your theater class, for example, may have rehearsed for months and got every line down perfectly. But the night before you open, half the cast comes down with the flu. Or your star pitcher breaks an arm right before the big game. Or your dad has to attend an out-of-town meeting the same week you all were flying to Disney World.

> **Life doesn't always work out precisely as planned—no matter how well you think things out, something comes along to challenge you.**

People who are not adaptable fall apart at the seams when life throws these kinds of curve balls. Die-hard entrepreneurs adapt. As a theater owner, for instance, you can't just close up shop if your cast gets ill. You'd lose money—and possibly your business. Instead, you might call in your backstage assistants who had memorized the lines and have them fill in. Or you might call in other actors, give them scripts to read from, and turn your production into an old-fashioned "radio show."

If your star pitcher broke an arm and you owned the team, you'd have to choose another player to fill in—and who knows, maybe he or she would prove to be a pro. And if you owned a business in which you had to send your best troubleshooter (your dad) on a rush job to Omaha, Nebraska, instead of to the client who was expecting him in Orlando, Florida, you might have to offer the Orlando client a discount on his next order to keep him waiting patiently and keep him happy.

That's what business is often like and why people who can't adapt frequently fail. Sometimes adaptability leads to new ways of doing business that are even better than the old. Your "radio show" might prove to be such a hit that you do every production that way from then on. Your substitute

Hot Tip

Adaptability isn't just adjusting to crises. It can also be expanding your business by adapting to your customers' needs. Shawn Himmelberger, 19, of Mud's Lawn Care, started off doing landscaping. But when he realized his customers also needed their driveways cleared of snow, he plowed right in.

pitcher might lead your team to the World Series. And the client who gets a discount to keep him happy might decide that your company handled the situation so well that he gives you three huge new orders.

How do you know if you've got adaptability? Think of situations in which you had to change gears at the last minute. Did you: a) dig in your heels, make a fuss, and refuse to think your way to a solution? Or: b) find a way around the problem?

If your answer is "a," don't worry—you can learn adaptability. Why not start now by thinking of what you might have done to solve that problem? Because another cool characteristic of entrepreneurs is learning from your mistakes. (If you can pick up a lesson from them, mistakes don't feel so awful.)

◀ Risk-Taking ▶

Entrepreneurs, by nature, are risk-takers. If they weren't, they would go to work for somebody else—because starting your own business is definitely risky. You run the risk that people won't take you seriously, that you won't find any customers to buy your products or services, that you'll lose the money you put into the company.

People who are afraid to get out there and risk it all, go out and get jobs in somebody else's company. They let somebody else worry about where to find customers, how to pay the bills, and how to adapt when life throws those curveballs. Of course, they also let somebody else have all the fun—making creative decisions and lots of money.

How do you know if you're a risk-taker?

That's what nonrisk-takers don't realize. They also fail to realize that working for someone else is risky, too. If your boss's company goes belly-up, you're out of a job. If your boss decides to cut back—like hundreds of companies did during the '90s—you're out of a job. And if your boss decides not to give you a raise or to change your schedule so you work only a few hours a week, then even if her company shines, you don't.

Entrepreneurs have a tremendous advantage over employees, even if their businesses fail. They're creative, adaptable, visionary and can pick themselves up off the floor of failure and start over again. People with employee-only mind-sets often find themselves unable to cope.

How do you know if you're a risk-taker? If you've done theater, dance or athletics, you probably are. It's not easy to perform in front of an audience—there's always the risk of failure. And the fact that it's public makes it even scarier. But if you've done it, you get an "A" for risk-taking. If you've entered into any sort of competition, like a science fair, art festival or soapbox derby, you're a risk-taker. And if you haven't done any of these things but have the will to start your own business, you're definitely a risk-taker.

◀ Confidence ▶

Entrepreneurs need lots of confidence—if you're going to take a risk and lay your money, reputation and time on the line, you need faith in yourself and your abilities to carry you through. It's another side of creativity—the part that convinces you to start painting that picture, pulling together that crazy Web site, or donning that team uniform.

When you own your business, you must have the confidence to believe you can make your vision a reality—that you can turn strangers into customers, adapt to unexpected and stressful situations, and keep things running smoothly.

Even though parental units contribute a lot to your confidence or lack thereof, it's really all up to you. Even people with perfect families—TV sitcom all-star types—don't always display the right stuff. You have to reach down inside and tell yourself you can do it. And then believe it.

Having confidence doesn't mean that entrepreneurs walk around with their chins thrust forward and their noses in the air. Everybody has times when they feel that life is tough and they just can't make it. But true entrepreneurs have enough faith in themselves and their businesses to keep going. They usually find that by the next day or week or month, they've slogged through their problems and managed to succeed.

Hot Tip

"Be open-minded and believe that you can do anything," advises Donna Sayers, who started DJ's Catering Service two years ago when she was 16. "Any kind of obstacle that might come to you won't make that much difference."

How do you know if you have confidence? Do you believe in yourself? If you don't have that faith, take a look at all the things you've already accomplished in life, from getting good grades to caring for younger brothers or sisters or learning to drive a car. Give yourself a pat on the back. Stick that chin in the air. And keep reading this book. You can do it!

··· personalized confidence ·········

In 1951, Lillian Vernon started her mail order business at her kitchen table. With $2,000 of wedding gift money, the 21-year-old pregnant housewife bought an initial supply of leather belts and handbags and placed an ad in Seventeen magazine. Fashion accessories by mail wasn't a unique idea, but the fact that Lillian personalized each order with the buyer's monogram was.

Photo Courtesy: Lillian Vernon Corp.

Lillian took in $32,000 in orders on that first ad—today, Lillian Vernon Corp. publishes eight different catalogs with more than 700 products in each. In 1999, the company had revenue of $241 million. Lillian, who's still at the helm of the mega-mail order group as CEO and chairman, says she knew with absolute certainty that teenagers would go for monogrammed items that made them feel unique. That's confidence.

◀ Drive ▶

In this case, drive doesn't have anything to do with getting behind the wheel of a car. Instead, it means being single-minded—having the ability to set yourself on a course and keep going until you get there. You can't be flighty or flaky—one of those people who wants to be an astronaut today and a dental assistant tomorrow—if you're going to run your own business. You have to decide on a game plan and stick with it.

Some people have a really hard time with this concept. They think starting a business might be sort of a hoot and they're all excited about it—for a short while. Then they lose interest and let all their plans ooze away to nothing. They may never actually get that business up and running. If they do, they don't follow through with promises, and they lose first customers and, eventually, the business.

True entrepreneurs, however, sink their teeth into their goals like a mad dog hanging onto a pant leg. They'll work—and work hard—to do everything necessary to get their business started, attract customers and then keep them. That's drive.

How do you determine if you have drive? If you've set yourself a goal—from sewing a dress to setting up a Web site to passing a midterm—and you've stuck with it even through the tough parts, you've got drive. If not, you can develop it. Start by going through this book and putting what you learn into practice.

◀ Competitiveness ▶

You know what it is to be competitive. Sometimes it's considered a good thing, like in sports or other contests. Occasionally, it's thought of as a negative trait, as in somebody who's not a team player.

When it comes to entrepreneurship, competitiveness is definitely a plus—it's one of the hallmarks of business. Think about it. McDonald's is in competition with Burger King and Wendy's. America Online is locked in deadly competition with Microsoft Network and Prodigy. Kmart goes head-to-head with Wal-Mart. These companies—and every other firm out there—have to constantly compete for customers' dollars or they'll be out of business before they can blink twice.

Hot Tip

"Three main points helped me become who I am," says Robert Sek of ID Enterprises. "One was my willingness to learn. One was my passion to come up with an idea and create something. And the last one, which helped me as much or more than the other two, is my perseverance—my drive and my ability to not let things stop me."

As an entrepreneur, you need to have the same competitive spirit—that desire to do better than the other guy and win the customers. Not a negative, cut-throat, killer instinct but a healthy rivalry. Successful entrepreneurs throw themselves into competition again and again until they win—they're not afraid to test their business skills, their creativity and themselves.

> As an entrepreneur, you'll need to have competitive spirit—that desire to do better than the other guy and win the customers.

How do you know if you're competitive? If you've entered into any sort of contest or competition, you get an instant "A." If you're the shy, retiring type who doesn't like to attract attention or hates any sort of conflict, then you haven't

Sowing The Seeds Of Business

Jason Smith has two businesses. He works with his father as the "son" half of Mike Smith & Son Farms in Hanover, Pennsylvania, and also has his own business selling corn and soybean seeds to local growers. He started his dealership in 1997 at age 18. "I've really grown in size," Jason says. "The interest I've created has really helped the business take off."

Jason started with a specific goal in mind. "My last year of high school, I was looking for something where I'd be home but communicating with the local farm community," he explains. "Just playing around on the Net, I came across an opportunity from a seed company. They were looking for dealers on the East Coast. I sent them an e-mail, and things took off from there."

Start-up costs for the business were minimal. Customers pay Jason for the seeds. He deducts his commission (the money he earns from sales), and sends the balance of the payment to the grower. "There really is very little money upfront," the 19 year-old says.

Jason's first customers were people his father knew. "I went up and talked to them and word spread," Jason says. "My name in the Hanover agriculture community is getting around. Customers see me out here helping Dad all the time. Having a background in your industry is important."

In 1999, while he was still in high school, Jason earned about $22,000. He estimates his revenues for 2000 will push $35,000 to $40,000. And he works hard to earn it.

"**My friends** tell me that I look more at the future than just what's at hand," Jason says. "I'm not worried that I have to make $50 to go party. I'll make $500. That way, I can go have fun and still have some left over."

"My friends tell me that I look more at the future than just what's at hand," Jason says. "I'm not worried that I have to make $50 to go party. I'll make $500. That way, I can go have fun and still have some left over."

Photo Courtesy: Mike Smith & Son Farms

quite grasped the spirit of competition. Remember, it doesn't mean pitting yourself in armed battle. It's having the self-respect and confidence to believe you can win—and then getting out there and trying.

> **Realize that it takes time to build a business, or just about anything else worthwhile, and that the only way to get there is to keep going—to persevere.**

◄ Perseverance ►

Perseverance is drive squared. Drive is having a shining goal in mind and reaching for it, like saying "I'm going to climb Mount Everest." It sees you through getting a passport and permission to make the climb, raising money to buy equipment and fly to Tibet, and setting up your base camp at the foot of the mountain.

Perseverance is what keeps you slogging on hour after hour, day after day, through brutal weather and flagging spirits, until you reach the top. It's sheer willpower, the mystery trait that keeps you going through the all the tough, dreary, generally unexciting and unfun parts of a project until you reach your goal.

For an entrepreneur, drive is like saying "I'm going to have a clothing design business and make $500 a month." Drive sees you through designing your garments, writing your business plan, getting a loan, and finding stores to buy your products. Perseverance is what keeps you working on your designs even when it seems no one is interested and the quality that keeps you going from store to store until you find those willing buyers.

How do you determine if you're a persevering person? Think back to all the times in your life when you have kept at a project until you suc-

Hot Tip

Mistakes and misfortunes can actually be a bonus. "I've learned that when you make mistakes, that's good," says Jason Ryan Dorsey, who started Golden Ladder Productions three years ago at age 18 and now is on a presidential advisory committee. "The periods in my life when I've learned the most are when I've made mistakes and struggled to stretch my comfort zone to take in new information I'd misunderstood or overlooked."

sweet success

Milton Hershey opened his first candy-making shop in Lancaster, Pennsylvania, in 1876 at age 18. It failed after six years. But Milton was not a quitter. Four more candy-making attempts in four more cities also resulted in failure, until he finally struck gold 10 years later with his own successful caramel company.

His gooey confections morphed into the ultimate sweet smell of success when Hershey began producing chocolate coatings for his sticky caramels and then all sorts of other chocolates and cocoas. Today, Hershey, Pennsylvania, the town Milton founded for his company, is a town devoted to chocolate, where even the street lights look like Hershey Kisses.

Photo Courtesy: The Hershey Foods Corp.

ceeded, even when you thought you would never make it. Maybe it was getting through a year of algebra with an actual decent grade. Or helping your parents remodel your house. Or rebuilding the engine on that old clunker that now runs great. Or practicing making your mom's famous spaghetti sauce until it tastes just as good as hers. These are persevering pluses.

If you're—honestly—a quitter, the type who gives up when the going gets tough, don't quit now! There's hope. Are you afraid you'll fail so it seems easier not to keep at it? Do you get bored halfway through? Are you impatient and want immediate results?

If any of these describe you, teach yourself to look beyond these sticking points to the prize of your goals. If you're afraid of failure, stop worrying about it. Entrepreneurs fail all the time. But, as we've said, they pick themselves up and try again. And eventually, they do succeed—often brilliantly. So each "failure" is really just another stepping stone to success. If you get bored, or you're impatient, keep your eye on that prize. Realize that it takes time to build a business, or just about anything else worthwhile, and that the only way to get there is to keep going—to persevere. Then force yourself to stay on track. You can do it!

◀ Integrity ▶

Integrity is honesty. It means being fair and ethical with your customers, your vendors or suppliers, your lenders and even your competitors. If you make shady business deals or fail to treat people fairly, sooner or later it all comes back to haunt you.

Say your customer overpays you. You told him your price was $50, but he hands you $60. As an entrepreneur, you'll politely tell him he made a mistake and give him back his extra $10. Why? First, if he realizes later that you let him overpay and never said anything, he's not likely to use your company again. People don't like to be cheated. Second, once he realizes he's been cheated, he won't recommend you to anyone else. And third, integrity makes a terrific impression. When that customer sees how you handle the situation, he'll be delighted. He'll not only use your company again, but he'll brag to his friends about how good you are. And they'll buy from you.

Remember that what goes around comes around.

How do you decide if you've got integrity? Think about how you would handle the same situation. If you'd hand back the overpayment, give yourself a gold star. If not, you need to reconsider. How would you like to be treated? What would your reaction be? Remember that what goes around comes around—the way you handle customers is the way you'll ultimately be handled yourself.

◀ Discipline ▶

You might think discipline refers to punishment. But in this case, it's not (although sometimes it might feel like it). Instead it's yet another facet of drive and perseverance. It's the ability to set a schedule and stick to it, like doing your homework every evening between 7 and 10, when you'd rather be out doing almost anything else.

As an entrepreneur, you need discipline to get projects done for your clients when you promise they'll be done. Say you tell a restaurant owner, for instance, that you'll have the walls painted in time for her grand opening. She's counting on you. So you need to be able to get yourself over to her place on a consistent basis until the job is done—on time. You can't let yourself get distracted by friends who want you to go fishing or to the movies or get waylaid watching a ballgame on TV.

If you don't get the job finished on time, you lose the restaurant owner as a customer. And you potentially lose other customers, too. If you do it right, she'll probably recommend you to other business owners. But if you screw up, she's not going to refer you to anyone. Plus, you lose your own self-respect.

People with little self-discipline make better employees than entrepreneurs because they can't complete a project by a deadline or stick to schedule unless somebody else (the boss) sets that schedule and stands over them to enforce it. This is OK. There's room for lots of different kinds of people in this world, both leaders and followers.

But if you want to be an entrepreneur, you need to be the leader, goal-setter and inner disciplinarian.

How do you know if you've got what it takes? Take a look at how you handle schedules and deadlines. Do you do your homework without a lot of outside motivation? Or do you have to have your parents crack the whip? Do you turn in school projects on time or late? How about things like soccer practice or ballet lessons—are you usually ready to roll on time, or does somebody have to drag you out the door at the last second?

If you discover you're not tops in the discipline department, you can develop it. Why not start by scheduling time to go through this book and complete each and every Business Brainstormer work sheet?

◄ Enthusiasm ►

All die-hard entrepreneurs have enthusiasm for their businesses, whether it's bug-hunting or beauty makeovers. If you weren't enthusiastic—if you didn't take delight in your products or services and in running the company—there wouldn't be much point in having a business. Sure, earning money and being your own boss are pretty cool, but if you

Hot Tip

Discipline can pay off in more ways than one. "I worked on Christmas Eve," says Kiera Kramer of Parties Perfect. "I felt bad because my customer really needed someone to work, and I wasn't sure if I could because I had to go to church with my family. I ended up working, and because it was a holiday, I told my customer my price was $15 per hour even though a regular party is $10. She wound up paying me something outrageous like $35 per hour."

don't really enjoy bug-hunting or beauty makeovers, and you don't like being a businessperson, you probably won't succeed. Just as you do a lot better at the subjects you like in school, you'll do much better as an entrepreneur if you love what you're doing.

One reason is that if you aren't enthusiastic, you'll have difficulty finding the drive and perseverance to see you through the tough times. Another is that enthusiasm is catching.

Hot Tip

If you're excited about your product or service, your customers are apt to get excited, too—which will make them want to buy from you.

If you start a recycling business but think used aluminum cans are boring or gross, then your customers will probably turn up their noses, too. But if you believe recycling is cool, that it will save our planet and possibly our lives, that it's inexpensive, clean and healthy, then who could say no? Your customers will have to agree—your enthusiasm will win them over.

How do you know if you're enthusiastically inclined? If you're the type who gets excited about projects—anything from camping trips to neighborhood beautification to planning a party or restoring a car—then you've got it.

If you're one of those people who can't seem to get excited about anything, maybe you haven't found your niche—your particular talent—yet. As you go through this book, you'll have lots of opportunities to explore what your likes and interests are and how you can turn them into a business. And that's something to get enthusiastic about!

Hot Tip

Amy Beaver has run a candle-sales operation with her brother since they were 7 and 9 years old. "Owning our own business taught us responsibility," Amy says. "Suddenly, you were there in the adult world and you had to do mature things. It woke us up to a lot more. A lot of kids today don't get the responsibility part—but it really helped us out a lot."

◀ Independence ▶

Entrepreneurs are independent by nature. They're leaders instead of followers and generally more delighted with their own company than with a group. As an entrepreneur, you're the boss—the person who bears the creative brainstorm, makes the decisions and keeps the company going with drive and perseverance. You'll have friends, family and other mentors to lend advice, but it's basically all up to you. There's no employer to tell you what to do or when—or even how. So you have to be independent.

Employees are not particularly independent. They may not like the idea of being bossed around, but they don't do well at thinking on their feet, making decisions or planning strategies. Entrepreneurs, on the other hand, usually detest the thought of being bossed. They like to be in the driver's seat—in control and in charge—and making their own version of Independence Day every day.

How do you know if you've got the independent spirit? If you've done odd jobs for neighbors to earn extra money, you're already an independent-minded entrepreneur. If you've planned and carried out projects on your own, from cleaning the garage to surprise your parents to designing your own greeting cards on your computer to collecting and selling trad-

queen of arts

Greeting card queen Mary Engelbreit always knew she wanted to be an artist—specifically, she wanted to illustrate children's books. She began her career as an entrepreneurial artist selling cards to a local shop for 25 to 50 cents each when she was in high school. After working at an art supply store and a newspaper, Mary decided to test her dream and in 1977, took her portfolio of drawings to publishers in New York.

No dice—nobody wanted to hire her as an illustrator, and one art director suggested she do greeting cards instead. Mary was crushed. But she picked herself up and became a card design sensation. Mary's card and product empire, Mary Engelbreit Enterprises, at recent count earned $100 million. Plus, by going independent and doing it her way, she got what she wanted to begin with—she now illustrates children's books, too!

The ThirTeen Traits Of The Entrepreneur

Go down the list of entrepreneurial right-stuff characteristics. Place a star next to the ones you've got and a check beside the ones where you might need work.

1. Vision _____
2. Creativity _____
3. Adaptability _____
4. Risk-Taking _____
5. Confidence _____
6. Drive _____
7. Competitiveness _____
8. Perseverance _____
9. Integrity _____
10. Discipline _____
11. Enthusiasm _____
12. Independence _____
13. Thriftiness _____

ing cards, you're independent. If you've never conceived of any sort of project on your own, now's the time to start.

◀ Thriftiness ▶

Our last—but not necessarily least—entrepreneurial trait is thriftiness. This is the quality of spending money wisely, of saving and being economical. Smart businesspeople don't spend every dime they earn on themselves. Instead, they reinvest that money in their company, buying more or better equipment, or services like advertising, or hiring employees so they can expand. We're not talking Scrooge, an example of thriftiness run amok because he never spent a penny on anything, but of using your income wisely instead of splurging on every CD, skateboard or expensive pair of jeans that catches your eye.

Entrepreneurs also tend to be thrifty when starting their companies. Instead of running out and buying a brand-new 8 zillion GB computer "for the business" before they've earned their first dollar, they might make do with the one they've had until the company can afford to purchase a new one that it actually needs.

How do you figure out if you're thrifty? Does your money burn a hole in your pocket, or do you have a tidy nest egg saved for something you really want? If you're a saver, you're thrifty. If you've got singe marks in your clothing from your cash burning holes, not to worry. This book will teach you how to use your business funds wisely.

Chapter Two

Visions And Dreams

Now that you know you have the right stuff to be an entrepreneur, what's next? Choosing your business. Some businesses start off with a vision or a dream, some begin by fulfilling a need, and others start off with a burning desire for independence. In this chapter, you'll discover how to brainstorm ideas, uncover your talents and put them to use. We'll explore and conquer the fear of failure—or even success—that keeps people from going ahead with their plans. Then it's on to Market Research Mania—from focus groups to person-on-the-street surveys and how to determine if that business brainstorm will flop or soar.

Trading Dollars

Before you sit down to dream up a company, you should know what a business is. You might think it's as simple as one person buying what another person or company has to sell, which is true—sort of. More specifically, a business is a trade, or exchange.

When you trek over to your local taco stand and order a burrito, you're trading your dollar-and-change for a tortilla stuffed with beans. It's exactly the same principle as when you trade your Minnie Mouse alarm clock for your friend's official "Star Trek" watch. You make the trade because you both consider it a fair exchange—she gets an object she wants by handing over an object you want. And you both agree the clock and the watch have the same value. It's not like one of you gets a stick of gum and the other gets the collectible.

When you are standing in the order line at the taco stand, it's the same thing. You are trading your money for that burrito, and you and the taco stand agree it's a fair exchange—a burrito dripping with cheese and sauce and your dollar-and-change have the same value.

That's what business is—selling a product or service at a price customers see as a fair trade for their dollars.

◄ Popsicle Prices ►

Let's say, for instance, that you are selling Popsicles from a cart on a blistering hot summer afternoon. You're at a ballgame, where everybody's about to drop from the heat, and you're the only vendor there. You can charge $3 per Popsicle and probably sell them all because people figure the cost of cooling off with your products is worth three dollar bills.

Hot Tip

Business camps can be a good way to learn entrepreneurship tips and meet other kids who are into the biz whiz thing. Kiera Kramer attended Camp Start-Up, which is run by an organization called Independent Means that teaches girls about entrepreneurship. "I saw an ad for it in a magazine," Kiera says. "I was interested in business and thought it would be a good thing I'd like to try. The camp was really great." (Interested? You can find contact information for Camp Start-Up in "Reach Out and Resource" on page 297.)

But if there are dozens of other Popsicle vendors roaming around, you'll probably only be able to get 50 cents each because there's plenty of *supply* to meet customers' *demand*. Now, if you want to get that higher price for your product, you'll have to do something different to make people think it's worth more money. Maybe you could have the team insignia carved into each Popsicle, give away a bag of popcorn with each purchase, or pass out glow-in-the-dark team bracelets—something to make people see your products as more valuable than your competitors'.

Change the picture and say you're not at the ballpark in the heat of summer but standing on a windy, sleety street corner in the dead of winter. You probably couldn't get even 50 cents for a Popsicle. You'd have plenty of supply but no demand.

Peddling Products And Selling Services

Of course, you can dream up companies that peddle lots of things besides Popsicles. All businesses sell either *products* or *services*. Products are objects like Beanie Babies and Bugs Bunny comic books. Services are activities you do for your customers, like lawn mowing, party planning, errand running and pet-sitting. Doctors, dentists, barbers and plumbers provide services—you don't go out and "buy" a checkup, a tooth filling or a drain roto-rooting like you would a book or a videotape. Supermarkets, car dealers, coffee bars and CD emporiums provide products—tangible objects from cans of soup to minivans to the greatest hits of the '90s.

Whichever you choose—product or service—you're still selling them to customers, who can also be called *clients* or *consumers*. When you call a person a consumer, you're usually talking about him in very general terms, as in the hypothetical average Joe who might (or might not) buy or *consume* your worm-farm-in-a-box or your iguana feeding service.

◀ A Jewel Of A System ▶

If you choose to deal in products, you can decide to go into *manufacturing, wholesale* or *retail*. Manufacturing is where you make that product, and it can be as high-tech as making computer microchips or as old-fashioned as stringing beads for bracelets. You can then sell directly to the public, like Dell does with its computers or like jewelry designers often do at crafts fairs. Or you can sell to *wholesalers*, who buy large amounts of products and then sell them to *retailers*, who then turn around and sell smaller quantities of products to consumers.

Let's say you're a jewelry wholesaler. You might attend a gift show where lots of crafters—the manufacturers—display their wares, hoping to attract wholesale buyers. You find a bracelet you think will be a hot seller—it's classy and trendy, and you can buy a hundred inexpensively. So you do. Then you take a sample bracelet to the retailers—the gift and clothing shops and drug stores in your town—and ask for orders. These retailers buy a dozen or so of each bracelet, mark up the price from what they paid you, and then sell them to their customers. It's called the chain of distribution, and it's a jewel of a system!

Hot Tip

An entrepreneurial rule-of-thumb is "Buy low, sell high." What this means is that you have to shop around—buy your wholesale goods for the lowest price you can find and then sell them for as high a price as you think your customers will pay.

Defining Your Market

To be successful in business, you must not only have a product or service to sell but your own special market, one where a genuine need or desire for your products or services exists and one with a large enough number of people to sell to. Deciding on these factors is called *defining your market*.

First off, the products or services you sell must be something you know and are enthusiastic about. If you're an avid hiker, and you want to sell products to other hikers or teach children the joys of trekking in the woods, great! Get tramping! But if you hate hills and the thought of the woods makes you itch from imaginary ticks and poison ivy, then make tracks to something else. Or else you'll likely fail. Instead, you need to find something you understand and enjoy.

Second, you must have a customer base to draw from. If you find flies fascinating and you have a huge collection under glass, that's swell, but you're not going to find many people who will want to buy fly merchandise. If, on the other hand, you're into fly *fishing* and you plan to sell your specially made lures, you'll have a huge number of enthusiasts all over the world from which to draw.

If you plan to offer a landscaping service, you won't need a huge customer base because this is labor-intensive—you can only do so many yards a week. But if you live in a concrete jungle of apartment buildings with not a lawn in sight, you'll be in trouble—unless you switch to starting window boxes for people.

Thinking Business

Now that you know what the pros know in terms of business basics, you can start thinking about the business you'd like to own. You might already have an idea. Some people know from the time they're very young that they want to be artists, musicians or gardeners. For them, it's pretty easy. All they have to do is narrow down exactly what they plan to sell. An artist might decide to design and sell greeting cards or pottery or painted furniture. A musician might start a rock band or give piano lessons. And a gardener could raise and sell organic vegetables or design gardens for homeowners.

You might have a similar situation—a talent and a passion for a particular craft. Maybe you've known forever that you're a writer, an automotive whiz, a computer genius or a cooking fiend. If so, take it away!

Donna Sayers, 18, started DJ's Catering Service in 1997 to do what she loves best—cooking. "I always wanted to own my own restaurant," the Brooklyn, New York, teen says. "But because that would cost thousands of dollars, I realized the most feasible thing was a catering business.

"Pick something that you absolutely love to do. Definitely pick something you think has a viable market but also pick something you love to do. For the time and effort and money and strain that's going to go into it, if you don't love it, you work as hard to get the outcome."

Hot Tip

You can make a lot of money with creative materials—if they become popular—by licensing them to various manufacturers. All those T-shirts, jammies, toys and other knicknacks that feature Warner Bros. cartoon characters like Bugs Bunny, for instance, are licensed products. The pajama manufacturer—like the makers of the other products—pays Warner Bros. for the right to put Bugs on their clothing.

Tweak An Idea

Some entrepreneurs start off with a vision or a dream, an idea that just about forces itself into existence. Thomas Edison, for instance, barely slept until he'd given birth to the light bulb. Dave Thomas lived and breathed hamburgers for decades while he pioneered his Wendy's fast-food chain. And the two Steves—Wozniak and Jobs—invented the Apple computer out of their vision of a personal computer for the home.

Newbie entrepreneurs often believe that the only way to go is with a product, and that to start off with a new business they have to come up with something completely new and radical—something the world has never seen before. Like a personal computer when nobody but university and government workers had access to computers or a light bulb when the world was lit by gas lanterns.

Think again. As you know, you can sell services as well as products—

Do You Believe In Magic ?

f you're looking for a magician, you don't have to try to find your way to the Hogwarts School like Harry Potter did—instead, go to Shawn Gollatz, who's in the business of making magic. A professional magician and balloon sculptor, Shawn performs at birthday parties, company picnics, winter holiday affairs and any other events that require enchanted entertainment.

The 18-year-old from Milersville, Pennsylvania, has been performing professionally for about three years, although he's been into magic since he was 8. "I started out doing magic for my family and friends," he says. "A friend of a friend knew someone who needed my services, and it started out like that."

The teen illusionist's first show for a public audience was at the Magicians Alliance of Eastern States convention, where he took first place in the junior competition. "That was my first real inspiration," he says.

Shawn has succeeded admirably, mastering not only the art of entertainment but winning grand prize as Young Entrepreneur of the Year in a local competition. Besides all that, Shawn's company, Jest Entertainment—which he began in 1997—earned almost $20,000 in 1999, with expenses of only about $300 for business cards.

"The key thing I learned came from a friend in magic who convinced me to get myself booked in a restaurant making balloon sculptures for the guests while they ate their dinners," Shawn explains. "This provided me with a guaranteed weekly income. Not only that, it provided me with a chance to meet about 300 new faces a week and personally give them a one-on-one taste of the business. If they asked for a business card, I had one ready. Then I'd get calls for individual shows or birthday parties."

> "The key is to find creative solutions to your problems and never be afraid to start small."

Shawn's advice to newbie teenage entrepreneurs? "If you can, find something you like doing," he says. "If you can't decide, find out what consumers want and fill it. Avoid second-guessing yourself. Everyone runs into trouble with either money or finding work along the way. The key is to find creative solutions to your problems and never be afraid to start small."

Photo Courtesy: Jest Entertainment

and neither one has to be new at all. Just tailored to your particular market. Take a look at what's already out there and decide how you can tweak it a little and make it fit your personality and your community.

Jason Upshaw, 21, of Second Gear Bicycles in Cambridge, Massachusetts, decided at 15 to open a secondhand bike sales and repair shop because he knew people in his neighborhood needed and wanted bikes but couldn't afford them. He realized that by giving new life to old two-wheelers, he could also give his neighbors the joy of spinning down the street on their very own wheels.

Anna and Sarah Levinson of Los Angeles started Ripe cosmetics because they loved designing colors and they'd put together hues people in their area wanted to buy.

Bronx, New Yorker Jasmine Jordan began publishing *Tools for Living* magazine in 1996 when she put together two related ideas. "I've been a writer for a number of years, since the age of 5," the 16-year-old says. "And it's just something that I always wanted to do. I didn't set out to do a big-time magazine. I wanted to have fun doing something I really loved and that I was good at." Then Jasmine hit on the idea of a publication that would publish the work of other kids who like to write but have a hard time getting published in adult magazines.

> **Take a look at what's already out there and decide how you can tweak it a little and make it fit your personality and your community.**

"It started as a little book, no graphics," Jasmine explains. "I did it on my little computer and showed it to my brother. He liked the concept of a magazine. He did the graphic design for me, and the magazine was basically born."

Kiera Kramer dreamed up her business when she noticed that her parents couldn't enjoy their own parties because they were too busy shuttling back and forth from the kitchen. So she started Parties Perfect, a company that does serving and clean-up for party-givers so they can get out of the kitchen and into the swing of things.

There are all kinds of other ideas out there, just waiting to be envisioned, tweaked and then turned into reality—by you.

Brainstorm Central

So how do you come up with hot ideas? You *brainstorm*. This might sound like a science fiction scenario in which a mad scientist lights up somebody's life by zapping his head with lightning. But it's actually a business technique in which people gather around a conference table (usually littered with coffee cups or cans of soda) to think up new ideas or solutions to problems.

Brainstorming is often used by advertising agency people to dream up new commercial campaigns, by scientists to come up with new applications or ways to use computer programs, by TV writers to devise thorny new plots for soap opera heroines or hilarious gag lines for sitcom characters, and by businesspeople to figure out how to solve knotty problems, from marketing to finances.

The point of brainstorming—and the part that makes it really fun—is that it doesn't matter how off-the-wall or impractical your ideas are. The important thing is to get the ideas out there, verbally if you're working with friends or partners, and on paper if you're operating alone.

a dell-icate idea

Michael Dell, the man behind Dell computers, started out selling PCs out of his dorm room at the University of Texas. His brainstorm was the concept of custom-building computers for consumers and selling directly to them. He figured that letting people "design" their own PCs would be a draw and not having to go through stores—which makes computers more expensive because of retailers' markups—would be another draw.

Dell was right. The company he founded in 1984 now boasts sales of more than $40 million per day just by phone and the Internet. That's not counting in-person sales to corporate and institutional customers. The company's four-quarter (meaning four three-month periods or one year) earnings at most recent tally was $25 billion. Not bad for a guy who started in a dorm room.

Photo Courtesy: Dell Computer Corp.

Not having to worry about "thinking inside the box" or thinking in conventional terms makes all the difference. You are free to really let your imagination soar. One idea leads to another and, before you know it, those off-the-wall notions have become workable, exciting inspirations.

◄ Starting Points ►

So here we go. Begin with these brainstorming starting points. We've provided a work sheet for personalized scribbling on pages 40-41. Use it to plot your visions, dreams and talents—both hidden and not-so-secret—and start designing your own custom-tailored business. Then add anything else that strikes a spark of creativity or interest (or both) in your mind:

▶ **List the businesses or careers you find fascinating.** A job as a disc jockey, for instance, could translate into a business as a mobile DJ, playing recorded music at parties and other events. You can turn your fascination into a business like Shawn Gollatz, who thought being a magician was the most fascinating occupation in the world and turned his magic into his company.

▶ **List your interests, passions and pastimes.** If you love animals, you could go into business as a pet valet, aquarium specialist or horse trainer. If you're a movie buff, you might start a movie research library. If you're a Net surfer or computer whiz, you could have a Web site design business or a dotcom business selling products online, or become an information broker, researching projects for clients online. Don't leave anything out—the Levinson sisters, for example, have made a thriving business out of "playing with" cosmetic colors.

▶ **List your skills and talents.** Maybe you're a genius with children or cars or sailing or surfing (the ocean or the Internet.) Again, don't leave anything out. Even talking on the phone is a talent—you could start a referral business, putting callers in touch with baby-sitters, college apartment roommates, or some other necessary commodity. Or you might start a telephone market research survey business.

You're free to really let your imagination soar.

▶ **List any odd jobs you've done or are already doing** for pocket money or allowance that could be the seeds of a business. This could be housecleaning, table-setting or lawn mowing. Shawn Himmelberger, 19, of Port Clinton, Pennsylvania, turned weekend work mowing neighbors' lawns into a full-time landscaping service. Laying an elegant table could become a business as an etiquette instructor, teaching kids and even adults how to set a proper table and use proper dining manners. That's what Jasmine Jordan does in addition to her publishing business. Or it could become the seed of a party-help business like Kiera Kramer's.

▶ **List any products or services you think your community could benefit from.** This could be anything from after-school care for children to a vegetarian breakfast bar to a community garden to a used bicycle shop like Jason Upshaw's.

···rainy day company···

One way to serve a need in your community—or in the world—is with a nonprofit company. Nonprofits, like rainy-day friends, are there when you need them, helping solve the world's ills in any number of ways—by providing shelter for the homeless, food for the hungry, natural environments for the world, or dreams come true for acutely ill children, to name just a few. The Red Cross, Habitat for Humanity, Make-a-Wish Foundation and The Nature Conservancy are all nonprofit organizations.

They're called nonprofit organizations because their main goals are not to earn profits for the sake of making money—although that helps the cause—but to benefit society. All profits that don't go into maintaining the business—like paying salaries to key people and paying for rent or supplies—are used to help carry out the company's mission.

The new buzzword for going nonprofit these days is "social entrepreneuring," and it's a hot concept. As a teen businessperson there are other nonprofit groups, like Youth Venture, whose goal is to help you—with both money and advice—to be a social entrepreneur and make your world, your town, your local park or even your school a better place. Read more about this group on 296.

◀ Recurring Themes ▶

After you've finished your brainstorming session, go back over your work sheet and see what ideas stand out. You may discover that the things you've put on paper have a recurring theme—maybe everything has to do with computers or kids or creating artwork.

You might realize that you have a real knack for painting or planting or even shopping. These talents could be the seeds of several businesses, from personal concierge, a business that finds everything from concert tickets to birthday cakes for ultra-busy clients, to flea market guru, where you buy and sell collectibles.

You might put two and two—or two and four—together and hit on the very thing your community could desperately use.

The Unknown Factor

Entrepreneur wanna-bes sometimes don't get beyond the wishful thinking stage, paralyzed by the fear of failure—or even success. They are so terrified of the unknown, the thought of all those monsters that might be lurking in the unforeseen future, that they refuse to start. Don't let this be you.

If you think there is a lot of work involved in becoming an entrepreneur, you're right. But you wouldn't be reading this book if you weren't ready to tackle the tasks. And doing it for yourself—with your family's pride and support as you go—puts a different spin on things. Being an entrepreneur is tough—but fun. Working for yourself, setting your own goals, then meeting and even exceeding them is far more exciting than any employee or allowance-receiving kid can imagine.

As for those fears: A little fear of the unknown is healthy—it keeps you on your toes. But fear to the point that you give up before you've begun is unfounded. You won't have a crystal ball to absolutely, positively guarantee success. But you don't have one in school or sports, either.

A Cool Idea To Keep Warm In The Winter

K-K Gregory's company began as the result of playing in the snow. "When I was 10 years old, I was playing outside with my brother," explains 16-year-old K-K from Bedford, Massachusetts. "My wrists were getting cold in between my jacket cuffs and the cuffs of my gloves. I was tired of that happening, and I wanted to fix it. We had some scraps of Polartex fleece laying around the house, so I decided to make a tube out of that to protect my wrists. I thought if it wasn't anchored to my hand somehow, it probably wouldn't work very well. So I cut holes for my thumbs, tried them out, and they worked great.

"The following weekend we had a Girl Scout troop meeting. We were going sledding, so I made 12 pairs—one for each person in the troop. They loved them and thought they were awesome. They said, 'Sell them and make some money off them.' I thought 'All right, sounds good!' "

And that was the birth of Wristies. "One girl's dad was an inventor, and he knew a good patent attorney," K-K says. "Another girl's dad owned a bike shop, and he was the first to buy the Wristies for his store. (See Chapter 3, page 86 for information about patents.) It wasn't very many (about a dozen), but it was a big thing to us because it was now a business."

Wristies has gone on to sell far more than a dozen pairs—K-K has received orders for thousands at a time, notably from TV network QVC and store-chain Brookstone. It took a couple of years for the business to get off the ground and get some major accounts. K-K and her mom—who helps out with everything from sewing Wristies to attending sales meetings—shopped department stores to find glove companies and their manufacturers, then pitched their product (which now includes a line of heated Wristies).

Photo Courtesy: Wristies Inc.

> "We were going sledding, so I made 12 pairs—one for each person in the troop. They loved them and thought they were awesome. They said, 'Sell them and make some money off them.' I thought 'All right, sounds good!' "

▶▶ Business Brainstormer

Brainstorm Central

1. List the businesses or careers you find fascinating.

_____

_____

_____

2. List your interests, passions and pastimes. Don't leave anything out!

_____

_____

_____

3. List your skills and talents.

_____

_____

_____

4. List any odd jobs you've had or have that could be the seeds of a business.

_____

_____

_____

5. List any products or services you think your community could benefit from.

_____

_____

_____

Continued on next page

Continued from previous page

6. Write down anything else that sparks brain waves—businesses you've seen on TV shows or movies, companies you've read about in magazines or books, projects your family or friends are involved in that could lead to a business you'd like.

_____

_____

_____

_____

7. Now go back over your lists. Does any one subject, interest or passion leap out? Do you see a recurring theme? If so, list it (or them) here:

_____

_____

8. Can one or more of these become a business? If so, write it (or them) down here:

_____

_____

9. Now—if you can—narrow down your choice to one business and write it down here:

_____

10. If you chose a business, congratulations! If not, set this list aside while you go through the rest of the book, and use the lines below to jot down new ideas:

_____

_____

_____

_____

Whether we like it or not, life isn't like that. That's what makes it exciting. And remember the risk-taking trait—a large part of the entrepreneurial edge is being willing to take a chance.

◄ Miracle Ideas ►

What if you've gone through all the brainstorming, decided you're not afraid of failure, and still haven't come up with the miracle idea that makes your heart beat faster? Not to worry.

We'll have more thoughts—which will fire up more ideas—as we go through the book. And we've got those 21 terrific businesses in the bonus book found on page 205. You can decide on one that sounds like a winner, and then tweak it to fit. Or turn it upside down. Any one of those businesses—or the ones run by the teen entrepreneurs we interview throughout this book or the adult ones we explore in sidebars—can lead you to a totally different idea. So while you're reading, keep those brain neurons firing.

Hot Tip

"Don't be afraid to fail," says Jason Ryan Dorsey of Golden Ladder Productions, a book publishing and training company. "Michael Dell—the founder of Dell Computers—told me that. Learn from your mistakes."

Market Research Mania

Once you've decided on a business, your next challenge is conducting *market research*—which is another facet of defining your market. Market research helps you determine whether the audience for your product or service really does exist and helps you refine your product or service so it will be the most appealing to that market.

Say you've decided to go with flower power and sell planted window boxes to urban New Yorkers. Market research will help you find out if enough New Yorkers really want window boxes to give you a market, what kind of plants and window boxes they would buy (large? small? with flowers? or herbs?) and how much they'd be willing to spend.

◄ Planning For Success ►

This is exactly what Robert Sek of ID Enterprises in Austin, Texas, did. "When I was 17, I decided I wanted to start a company over the Net," Robert says. "I realized that whenever I went to conventions, companies all had security badges. But there were no central locations where they could go and purchase badges or ID cards. With that in mind, I started thinking about places around my area that dealt in that kind of product.

"So I went to different security stores, and spoke to them and got a lot of information," explains Robert, now a 21-year-old business economics major at the University of Texas. "Since I was 17, they really didn't take me too seriously as a threat. Then I'd go around and acquire information on products and equipment. They thought I was a naïve young high school kid."

They were wrong—Robert was young, all right, but not naïve. And he was onto something big. "Then I realized that if I started offering this as an option on the Net, I could potentially reach everyone in the nation," Robert explains. "After two years of researching everything from the legalities to accounting to product development to Web site design, I figured everything out and started production my freshman year in college when I was 19."

Robert's intensive planning paid off. His company is worth a cool half million dollars and has enabled him to buy not only his own car but his own condo—pretty cool for a guy who didn't even tell his parents he was planning a company until he'd already been running it successfully for almost a year. "I didn't want to tell them because they would have the same reaction as everyone else," Robert says. "They'd be another nay-sayer. And my parents could have more influence over me. I also thought that if I failed they would never know and then they wouldn't be disappointed."

Hot Tip

Part of market research is looking at the demographics of your niche customers and your area—the social, gender, age and economic make-up of your target population. If you're selling pink Doc Marten-style boots, for instance, your ideal demographic population will be female teens and Gen Xers who probably live in a sophisticated, urban area and can afford the price.

Hot Tip

"Don't be afraid to call people or to ask questions," says Jason Smith, 19, a Hanover, Pennsylvania, seed and grain dealer. "I'm polite, but I'll walk up to someone and just ask. That's what people like. But if you have an attitude, forget it—it's not going to work."

fortune from failure

One of the most important factors to business success is something you might never guess: failure. Many prosperous entrepreneurs say previous business failures—more than anything else—helped fuel their current successes.

The old saying about learning from your mistakes may be a cliche, but thousands of successful business owners have done exactly that. Instead of letting failure crush them, these entrepreneurs profited from the experience, gaining valuable lessons they couldn't have learned any other way.

Failure hurts—a lot—but it also challenges and motivates you to pick yourself up, dust yourself off, and try again. In a way it's like learning to ride a bike. You probably took a few tumbles before you figured out the correct mix of speed and balance. And you may have scraped your knees or elbows and shed a few tears. But you didn't give up—you kept at it until all of a sudden, you were flying down the street, feeling free and swift as an eagle. Business failure and ultimate success works the same way.

And remember, there's a big difference between failing and being a failure. The true failure simply gives up. The wise entrepreneur learns from her mistakes and ultimately succeeds.

◄ Hello, Hello ►

So how do you conduct your own market research? Basically, you ask. One way to do this is with telephone surveys. You can gain valuable information, but it's not always easy. Some people will be delighted to answer your questions, but others may just hang up. In this age of telemarketing, when people are bombarded with callers selling everything from credit cards to sun rooms to spa memberships, lots of folks are leery of calls from anyone they don't know. Unless you have a thick skin, it can be difficult to make *cold-calls*, the term for unsolicited calls to strangers.

The solution is to target a specific audience—people you already have some connection with. You might use your church or temple roster. Then, even if you don't know the person you're calling, you can say something like "Hi, my name's Jen Jacobs, and I'm a member of your church. I'm planning on starting a business, and I'd like to ask your opinion on a few items." Sharing a common church makes the person feel she knows you, making her more likely to answer your questions.

Where else can you get phone numbers? Find a group associated with your target market. If you belong to an association or organization—anything from scouting or an astronomy club to a zoo volunteer program, you've got it made. If you're going the window box route, you might call adults in your organization who qualify as potential customers, or ask to talk to the parents of kids in your group. If you were planning to sell a special car log you designed for vintage auto fanatics, you'd call people in your car club as well as in other car clubs around your region.

Hot Tip

If you're the type who gets tongue-tied at the thought of picking up the phone and talking to someone you don't know, try this: Write down your opening lines, like "Hi, My name is Alex Anderson, and I'd like to ask you a few questions about. . ." Then make a list of your questions. Just having something to read from can be a major tongue-detangler.

◀ Up Close And Personal ▶

Another market research way to go is to get up-close and personal with a *focus group*. This is an informal get-together between you and a selection of potential customers, usually about five to a dozen people. You can invite them into the living room or den or host your focus group in the school library or church hall—after, of course, getting permission from the proper authorities.

Make sure the people in your group are the ones you want to reach—use the same criteria you use for telephone surveys. If you're targeting working adults for that window box business, for instance, it won't do you any good to invite Mrs. Zebling next door, who's retired and spends all her days in her huge terrace garden. She won't need or want your serv-

Hot Tip

Your parents or brothers or aunts might belong to groups with lists of people you can call. Or you might be able to start by talking to their colleagues at work. When you mention your relative's name, that's your foot in the door.

ices. The people you've chosen—the ones who represent your target market—will usually want to attend your focus group for one or more reasons: They know you or your parents, they are interested in the business you're planning, or they like the idea of helping out a young person.

Hot Tip

Some market researchers head straight to the mall or supermarket. Armed with a clipboard, they approach shoppers and ask for a few moments to ask the questions on their list. Or they set up a card table and chairs where they can ask shoppers to sit down and fill in survey questionnaires. Some people will be too hurried to answer questions, but others find responding to surveys fun. This can be a good way to get a wide sampling of people, but make sure you have permission from supermarket or mall management first.

Once you have your group assembled, give them refreshments—which people always appreciate—and begin asking those pressing market research questions. Keep your questions focused on your objectives: deciding which products to choose (like asking if people would rather have petunias or tomatoes), how to price your products, and what your company name should be.

Hand out surveys that ask not only about your business but also about the group—their age range, income level and interests. For your window box business, you'll also want to know things like how many windows they have that boxes could fit outside of, whether they would prefer to take care of their own flowers or have you do it for an additional fee, and what sorts of plants they like.

If you were conducting a focus group for a different business—say dog training—you wouldn't be interested in which flowers people prefer. Instead, you'd want to know if their dogs have the habit of eating people and furniture, or peeing on them.

Have plenty of pens and pencils on hand and encourage discussion. You'll learn more than you might imagine. For an idea of what a survey might actually look like, take a peek at the sample on page 47.

◀ Just The Facts, Ma'am! ▶

Besides going directly to your potential participants for market research, you'll also want statistical information. If you're going to run a desktop publishing company targeted toward SOHOs, for instance, you'll

Market Research Survey
Window Box Business

1. How many window boxes or live planting containers do you now have?_____

2. How many window boxes or live planting containers would you like to have?_____

3. How many people reside in your household?_____

4. What are their ages?_____

5. What is your household income: ❑ Under $30,000 per year
   ❑ $30,000 to $60,000 per year   ❑ Over $60,000 per year

6. How much do you spend on average for plants or flowers each month?_____

7. Would you be interested in having a service that would provide window boxes full of fresh flowers and herbs and then water and maintain them on a weekly basis?_____

8. How much would you be willing to spend for a planted window box?_____

9. How much would you be willing to spend for weekly watering and maintenance?_____

10. Would you prefer to pay for windows boxes, watering and maintenance: ❑ by the week   ❑ by the month   ❑ twice a year

11. Would you prefer to have watering and maintenance done while you were at work or while you're at home?_____

12. Please comment on the name Flower Power (love, like, dislike or hate, and why)_____

_____

_____

13. Please comment on the name Petal Nirvana (love, like, dislike or hate, and why)_____

_____

_____

niche market niceties

When you decide on your target market, you're also developing your market niche. This is your special corner of a larger market. If you sell vegetarian hot dogs, for instance, your niche market is not the wide world of people who buy and eat wieners, but the smaller, more focused group of wiener-eaters who are vegetarians, too.

If you sell power bead bracelets, your target market is not just everybody who buys bracelets (which could be Tinkerbell bracelets for toddlers to gold bangles for grannies) but New Age-influenced people who believe—or can be taught to believe—that different gemstones have specific powers.

This is an important consideration because while you could probably easily sell power bead bracelets at any teen-oriented or Gen X store, you'd probably have a hard time peddling them to stores where grandmothers shop.

want to know how many small or home businesses there are in your community. If you plan to write and sell a book chock-full of fund-raising ideas for private elementary schools, you'll need to know how many private elementary schools there are in the United States, in the Midwest, for instance, or in the city of St. Louis. The answers will give you an idea of just how many potential customers you will have and if that number is large enough for you to earn money.

You can get all this sort of information and much more from a variety of sources:

▶ **The public library:** Reference librarians are extremely helpful with this sort of thing. All you have to do is call and tell the librarian that you need to know how many small or home businesses there are in your town and how many private elementary schools there are in the area you want to target first. Or how many fly fish-

> **The answers will give you an idea of just how many potential customers you will have and if that number is large enough for you to earn money.**

erman or disabled children under age 14 there are in the United States—whatever you need to know. She'll look up the information and call you back with the answer. Or you can go into the library and dig through books of statistics yourself, unearthing more facts and figures than you could use in a quadruple round of Trivial Pursuit.

▶ **The Internet:** A world library at your fingertips! You'll have access to all sorts of stuff without ever leaving your desk. For starters, check in with the U.S. Census Bureau at www.census.gov and the Department of Commerce at www.doc.gov.

▶ **Organizations and associations:** What better places to go for information on your specific market? If you're targeting senior citizens, for example, you could contact the American Association of Retired Persons for a count of its members; for a count of primary school teachers, you'd talk to the folks at state and regional teachers' associations.

yahoodling the web

What's a klutz, a bumpkin and also a powerhouse of a Web guide? If you said Yahoo!, you're right. The mega-Net guide was born in 1994 as the brainchild of Jerry Yang and David Filo, 26- and 28-year-old doctoral candidates in engineering at Stanford University in California.

David and Jerry first conceived of their guide as a way to keep track of their personal Web surfing paths. But it soon morphed into much more as the pals tweaked it into a software program designed to help other surfers navigate the Net with ease.

The pioneering duo called their site Yahoo! because they say they considered themselves yahoos. But then they liked oddball names—Jerry's workstation was called Akebono and David's computer went by the name Konishiki, both famous Hawaiian sumo wrestlers.

In 1995, David and Jerry moved Yahoo! to the computers at Netscape Communications. Today, the site that started as the hobby of a couple of self-styled yahoos has more 120 million users worldwide and is a mega-stock on Wall Street.

Photo Courtesy: Yahoo! Inc.

◀ Shopping The Competition ▶

No matter how well you target your market and plan your business, you're going to face some sort of competition. This is OK—a little competition is healthy. If you do your homework properly, your company will shine despite—or because of—your rivals' lights.

The time to scrutinize those rivals is during your market research phase. What are they doing that's absolutely perfect? What can you successfully copy? What are they doing that you can do better? What can you offer that will draw customers away from them and to you? How can you answer all these questions? By performing these research tasks:

> ▶ **Shop the competition.** If you plan to design and sell T-shirts, go to the mall and look at all the other T-shirts on the racks. Study them. What works? What doesn't? And why? How are they priced? Ask the store owner or manager, or even the sales clerk if he or she seems sharp, what designs, fabrics and price ranges sell the best. If you're going to train dogs, call other dog trainers to find out what specific services they offer and what they charge. Ask what their most popular services are.

> ▶ **Investigate and inspect the advertising done by every other company that's similar to yours**—fliers that come in the mail, local newspaper or TV ads, even mail order catalogs. What products or services do they offer, what do they charge and how do they promote themselves? Decide what you think works the best and why.

> ▶ **Talk to the owners of businesses similar to yours.** Other business owners within your community may not be the best ones to approach because they might see you as competition. But it's perfectly OK to call people in other areas. Ask if you can schedule a time convenient to the entrepreneur to ask some questions. Most will be happy to oblige.

> ▶ **Identify all potential competition.** *Every* business has competitors. Even if there's no other window box business in your town, for instance, garden centers and florists can be competition. Potential customers might find it easier or cheaper to buy from these places

> No matter how well you target your market and plan your business, you're going to face some sort of competition.

than from you. Or you might be the only professional dog trainer in town, but the community recreation center might offer a course— that would be your competition.

▶ **Surf your competitors' Web sites.** Again, study what your rivals are doing locally, nationally and globally, and decide what works and what doesn't. Then figure out why.

Chapter Three

The Rock-Solid Foundation

O K, you've done your market research. You've decided on your target clients and your niche market. That's terrific! But there's more to a brilliant business than a 100 gigawatt bulb of an idea. In this chapter we'll explore how to build a rock-solid foundation from sole proprietorships to partnerships to corporations. You'll learn how to choose a business name that's really cool, how to stay legal with government types and decide what equipment you may need.

Clues And Impressions

Customers form an idea of the type of business they're dealing with from lots of large and small clues. If the business is a typical retail one, they look at the store's exterior. As soon as they walk through the door, their impressions are strengthened by the store's layout and displays.

If your business is a service one, where you go to your customers, then their first impression comes from other clues—the way you answer the phone, the way you dress, a T-shirt or polo shirt you wear that sports your company name and logo or your name and logo on your company car or truck (if you have one).

Name That Business

One of the most important customer clues comes from your business name. It can be cute, trendy, businesslike, elegant or down-home. But since it will immediately convey an idea of what you're all about, you want it to be right.

Your business name can reflect your products or services—for example, Dream Time Cuddle Company for a business that makes stuffed animals for young kids or Seniors' Sneakers Errand Service for a business that runs errands for senior citizens. Just make sure your company's name doesn't limit you. If the stuffed toy company decides to branch out to include tricycles a few years down the road, its name may no longer accu-

at first glance

Besides your name, your customers will get valuable first-impression clues about your company from your visual image. This means that the colors, graphics, typefaces and paper stocks you choose for everything from stationery to brochures to mailing labels is vitally important to how they perceive you.

If your company focuses on kids, for instance, go all-out for a logo that says "children": bright primary colors and a bouncy, exuberant type style. If you're talking landscaping, splash your materials with green images—flowers, trees or leaves.

You can design just about everything with your trusty desktop publishing program. But keep in mind that you're selling not only your special expertise, energy level and character, but an image of solid trust, too. You want potential clients to know they're in good hands when they hire you.

Have friends or family look over your designs before you commit to a print run. Do they see typos? Amateur quality? Or do they catch the sparkle of a true professional?

rately reflect its products. And if Seniors' Sneakers flexes its wings and starts running errands for young professionals as well, it will have to change names, too. When a company undergoes a name change, it risks losing its carefully built customer base.

◄ Too Clever ►

A clever name is good advertising—it helps you stand out from the crowd and helps people remember you. But don't choose a name that's so completely clever that people can't tell what you're selling. Just for Kicks might be a cool name for a dance studio that teaches customers to kick up their heels, but nobody's going to figure it out without coaching. Of course, if you add "Dance Instruction" to the name, you've got it made.

You should also avoid calling your business something like Larry Lingerberger Associates (especially if your name isn't Larry Lingerberger). The reason, again, is that it doesn't give people a clue as to what product or service you're selling. A name like L.L. Bean Sprouts & Things—for organic produce—will be clearer and more interesting.

The Totally Fictitious Business Name

Once you decide on a business name, you'll need to register it in your local area or state. You do this for three reasons:

1. It insures that no one else in your local area is using the name and gives you dibs on it.

2. It makes your local authorities happy. Most cities or counties require that you have a fictitious business name or dba (doing business as) license. This way, they can keep tabs on you for tax or other licensing purposes, and you go on public record so anyone can look up the name of your company and find out who it belongs to.

3. Most banks won't allow you to open a business checking account—one with your company name, which gives you

> **Hot Tip**
>
> Why use a dba? Because it tells anyone who wants to look it up that you're, for instance, Casey Jones doing business as (or under the name of) Choo-Choo Charlie's Collectibles.

▶▶ Business Brainstormer

Name That Business

List three ideas based on the products or services you plan to provide (e.g., children's clothing, custom menu design, aromatherapy products):

1._____

2._____

3._____

List three ideas based on your niche market (e.g., affordable children's special-occasion clothes, exclusive designs for the small restaurateur, aromatherapy for the office environment):

1._____

2._____

3._____

List three ideas combining a favorite theme with your special niche (e.g., Tea Party children's party clothes, Table for Two menu designs, The Tranquil Desk aromatic office products):

1._____

2._____

3._____

After you've decided which name you like best, ask yourself a few important questions:

▶ Have you said it aloud to make sure it's easily understood and pronounced? (Does your family like it? Have you had a friend call to see how it sounds over the phone?)

▶ Have you checked your local Yellow Pages to make sure the same or similar name is not already listed?

Continued on next page

Continued from previous page

▶ Have you checked with your local business authority to make sure the name is available?

▶ Have you registered your domain name if you plan to have a Web site?

▶ Have you started your trademark search if you plan to conduct one?

credibility among suppliers and others—unless you can show them your fictitious business license.

◀ Suitable For Framing ▶

Getting your dba is easy, but the process varies a bit in different regions of the country. In the state of Florida, you call the Secretary of State's office to check on up to three potential business names. When you hit on one that hasn't already been taken, the Secretary's office sends you a registration form. You mail back the completed form, the registration fee and a form from your local newspaper verifying that you have advertised your dba for one week. In return, you receive a certificate listing your business on an official certificate suitable for framing.

In other areas of the country, you might simply go down to your city or county clerk's office, thumb through a big book of business names, and then complete the registration procedure at the clerk's window.

It generally costs $10 to $100 to file your dba—and in some states the newspaper will do the filing for you for a small fee.

Hot Tip

If your first-choice domain name has been taken, get creative. But not so creative that your domain name has no relation to your company name. If your company is called Backwoods Tours, for instance, and there's already a www.backwoods.com, try something like www.we'rebackwoods.com or www.bwoods.com.

◀ Eminent Domain ▶

If you plan to have a Web site, you'll also need to register your *domain name*, that part of a Web address that comes after the "www" and allows people to access your site. Like trademarks and local dbas, no two companies can share the same domain name. You'll have to think up several versions of the name you want in case your first choice has already been taken.

Here's what you do: Open your Web browser and type in www.networksolutions.com. Now you're in (you guessed it!) the Network Solutions Web site, which is very user-friendly—and fun! Check to see if the domain name you chose has already been taken. If it has, choose another. When you find a version that's available, register it online. The cost is $70 for two years of registration, or $119 for a two-year reservation (in case you want to reserve a name but you don't plan to use it right away).

Foundation Fundamentals

Just as in building a house, you must have a solid foundation on which to build your business. In this case, it's not a basement or a concrete slab or even tent stakes stuck into the soil but the type of legal structure you go

the voice of mickey

All you have to say is "Disney" and images of fairy tale castles and talking mice come to mind. But once upon a time, Disney wasn't an entertainment empire but the name of a young entrepreneur.

Walt Disney started out as a commercial artist at age 18, not long after adventuring onto the battlefields of World War I as a teenage ambulance driver. With the war over, he set his sights on drawing, working for a couple of different companies. He felt he could do better on his own than as an employee and by the time he was 21, he had started his own animation studio in Kansas City, Missouri.

It failed a year later, but Walt persevered, opening a new studio in Hollywood. In 1928, Walt and his key animator, Ub Iwerks, introduced the world to Mickey Mouse, who starred as the title character in a film called "Steamboat Willie." (Trivia tip: Walt Disney was the voice of Mickey until his death in 1966.)

Today, Walt's animation studio is an entertainment powerhouse and a name that means fun and enchantment to people all over the world.

···the name of the game·········

Making sure you're the only one with your business name is important. Imagine how awful it would be if—after you'd worked long and hard to develop your business—you discovered that another company had your same name. Customers might call them, thinking they were calling you, and you'd lose business. Or customers might hear bad things about the other company and not call at all. It could be rough.

Most smaller companies register a dba with their city or state and consider it a job well done. But companies that plan to go national or global take it a step further and go for a trademark, which is similar to a dba but guarantees that you're the only Fantasia Ferret Farm in the country.

You can do a trademark search and registration on your own with guidance from the U.S. Trademark and Patent Office, or you can hire an attorney or a trademark search firm. If you decide to do it yourself, you can contact the U.S. Patent and Trademark Office at www.uspto.gov.

with. And you have to choose one. The Internal Revenue Service, or IRS, which makes sure you pay your annual taxes, insists that you have a specific structure. You can decide on a *sole proprietorship*, a *partnership* or a *corporation*. Many small businesses choose the first option, the sole proprietorship, because it's the least complicated and the least expensive. If you decide to go this route, you can switch to another format later on if you like.

But before we get ahead of ourselves, let's check out the pluses and minuses of each:

◄ The Soul Proprietorship ►

The sole proprietorship is the simplest structure, and as its name implies, it usually consists of one person—the owner who pours heart and soul into the business, monitoring its growth and making it work. All you have to do to be officially counted as a sole proprietor is to file your fictitious business name or dba. So it's fairly inexpensive—which is a plus.

Another plus is your tax *consequence*, or payments. The IRS can be extremely demanding when it comes to taxes. In some business structures you have to pay taxes on the money your company earns and then pay them again on the same money because the IRS counts it as your personal income as well as your company's income. As a sole proprietor, however, you get off pretty easily. You only get taxed once.

A third plus to the sole proprietorship is that since you're the only owner, you call the shots. You get to make all the decisions, and you don't have to consult with anyone unless you want to.

The minus of this business structure is that you're fully responsible for everything that has to do with your company. If Choo Choo Charlie's Collectibles racks up thousands of dollars in debts, the creditors can come after you. They have to go through a lengthy court routine to do so, but they can take your savings, your car, your house or your inventory.

If a customer decides to sue Choo Choo Charlie's Collectibles because he tripped over a train in your shop and conked his head, you're the one who'll face the music because you are Choo Choo Charlie. And again, that customer will have to take you to court, but if he wins, he can take everything.

◄ Howdy, Pardnership ►

If you go into business with a friend or family member, you might want to consider structuring your company as a partnership. Partnerships come in two flavors, *general* and *limited*. A general partnership is pretty much like a sole proprietorship, except, of course, that there's more than one of you. Both (or all, if there's more than two) partners manage the company, making decisions and calling the shots. You might divide the labor so that one partner handles the creative end, like designing Web sites, and the other handles the business end, like finding customers and paying the bills. That's up to the partners. The IRS doesn't care who does what.

When tax time rolls around, both partners pay only once—just like in a sole proprietorship. That's a plus. And if anybody decides to sue because of unpaid debts or because they got conked on the head, both partners are equally responsible. That's a minus.

A *limited partnership* consists of general and limited partners. The general partners run the company, making all the creative and management decisions, paying the bills and sweeping the floors or whatever is necessary to keep the company going.

Hot Tip

Most states require you to pay annual taxes, just like the IRS does. Make sure you find out if yours does well before April 15—tax deadline day—rolls around!

In The Security Zone

Robert Sek is the mastermind behind Austin, Texas-based ID Enterprises, a thriving business that sells security badges and ID cards online—everything from the most basic styles to encoded and holographic models. Now 21, Robert began researching his company at age 17 and threw open his "virtual" doors two years later. He quickly discovered that all the planning had been worth it.

"We attended a convention in Las Vegas and got a lot of publicity out of that," Robert says. "People in the industry didn't have anyone to go to for this type of product. They had to create everything for themselves for a convention or expo. So it's basically within the loop and just kind of caught on like fire.

"The unique thing about the company is that I did zero advertising and zero marketing. The company grew exponentially. At first it was really slow. Then through word-of-mouth it became pretty successful and pretty well-known." So much so that the University of Texas student keeps nine independent contractors busy turning out products.

"**People** in the industry didn't have anyone to go to for this type of product. They had to create everything for themselves for a convention or expo. So it's basically within the loop and just kind of caught on like fire."

Robert structured ID Enterprises as a sole proprietorship, which gives him the freedom to move on when he's ready without having to consult partners or shareholders. He's temporarily taken down his Web site while he prepares to sell the company to some of his employees. Why? "I'm working on some really big ventures now that are taking some of my time away," he explains.

But don't think the security badge star has turned up his nose at his mega-successful company or what it took to get there. Thanks to his business, Robert says, he was able to buy a car and a condo. "Three years ago, I didn't have those," he says. "It's important to stop and look back and remember where I was."

Photo Courtesy: ID Enterprises

···a taxing matter····

It's a fact of life that everybody pays taxes and that everybody hates to do it. Most people consider paying taxes to the federal government—the IRS—as about the same as paying money to a medieval lord so he doesn't chop your head off. They think of it as hard-earned money taken out of their pockets for no good reason.

The money you pay as taxes actually goes toward lots of programs the federal government provides: highway repairs and improvements, housing for seniors and the poor, military equipment and personnel to defend the country, funding for arts programs, and much, much more. Taxes are basically the same thing as if you paid your parents an allowance every year that went toward paying for your house, the family car, vacations and electric bills.

It can get very complicated but on a basic level, individuals and companies pay different tax rates, depending on how much they earn. People with small incomes pay a smaller percentage of their earnings than people with large incomes.

It's important to pay your taxes. If you don't, you won't lose your head, but you will pay stiff penalties. And the IRS, like Dudley Do-Right, always gets its man.

The limited partners are investors—they put up some of the money to get the company started and share in the profits—but they don't have any control over operations. And they don't have the same liabilities as the general partners.

Take a close look at the opening credits next time you go to the movies. Motion pictures—which cost millions to make—are often funded through limited partnerships. Unless you're making a big-budget film, you should steer clear of limited partnerships. You have to file all sorts of legal documents and do lots of other paperwork that's not fun—and it's easier and cleaner to draw up a general partnership.

◄ Going Corporate ►

If you don't want to worry about the financial and legal consequences of a sole proprietorship or a partnership, you might want to consider forming a corporation. You don't have to do it immediately—in fact, you can't legally do so until you're 18 without your parents' co-signing the papers. But you can go this route—just as Elise Macmillan of The Chocolate Farm, her brother Evan of netINVENT and K-K Gregory of Wristies have done.

If and when you do choose to incorporate, you—as either a one-person company or with partners—file papers with the state that give you legal *incorporated* status. It takes time and money to incorporate, and you have to re-register (and pay another fee) every year. And it's complicated—you might want an attorney to decipher the rules and regulations.

But a corporation is an entity in its own right, completely separate from you. So if somebody decides to sue because the company owes thousands of dollars or they fell and conked their head, they can only go after

··· married to a monster ············

A partnership can be a magical relationship that gives birth to a terrific company. Or it can be like being married to Frankenstein's monster (or his monster bride). Some would-be entrepreneurs strive for a partnership because they think running a business will be easier if they have help. That's not always true.

In a partnership, like in a marriage, both partners must do their share to keep things going. They need to have the same vision or be able to come to an agreement if things differ. It's OK if one partner is a creative dreamer who invents terrific products but can't add even with a calculator and the other is a die-hard accounting whiz with no imagination—as long as their styles mesh. But if one wants to funnel all the profits into the first hamburger joint on Jupiter and the other insists on using it to add an outdoor patio—or on paying herself so she can go on a Hawaiian vacation—the partnership is in trouble.

If you decide to form a partnership, make sure your partner is someone you can work with over the long haul. Talk about your ideas for the company, both large and small. Decide who has what responsibilities. Then draw up a partnership agreement that details how much money each partner will contribute, how and when you'll distribute earnings, and what each person's responsibilities are. You should also explain what happens to the company and the profits if one or both of you decides to bow out, and who—like a teacher or other mentor—will act as a mediator, or dispute settler, if you can't come to an agreement on certain matters.

the corporation's assets and not yours. Your savings are safe. Another plus to the corporation is that it can sell *stock*—shares in the company—to raise money.

There are several kinds of corporations, including *S corporations* and *LLCs*, or *limited liability corporations*, that give you various tax options—you should consult an accountant for advice on the one that's best for you.

Contract Smarts

While you're setting up the structure of your business, you should also consider consulting an attorney to help you get contract smart. "You might have an attorney draw up some basic contracts," says Jason Ryan Dorsey, whose company, Golden Ladder Productions, publishes books

stock smarts

Selling stock is a complicated step, for which you'll need an attorney, but here's basically how it works: You decide you need money to finance your business, so you offer 100 shares in your company at $10 each. Each person who buys a share is actually buying a $1/100$th ownership in your company and is now called a shareholder or stockholder. Along with the share, each stockholder gets one vote at stockholder's meetings. If your brother buys one share, he gets one vote. If your neighbor buys 10 shares, she gets 10 votes. You get $10 for each share you sell.

The main reason people buy stocks is not for the votes but for the money they might make later. Investors hope that your company will become so successful that your stock will rise in popularity—and in value. That $10 share they bought yesterday might be worth $50 or even $100 next year, or in 10 years. They can then sell their stock for a tidy profit or keep it as a sort of savings account.

When a company makes a certain amount of money, it pays some of it back to the shareholders in the form of dividends. You might, for example, pay $1 for each share. Your brother will get a check for $1 and your neighbor, with 10 shares, would get $10. You, of course, get a company people believe in and the money to finance your business—which will make you more money.

and training materials. "I learned that the hard way because I lost about $40,000 signing the wrong kinds of contracts.

"So we sat down with an attorney and paid him for half an hour and he showed us about contracts," Jason explains. "It's so important that you have a contract whether you clean someone's house or have a large business that deals in thousands of dollars every day. Contracts are part of the adult world, and they should be a part of all business worlds. That way no one gets mad. A contract is not a signal that you don't trust someone but a sign of respect. It's a sign that each of you agrees up front to do something for the other person.

"A contract should be simple, and it should be as detailed as possible specifically to what you're trying to do, what you each expect, and what's going to happen if the contract isn't fulfilled."

Government X-Files

OK, you've chosen a legal structure. You know all about paying those taxes to the IRS. But that's not all there is. The government can seem like a conspiracy of licenses to obtain, permits to file and other taxes to pay. And there's more than just a single government entity. Besides the feds, there are also city, county and state governments to deal with.

And it doesn't pay to ignore these sometimes mysterious entities. Like the IRS, local and state governments can get extremely cranky if you fail to follow the rules. So let's take them one at a time.

◄ In The Zone ►

You'll need to contact your city to get a business license, which gives you permission to operate within the city limits. You'll have to pay a fee—amounts vary among cities. And you'll come under the scrutiny of the city planning commission.

Cities and counties use *zoning* regulations, or *codes*, to plan what types of businesses can operate in which sections of town. This is to prevent things like an auto salvage yard setting up shop in the middle of a ritzy residential neighborhood or a rowdy bar or smelly manufacturing plant going in-between a park and a school.

When you file your application, the city planning or zoning department will check to make sure your area is zoned for the type of business you'll operate and that there are enough parking spaces to meet city codes.

living the good life

Martha Stewart is one of those celebrities that other people seem to either love or hate. Whichever way you feel about her, she's an entrepreneur extraordinaire. She learned gardening from her father when she was 3, cooking, baking and sewing from her mother and was taught the fine art of pie and cake baking from the retired bakers who lived next door in Nutley, New Jersey.

Armed with all these homemaking abilities, you might think Martha would jump right into the home arts. Instead, she started work as a model to help finance her college education and continued in TV commercials (for Breck shampoo, Clairol, Lifebuoy soap and yipes! Tareyton cigarettes) until her daughter was born in 1965.

Two years later, Martha started on her second career as a stockbroker. When hard times hit the stock market in 1973, she quit Wall Street and started restoring the historic farmhouse she still lives in. In 1976, she started her third career—a catering business—first with an old college friend and then on her own. In 10 years, the company—which Martha ran out of her farmhouse basement—had become a $1 million powerhouse.

But entrepreneurial Martha didn't stop there. Putting together everything she'd learned from all her careers and her childhood, she went on to open a retail store selling specialty foods and entertaining supplies; write books and articles on gardening and home arts; develop TV shows, CDs, a magazine, and a Web site; and sign on with Kmart for a special Martha Stewart line of products.

Today, shares in Martha Stewart Living Omnimedia Inc. are traded on the New York Stock Exchange—and her home arts history is a mega-multimedia success story.

Photo Courtesy: Martha Stewart Living Omnimedia

··the real thing·········

Every business needs a real accountant, not Mom or Dad, advises Jason Ryan Dorsey, who started his first business at age 8. "Call and tell them 'I'm 13 years old, I'm starting a business selling baseball cards [or whatever fits you]," Jason says. "I need an accountant, but I don't have much money. Can I come talk to you for 15 minutes?

"Most of it's pretty simple. Just having that accountant there to give you the right forms, tell you what taxes if any you're going to pay and help you put together a little bit of a budget is critical. All entrepreneurs should know about taxes because there's nothing worse than messing them up and the IRS letting you know that."

If your area isn't zoned for the type of business you have your heart set on, you'll have to apply for a *variance* or *conditional use permit*. This involves presenting your case before the planning commission in a sort of mini-courtroom drama. Variances can be easy to obtain as long as you can show that your business won't disrupt the character of the neighborhood.

If you plan to be homebased, you'll need to investigate your city's zoning ordinances carefully. Residential neighborhoods often have strict zoning regulations that forbid business use of the home. Not to worry, though—it's entirely possible to get a variance or conditional use permit and in many areas, people are becoming very supportive of homebased businesses.

◄ Permit Me ►

When you sell products as a retailer, you're required by law to add state and/or local taxes onto every sale you make. And then, of course, you're required to turn over those taxes you've collected to the state or local government. So before you open for business, you need to register to collect sales tax by applying for a sales license or permit. The amount of sales tax varies by state, county and city, so you'll need to

Hot Tip

"Because my business is Internet-based, there's no need to pay for rent and utilities outside of home," says Robert Sek. "I pondered having an office space, but there's no need to waste money on it—it wouldn't make my company more successful or productive."

check with the proper authorities to find out how much to charge your customers.

Many state and local governments let service businesses off the hook when it comes to sales tax. But some have recently changed their rules, so if you'll have a service business it's still important to check it out.

Don't think you can slip away without a permit. You may get away with it for a while, but the final outcome won't be pleasant. In some states, it's a criminal offense to sell without a license, and you can be held liable for any uncollected sales taxes if and when they catch you.

> **Don't think you can slip away without a permit. You may get away with it for a while, but the final outcome won't be pleasant.**

If you ship retail goodies out of state, like in a mail order business (which includes selling over the Net), be careful. Whether you collect sales tax or not depends on various factors like where you are and where you're sending your merchandise, so check with your accountant before you send.

As a bonus, some of this sales tax stuff can work to your advantage. When you apply for a resale license, you don't have to pay tax on materials, merchandise or supplies that you purchase wholesale to resell to your customers.

◀ To Your Health ▶

If you plan to sell food—either directly to customers as in a hot dog stand or catering company, or as a wholesaler—you'll need a county health department permit. This costs about $25 and varies depending on the size of the business and the amount and type of equipment you'll have. The health department will want to inspect your operation before it issues the permit, so make sure everything gleams.

◀ Counting On The County ▶

County governments often require the same types of licenses and permits as cities. If your business is outside the limits of any city or town, then these county permits apply to you. The good news? County regulations are frequently not as strict as city ones.

Techie Central

Some businesses require lots of equipment—others require nothing special at all. Your company's needs will depend on what type of business you go into and how you choose to operate. You might, for instance, start a lawn-care business with a really old-fashioned hand mower, or—like Shawn Himmelberger—you might decide to invest in a riding mower.

Although each company's needs will be different, there are some pieces of equipment every business will need sooner or later. We've provided a handy checklist (see page 75) of these items to help you determine what you already have on hand and what you may want to purchase—and how much you'll need to spend. This is important because figuring your start-up costs, including equipment, is an important part of launching any new business.

Die-hard shoppers may want to rush out and buy every item brand-spanking new, but remember—die-hard entrepreneurs are frugal. If you can use what you have until your company can afford to buy the newest model, that's OK. So now, checklist in hand, let's take a whirlwind virtual shopping spree.

Office Equipment

First up, let's take a look at your office equipment, the tools of the trade that will get your operation up and running and keep it going efficiently:

◀ Computer Star ▶

Every business should have a computer as soon as it can afford one. Your computer will be the star of your office setup and may well be your most important start-up purchase. If you already own a computer, you'll want to make sure it's capable of handling the tasks you'll assign it.

Your new computer should be a Pentium with a Windows 95 or Windows 98 operating system since this is what all but clunker found-at-garage-sale software packages are geared for. To run your software properly, you'll need 64MB to 128MB RAM, plus at least a 3GB hard drive, a CD-ROM drive, and a 56K modem.

You can expect to pay from $1,500 to $3,500 for a good name-brand computer with prices increasing as you add on goodies.

◀ Purring Printers ▶

A good printer is a must. You'll want to produce all sorts of materials—from advertising fliers to invoices, thank-you notes and contracts—and they all need to look polished and professional. The materials you produce will be a direct reflection of your company, so you need a printer that produces sharp, bold material.

Hot Tip

Monitors are often sold separately. You'll want an SVGA high resolution color display and a screen large enough to make long-term viewing comfortable. Remember that a few extra dollars spent up-front will save hours of squinting in the long haul. You can expect to dish out $200 and up for a solid midrange model.

Fortunately, really sharp printers are much less expensive now than ever before. You can purchase an LED, which virtually simulates the higher-ticket laser printer, or an inkjet, many of which can produce all the wonderful colors of commercial artwork. Color-capable models print more slowly than their black-and-white buddies, but if you'll be doing lots of marketing materials like brochures and newsletters, then color should be a consideration. You can expect to pay from $200 to $1,000 for a color inkjet or laser printer.

Hot Tip

Robert Sek's start-up costs were minimal because he spent a long time researching the special—and expensive—printers he needed for his ID card and security badge business. "What made it possible for me to buy a printer was the research I did," Robert says. "I found an inexpensive one that helped me start off. Then we turned a profit in one month and with that money, we upgraded to more sophisticated equipment. And now our equipment's top of the line."

◀ Soft On Software ▶

A dazzling array of software lines the shelves of most office supply stores, ready to help you perform every business task—design and print your own checks, develop professional-quality marketing materials, make mailing lists and labels, even act as your own attorney and accountant.

Most new computers come preloaded with all the software you'll need for basic office procedures. If yours doesn't or if you've lucked into a stripped-down hand-me-down, you may want to look into the following programs. You'll need a word processing program to write correspondence, contracts, sales reports and whatever strikes your fancy. A good basic program such as Microsoft Word or Corel WordPerfect goes for $60 to $220.

You may also want an accounting program such as QuickBooks or Microsoft Money to track your business finances. You can expect to pay $49 to $199 for your cyberspace checkbook.

For those polished marketing materials, you'll want a desktop publishing program, such as My Marketing Materials by My Software. It's user-friendly, with a lot of depth and a lot of breadth, multiple formats and multiple layouts. And it's customizable. You can expect to pay $29 to $49.

◀ Take A Message ▶

You also need someone to answer the phone. You won't be at your desk every minute, and a phone that goes unanswered is extremely unprofessional. A smart solution is voice mail, the phone company's version of the answering machine.

Like an answering machine, voice mail takes your messages when you're not in the office. If you have call waiting, a feature that discreetly beeps to announce an incoming call while you're already on the phone, and you choose not to answer that second call, voice mail will take a message for you.

Voice mail costs depend on your local phone company and the features you choose, but you can expect to pay in the range of $6 to $20 a month.

Hot Tip

Don't "enhance" your voice mail message with a cutesy script. It's not businesslike. Keep it simple. Give your business name—spoken clearly and carefully—and ask callers to leave a short message and a phone number. Thank them for calling and assure them that someone from your company will return their call as soon as possible.

◀ Phone Fun ▶

Now for the telephone itself. If you'll be homebased, you need to consider three things:

1. How many calls your business will probably receive
2. How many calls your family usually receives
3. How your family handles calls

If your business will be fairly low-key—you will have a few steady clients but not an unbroken stream of inquiries from potentials, or you will do most of your business on the Net—then you might consider starting out with your family's phone.

> **Customers who leave a message but don't hear from you will assume you don't care enough to respond, and that's very bad for business.**

If, however, your family is the gabby type, you'll want a separate line for your business. Otherwise, your customers will never get through to you.

Most teen entrepreneurs' families are very supportive and willing to help. But if no one in your family can remember to take or pass on a message, you'll definitely need your own line. Customers who leave a message but don't hear from you will assume you don't care enough to respond, and that's very bad for business.

If you decide to go for your own phone line, you should plan on

danger, will robinson

You should invest in a UPS, or uninterruptible power supply (not to be confused with UPS, the package service), for your computer system, especially if you live in an area where lightning or power surges are frequent occurrences. If you're a computer newbie, you may not realize that even a flicker of power loss can shut down your computer, causing it to forget all the data you've carefully entered during your current work session, or—the ultimate horror—fry your computer's brains entirely. With a UPS in your arsenal, you won't lose power to your system when the house power fails or flickers. Instead, the unit flashes red and sounds a warning, giving you ample time to safely shut down your computer.

If you'll be spending a lot of time on the Internet, you want to be sure that your UPS includes phone line protection. You can expect to pay $125 and up for one of these power pals.

spending $10 to $40 for a phone. Then you'll have the phone bill to consider. Costs depend on how many fun features you add to your telephone service and which local and long-distance carriers you choose. For the purpose of start-up budgeting, let's say you should allocate about $25 per line. You'll also need to add the phone company's installation fee, which should be in the range of $40. Check with your local phone company to determine exactly what costs are in your area.

◄ Serve And Protect ►

A surge protector safeguards your electronic equipment from power spikes during storms or outages. Your battery backup will double as a surge protector for your computer hard drive, or CPU, and monitor, but you'll want protection for those other valuable office allies, your printer and—if you have one—your fax machine. They don't need a battery backup because no data will be lost if the power goes out, and a surge protector will do the job for a lot less money. If you've got a fax machine, be sure the surge protector also defends its phone line. You can expect to pay in the range of $15 to $60.

Hot Tip

Even though your computer probably has an on-board calculator program, it helps to have a real calculator close at hand. You can do quick calculations without zipping around through cyberspace, and with the paper tape, you can check your work. Expect to pay less than $15 for a battery-operated model and $25 to $80 for a plug-in job.

◄ Official Furniture ►

Office furniture is an extremely optional item. It's important that your work environment is comfortable, but you don't need to buy a glitzy chrome-and-lucite desk, matching leather chair and sleek file cabinets. If you're homebased, it's perfectly acceptable to start off with an old door set on cinder blocks for a desk, an extra chair from the kitchen or garage, and an egg crate for your files.

And while we're talking files, don't forget that you'll need some office supplies, too. You probably have most of this stuff—like pens, pencils, stapler and scissors—on hand, either as school supplies or as items in the family junk drawer, so this is not a major expense. Take a look at the checklist on page 76 to double check your inventory.

◀ Just The Fax ▶

The fax machine is an optional item but one that you might want to consider when your business can afford it. Along with e-mail, it's the method of choice for communicating quickly and clearly with clients and suppliers. Many customers like to fax information back and forth, and as a savvy entrepreneur, you want to oblige. After all, the easier you make communications, the easier it will be for people to buy from you.

Shawn Gollatz bought a fax machine that doubles as a laser printer. "It's a very useful tool in sending out confirmations for jobs," the magician says. "As soon as I got done with a phone call requesting a show, I could fax a confirmation and a photo or some promotional information. Within 15 minutes of the phone call, customers could get the confirmation, sign it and fax it right back."

And don't forget faxing lunch orders to that deli down the street! Fax machines can be bought for $200.

Hot Tip

Never send a piece of paper out of your office unless you've kept a copy—if you or your customers have questions later, you'll know exactly what you sent. Print two of every document from your computer, keeping one as a file copy. Make copies of hand-written invoices and receipts with special two-part invoice and receipt books you buy at the office supply store.

▶▶ Business Brainstormer

The Teenage Entrepreneur's Office Checklist

Use this handy list as a shopping guide for equipping your office. It's been designed with the one-person home office in mind. If you've got partners, employees, or you just inherited a million dollars from a mysterious foundation with the stipulation that you spend at least half on office equipment, you may want to make modifications.

After you've done your shopping, fill in the purchase price next to each item, add up the total, and you'll have a head-start on figuring out your business start-up costs (which we'll get to in Chapter 5).

- ☑ Windows 98-based Pentium-class PC with SVGA Monitor, Modem, and CD-ROM $_____
- ❑ Laser or Inkjet Printer _____
- ❑ Software:
    Word Processing _____
    Desktop Publishing _____
    Accounting _____
- ❑ Phone with Voice Mail, or _____
- ❑ Answering Machine _____
- ❑ Uninterruptible Power Supply _____
- ❑ Surge Protector _____
- ☑ Calculator _____
- ❑ Office Supplies (See Mini-List) _____

Not On The Critical List:
- ❑ Fax Machine _____
- ❑ Copier _____
- ☑ Desk _____
- ☑ Desk Chair _____
- ❑ Filing Cabinet _____
- ❑ Bookcase _____

Total Office Equipment Expenditures $_____

▶▶ Business Brainstormer

The Office Supplies Mini-Shopping List

Computer/Copier/Fax Paper	$_____
Blank Business Cards	_____
Blank Letterhead Stationery	_____
Matching Envelopes	_____
File Folders	_____
Return Address Self-Stamper or Stickers	_____
Extra Printer Cartridge	_____
Mouse Pad	_____
Miscellaneous Office Supplies (Pencils, Paper Clips, Etc.)	_____
Extra Fax Cartridge	_____
Total Office Supplies Expenditures	$_____

Chapter Four

Get With The Plan

Every good entrepreneurial effort begins with a business plan—it helps you design your product or service and your company, spot potential pitfalls and entice investors. At first glance, it might seem daunting—like another version of the dreaded term paper—but it's extremely important. When you go to a bank or other investor and ask for funds, they'll immediately demand to see your business plan.

If you don't have one, you look unprofessional, unprepared and unworthy of their time, effort and money. But when you produce your business plan with a flourish, you look sharp, smart, professional and ready to be taken seriously.

This is your business baby, so it should be a fun and relatively painless process. "It's not really hard to do if you follow the models," says Ripe's Anna Levinson. "It's just writing down on paper the story of where your company's going and where you want to take it."

◀ The Plot Thickens ▶

So what exactly is a business plan? It describes your company goals in detail, the strategies you'll use to meet them, potential problems and how you'll solve them, the organizational structure of your business and the amount of money you'll need to finance it. Besides helping you get financing, a business plan helps you plot out every detail of your company so you know where you want to go and how you'll get there.

A business plan can be anywhere from five to 25 pages long, but it should always be neatly printed (from a computer) and be bound into some sort of folder—no paper clips or staples allowed.

Like those other legendary greats—the Seven Dwarfs and the Seven Wonders of the World—a great business plan has seven basic elements. Let's take them one at a time so you can see exactly how they work.

> A business plan helps you plot out every detail of your company so you know where you want to go and how you'll get there.

◀ Executive Suite ▶

The first section of your business plan is the executive summary. Although it comes first, it's actually the last section you write. This is because you don't find out all the details that go into it until you've written the rest of your plan. It's called a summary for a very good reason—it sums up in one page the essence of your business plan. You should include a bit of information on each section but not too much.

Hot Tip

When you are writing a business plan, see yourself as your own client. That's the advice of Kevin Colleran, the Internet marketing whiz. If you don't think you'd buy your product, chances are no one else will buy it, either.

The executive summary is sort of like the coming attractions at the movie theater. In the movies, the trailer gives you the flavor of the film: whether it's a comedy, romance or spooky thriller, what the story line is, and who the stars are. Its purpose is to spark your interest so you come back to see the movie as soon as it hits the theater.

In your business plan, the executive summary gives the reader the flavor of your business: what your product or service will be, how you'll sell it, how much money you plan to make, and how much you need to get started. Its purpose—like the movie trailer's—is to spark the readers' interest so they turn the page and read the rest of the plan.

Lenders and investors are deluged with business plans and hopeful businesspeople every day. A lot of those plans aren't very well thought out, either, making these people skeptical of entrepreneurs. Your business plan has to really shine. You can't assume the banker will see through confusion or sloppiness to what you think you might mean.

The elements you will want to briefly cover are:

> Business description
> Marketing strategies
> Competitive analysis
> Design and development plans
> Operations and management plans
> Your legal structure—sole proprietorship, partnership, corporation or LLC
> Business financials

If you'll be running a personal chef business, for instance, your executive summary might look like the sample on the following page.

Hot Tip

"The biggest thing I learned about a business plan is that most people don't read beyond the executive summary," says Jason Ryan Dorsey of Golden Ladder Productions. "If there's one part you're really going to make good, that's it."

◄ In The Spotlight ►

The second section of your business plan is the business description. Here's where you give your sales pitch and let your business shine. Be sure to include these elements:

> Describe your product or service and emphasize any unique features that set it apart from the rest.

> Explain how your product or service will get to your customers and describe—if necessary—whether you'll go wholesale or retail.

> Describe your target market and how your product or service will appeal to and help your customers.

> Explain how you came up with your business idea.

Executive Summary

On-Call Mom will provide a service—preparing home-cooked ready to heat and eat meals for busy families and professional people. The business will come to clients' homes once a week to cook five nights worth of dinners for them in their own kitchens. Dinners will include entrees, side dishes and desserts and will be designed around the clients' food preferences.

The business will attract customers through attractively designed fliers that feature a discount coupon. These fliers will be hung on doorknobs and distributed to offices targeted through market research. The business will also be featured in a publicity story in the local paper.

The business has several types of competition: one other personal chef service operating in greater Spudville, fast-food restaurants, pizza delivery services and supermarket deli sections. The business has developed strategies to give it an advantage over these competitors. The first is competitive pricing, and the second strategy is stressing the physical and psychological benefits of sitting down to a healthy, home-cooked meal each weeknight.

On-Call Mom is a partnership drawn up in June 2000. The two partners have extensive experience in family style cooking as well as in accounting and desktop publishing.

The business projects annual revenues of $7,500 in its first year of operation. It will require start-up costs of $744, which will go to purchase groceries, pots, pans and utensils, food storage containers, business cards and stationery, paper for fliers, and to fund a neighborhood grand opening, as well as to pay for the routine business start-up costs detailed in the chart on page 91.

▶ Tell what you'll charge customers for your product or service.

▶ Explain how much financing you need and why. What will you do with the money?

If you'll be running an auto detail business, for instance, here's how you might address these points:

▶ Vehicle Spa will provide a service—traveling to clients' homes and offices to wash, wax and pamper the family vehicle. Besides the usual clean and wax, the company will also shampoo carpets, clean upholstery and polish chrome and tires. This business is unique because customers don't have to take time away from home or work to get their cars detailed.

Hot Tip
Use your business name in your business plan. This stresses that the business is a real and serious entity.

▶ Vehicle Spa will travel to clients' homes or offices on a weekly, biweekly or monthly basis, depending on customers' needs.

▶ The target market is families where both parents work and professional people who work long hours. It will also target seniors who like to have a clean and shiny car but can't do the work themselves.

▶ The owner came up with the idea from observing how difficult it is for busy professional people to keep their vehicles looking sharp while working long hours.

▶ Vehicle Spa will charge clients $10 per hour.

▶ The business seeks start-up funds of $450. This will allow purchase of a wet-dry vacuum, mini-carpet shampooer, buffer/polisher and cleaning and polishing supplies. It will also pay for business cards and fliers, a business license and a grand opening party.

Hot Tip
Word everything in the third person—instead of "I will," put "The business will"—which is proper lingo for a business plan.

◀ Market Smarts ▶

The third section of your business plan is marketing strategies. Here's where you put to work all that terrific information you uncovered during your market research phase. Use it to demonstrate to your readers that you've got great customer potential, and then explain how you'll nab those customers.

sear-ious entrepreneur

Back in 1886, Richard Sears (left) was a railway station agent in a small town in Minnesota with an eye not only for inbound trains but

for entrepreneurship. When a local jeweler received a shipment of watches that he hadn't ordered, Sears bought them, sold them to other station agents, and made such a tidy profit that he ordered more. He did so well that he opened a watch company, which he soon moved to Chicago. There he advertised for a watchmaker, and Alvah Roebuck (below) answered the call.

That was the beginning of a partnership that became Sears, Roebuck and Co. in 1893. They made their name selling by mail order to rural America, and by 1895 the Sears catalog weighed in at a hefty 532 pages, crammed with everything a shopper could want, from shoes and buggies to fishing tackle and furniture. A few years later, you could even buy a house from the Sears catalog, which replaced the Bible as the most widely-read publication in America.

Today you can't buy the house, but you can buy just about anything else you could want from Sears, Roebuck—the company started by two guys in their 20s that means retail all over the United States and Canada.

The points you'll want to cover are:

▶ Your market's size and structure

▶ Your market's growth prospects, trends and sales potential

▶ Where and how you got your market research information

▶ The strategies you'll use to get paying customers

▶ The number of customers you expect in your first month and first year

For a computer tutor business, you might handle these issues like this:

▶ There are more than 100 million Internet users in the United States with Internet traffic doubling every 100 days, which means lots and lots of people who need to be taught to use the World Wide Web. In Spudville, approximately 1,063 computers have been purchased in the past year. In Computer Guru's immediate neighborhood, there are 50 families with computers, 18 single young professionals with computers and 43 businesses with at least one computer. These figures show a large, well-defined market for Computer Guru's services in the community and in the country as a whole.

▶ The number of computers in the United States has increased 200 percent in the last 10 years and 98 percent in Spudville, so this is a growing market. With more and more individuals, families and businesses buying and relying on computers, the potential for a business that provides computer training is strong.

> **Hot Tip**
>
> The more researched your marketing strategies are, the better chance you have of winning investors or a loan—and of setting yourself an easy-to-follow road map to success.

▶ Market research statistics were obtained from the U.S. Department of Commerce. The demographics for Spudville and the immediate neighborhood were compiled from focus groups and telephone surveys conducted by the business owner. This research indicates there is a strong desire for Computer Guru's service in the area.

▶ The business will attract customers through attractively designed fliers that feature a discount coupon. Fliers will be hung on doorknobs and be distributed to offices targeted through market research. The business will also be featured in a publicity story in the local paper.

▶ Computer Guru expects to attract three clients within the first month of operation and will have 36 clients within one year.

Write this section using the same rules you used for the Business Description section and include everything that you think presents a strong case for your business.

◀ Competitive Edge ▶

The fourth section of the business plan is your competitive analysis. Here's where you give readers the scoop on your competition—who they are and what they do, their strong points and their failings. This is part two of your marketing strategies section because it's where you explain how you handle the competition.

These are the elements you'll want to discuss:

▸ Who your competitors are

▸ Their strengths and weaknesses

▸ The strategies that give your company an advantage

▸ Any special weakness among the competition that you can exploit

As the owner of an interior landscape (indoor planting and plant care) business, you might handle this section like this:

▸ Inside Gardener has three types of competition: the other interior landscape service in Spudville, florist shops and garden centers.

▸ The strength of the other interior landscape service is that it has been operating for two years and has developed a steady customer base. Its weakness is that it's expensive, charging $25 per hour.

The strength of florists is that people are used to calling them when they want fresh flowers for a party or other event. The weakness to this competitor is that it's very expensive and its flowers don't last long. In contrast, Inside Gardener will provide flowers and greenery on a permanent basis.

The strength of garden centers is that their plants are inexpensive and that people are used to shopping at them. The weakness, however, is that it takes time and effort to choose and plant these materials and then keep them alive and healthy—time and effort many working people don't have. Also, most people don't feel they have the skills to keep plants growing.

▸ The business has developed strategies to give it an advantage over its competitors. The first is pricing. While the existing interior landscape service charges $25 per hour and up, Inside Gardener's prices start at $7 per hour. This makes it affordable and appealing to potential customers. Second, Inside Gardener will provide plants that improve indoor air quality. In today's health-conscious world, customers will perceive this as an added benefit.

▸ The chief weakness among the florist and garden center competition is that it doesn't come to clients' homes or offices to care for plants on a weekly basis and replace flowers on a seasonal basis. The chief weakness of the other indoor landscape business is its high price.

Once you start the ball rolling, you'll be surprised at how many ideas come to you—and how creatively you solve them. Just make sure you

Paging All Profits

Richard Williams wasn't planning a business when he took a trip with his dad to the Motorola pager repair center in Dallas. But inspiration struck while he was touring the facility. "I noticed it was taking an ungodly amount of time to turn out simple pagers and costing people a lot of money," he recalls.

The Austin, Texas, teen was 14 at the time. He knew he could do better—and did. Richard contracted with repair technicians to cure ailing pagers in a snappy three-day turnaround time while providing the same warranty as Motorola. He then convinced pager-sales companies whose employees carry pagers to buy his repair services.

And that was the birth of EBS (for Electronic Board Service), a company that operates in four states and employs from four to 15 certified pager technicians, depending on current workloads.

Richard, now 19 and a college student, also manages to incorporate being the national president of DECA, a program that teaches kids about marketing and entrepreneurship, into his schedule of school and successful business. He wrote a business plan for his company for a DECA competition—which he won.

Writing the business plan wasn't hard, Richard says, just time consuming. "I already knew about the industry and where I wanted to take my company," Richard explains. "The way I wrote it was that I had a company. Here's what I've accomplished; we have our own niche market, and it's growing. I would like to secure funds to advance to this level and develop these products."

Richard worked on his business plan on and off for about a month. "The hardest part is predicting your financial projections, making sure you have an accurate five-year projection," he says. "I see a lot of business plans, and I think one thing that really turns investors off is that entrepreneurs don't write in accurate figures." Instead, they try to make the financial picture look too pretty. "It's not unusual to be minus in your first year in business," Richard counsels. "Investors understand that."

> **"I see a lot** of business plans, and I think one thing that really turns investors off is that entrepreneurs don't write in accurate figures."

Photo Courtesy: EBS

make yourself clear to readers. Don't assume they'll know what you're talking about—spell it all out.

◄ Design Studio ►

The fifth section is design and development plans. If your product or service is already developed, you can skip this section. But if your business centers around the creation or major redesign of a product—anything from a can opener you operate with one hand to windshield wipers for reading glasses to a thermal dog blanket—then this section is essential.

You'll want to cover:

▶ Your design and materials, including diagrams or blueprints to show what your product will look like and how it will work.

▶ How you'll develop your product—make it in your garage workshop, for instance, or pay a manufacturer to build it.

We can't use the personal chef business here, so let's say you've designed a device that alerts kids when their parents are within a block of

·· patently inventive ·······

If you plan to base your company on an invention, you'll probably want to patent it. A patent is like a trademark for a mechanical or chemical device—anything from a new kind of light source to a bio-chemically engineered new gene to a toy to an automotive engine to a radical new floor mop. With a patent on your invention, no one else can make, use or sell your brainchild without your permission for 20 years. That gives you plenty of time to make money from it without competition from invention thieves.

It takes a long time to file a patent—up to two years—and you must have a working model on hand. You can't go with a mere idea for a time machine or teleportation device—you must have the actu-al gizmo in operating condition. You must have drawings or blue-prints showing how it's constructed and how it works to file with the U.S. Patent and Trademark Office. And you have to conduct a patent search to make sure nobody else has already invented what you thought was your brilliant idea.

Because filing a patent is so complicated, you'll need to hire a patent attorney to help you with the task. But it can be well worth the effort—just ask Thomas Edison.

tupper bucks

You know it as something you stick leftovers in, then stash in the fridge. But did you also know that Tupperware was the invention of Earl Tupper of Berlin, New Hampshire, and the cornerstone of a corporation worth $1 billion in 1999?

Mr. Tupper began experimenting with his revolutionary plastics in the 1930s, but when World War II hit, Tupper found himself manufacturing plastic gas mask parts instead of packagings for leftovers. When the war was over, Americans came home from the front to start families and began buying refrigerators and freezers like mad. Earl Tupper set himself the task of answering a major consumer need—how to store food in all those fancy new refrigerators and keep it fresh.

He came up with the magic formula and introduced his products into hardware and department stores in 1946. But people who had been raised with glass refrigerator containers didn't know how to burp the lid and seal the food, and Earl's products did not sell well. Then in the late 1940s, the Tupperware party idea hit the market, and sales soared.

One of Tupper's first Tupperware party ladies was a single mom named Brownie Wise, and she was so brilliant at sales that Earl brought her aboard the company to help build and refine direct sales—the system of selling directly to consumers instead of through stores. More than half a century later, Mr. Tupper's invention and his company are still going strong with a Tupperware party started every 2.2 seconds somewhere in the world, according to the company's most recent figures.

home (so you can hurry and clean up the house). Here's what this section might look like:

▶ The Parent Alert will consist of a magnetic mini-transmitter encased in a simulated extra key holder. This can be hidden under the car and will send a signal to a converted pocket beeper, thus alerting the kid.

▶ The product will be developed in the business owner's basement workshop.

◄ Operation: Management ►

Section six of your business plan concerns your operations and management plans. Here you explain how your company will function on a daily basis. You describe the qualifications and responsibilities of the management team and any support people you'll need and how everybody will be compensated, or paid. And you discuss the capital, or funds, you'll need to keep the company running.

The items you'll want to cover are:

▶ Your qualifications and those of any partners. This is the place to talk about any background or experience that makes you or your team especially perfect to handle your particular business.

▶ Who on your management team is responsible for what

▶ Any support staff or employees you might have

▶ Who gets paid how much and when

▶ How much working capital you need to keep your wheels turning

Here's what all this might look like for a pet valet (pet care) business:

▶ Partner Devon Silver has been caring for dogs and cats since the age of 6. Besides her own black Lab dog and two Himalayan cats, she helps out with her mom's cocker spaniel breeding business. She took animal care and dog-training classes at Spudville Community Learning Center and volunteers several hours a week at Pets 911 Veterinary Clinic.

Partner Dana Golden is also very experienced with pets. Since age 8, she has been fully responsible for two golden retrievers and a Shetland pony and helps care for her family's cockatoo and tropical fish. Dana also excels at everything to do with computers. She tracks her family's expenses with accounting software and uses her extensive skill in desktop publishing to produce cards and newsletters.

▶ Both Devon and Dana will work with pets and shop for supplies and ma-

Hot Tip

Service businesses are usually labor-intensive, meaning you can only do so much without hiring help because to earn money you have to put in hours of labor in a single day. You can only cook so many meals or mow so many lawns on your own. In a retail or wholesale business, however, you can sell dozens or hundreds of doohickeys-in-a-box on your own.

terials. Dana will keep the books, tracking expenses and income, and will put her considerable desktop publishing skills to work in designing and printing business cards and fliers. Devon will handle sales and marketing.

▶ Because the business is labor-intensive, the partners expect to take on independent contractors after they gain six clients. Each contractor will handle three clients and will be paid $7 per hour.

▶ All income will be split into thirds—one-third to Devon, one-third to Dana and one-third going back into the company to pay off loans and for company growth.

▶ Pet Assistant will need to have a minimum of $50 on hand to enable it to purchase supplies and materials.

What do you do if you don't have any background or experience? Get creative. You might, for instance, explain that you've done lots of research into the personal chef business and have an arsenal of cookbooks and videos at your disposal. Or that your aunt, who has a catering business, will be your on-call advisor. Or that your grandmother, who's a world-class cook, has taught you everything she knows.

> **Don't make things up, but think about how what you do know applies to your business. You might come up with more than you imagine.**

Don't make things up, but think about how what you do know applies to your business. You might come up with more than you imagine.

◀ Financial Factors ▶

You knew it was coming—the math part, where you present your financial information. If you're a math whiz and you like nothing better than tinkering with numbers, then section seven of your business plan will put you in arithmetic nirvana. If, however, you are among the math-phobic, take heart. It's not as dispiriting as it might appear at first glance.

Besides, it's important. Your financial statements are the nitty-gritty of your business plan. They show potential investors that your company is capable of earning a profit, and they paint a picture of how much it can earn over a given period of time.

But let's take it one step at a time. Here are the items you'll need to include:

1. Your start-up costs (see sample on page 91)

2. Twelve projected monthly income statements—one year's worth. If you will go for a large loan, you will also need to do one for each succeeding year. (Take a look at the sample in Chapter 7.)

We'll explore all these financials in depth in Chapter 7 and discover how really unintimidating they are. For now, let's look at why you (and your banker or investors) want them in your business plan.

◄ Crank Up Costs ►

Your start-up costs consist of everything you'll need to get your company up and running. For the personal chef business, these would include those first few batches of groceries; pots, pans and utensils; food storage containers; business cards and stationery; paper for fliers; a neighborhood grand opening; a separate telephone and phone service. The partners already have a computer and software, but if they didn't and they needed it, that price would have to be counted.

If you're opening a shop, you'll have to add in rent and a security deposit for your storefront and utilities like electricity and gas. If you'll need special equipment—anything from a cash register to a delivery truck to a riding lawn mower to a digital camera—you'll have to count those items as start-up costs, too. If you design a product to be manufactured by somebody else, you'll have to add that in the costs as well.

Other start-up costs can include paying your accountant and attorney for consultations on setting up the company, insurance like workers' compensation and money to buy refreshments at focus groups.

Hot Tip

The more sophisticated—and expensive—your business is, the more financials you'll need. A house-cleaning service that plans to go after a loan of $500 will probably do fine by detailing its start-up costs and one year of projected income statements. But a biotech firm or a expensive start-up e-commerce business that will go after financing of $500,000 or $1 million or more will need to show several years worth of projected income statements.

Take a look at the sample start-up costs below, then use the business brainstormer on page 92 to pencil in your own start-up expenses.

◄ Calculating The Risk ►

You can see why it's important to calculate your start-up costs before you dash headlong into business. Knowing what you will need upfront helps you decide: a) whether you really need it immediately and b) how you'll get the money to pay for it. Entrepreneur wanna-bes who don't plan ahead often find themselves in trouble before they've even opened for business because they run out of funds before they reach "go."

Cosmetics entrepreneurs Anna and Sarah Levinson stress the importance of pre-planning your start-up, something they learned the hard way.

"When we started, we were so excited to take the company on a larger scale, we ignored a lot of the costs it was going to take to do so," Anna says. "It should be thoroughly researched if you're going to bring a prod-

On-Call Mom

Start-up Costs

Licenses	$ 50
Phone	25
Pots, pans and utensils	60
Food storage containers	25
Initial groceries	200
Grand opening	100
Attorney services	125
Miscellaneous postage	12
Internet service	20
Stationery/office supplies	60
	$ 677
Miscellaneous expenses (Add roughly 10% of total)	67
Total Start-Up Costs	**$ 744**

Know what you will need upfront.

▶▶ Business Brainstormer

Start-Up Costs Work Sheet

Professional associations	$ _____
Office equipment and furniture	_____
Market research	_____
Software	_____
Licenses	_____
Phone	_____
Grand opening	_____
Attorney services	_____
Accounting services	_____
Miscellaneous postage	_____
Internet service	_____
Web site design and marketing	_____
Stationery/office supplies	_____
Insurance	_____
Subtotal	_____
Miscellaneous expenses (Add roughly 10% of total)	_____
Total Start-Up Costs	$ _____

Note: You may not need everything on this start-up work sheet—and you might need to pencil in other elements that don't appear here. Tailor the work sheet to your business.

uct to the market. For everything you think it's going to cost, you need to add on a good cushion of 10 percent."

◀ The Cash Generator ▶

After you have dealt with start-up necessities, you go on to the income statement, which spells out your company's ability to generate cash. It projects things like *revenue* (which is your earnings), expenses and the *cost of goods* (which is your materials), like the disposable food storage containers used in the personal chef business. An income statement shows investors—and you— exactly what money will go into your business as earnings and what will come out as expenses.

What's left is your profit—the money you've actually made.

How do you make up an income statement for a company you haven't even started that hasn't yet earned anything (or spent anything)? It's not that hard—in fact, it's actually fun. What you do is take advantage of all that research you did. You know how much you're going to charge customers, and you know how many customers you expect to have. So if you multiply one by the other, that's your income. In the personal chef business, for instance, you know that at the end of your first month you should have three clients who will pay you $200 per week and 3 x 200 is $600. Then you multiply $600 x 4.3 (because there are roughly 4.3 weeks in a month) and your monthly income is $2,580. Easy!

> An income statement shows investors—and you— exactly what money will go into your business as earnings and what will come out as expenses.

Hot Tip

"Find a business that will cost you very little," Kevin Colleran advises. "Then keep tweaking it until it's almost free. Maybe you can be an intern at an Internet company, for example, so you can save on Web site costs or trade your product for advertising with a newspaper. Cut back your costs and barter, barter, barter." (A barter is an exchange of products or services.)

◀ Cool Tool ▶

You'll handle expenses the same way. You know from your research what your costs will be. Just pencil them in. Then add up all your expenses, subtract them from your income, and there's your profit.

The thing that makes this exercise exciting is that you can tell from this one piece of paper—the income statement—whether your company has the potential to make money. If you discover, for instance, that your expenses will add up to more than your income, you can stomp on the brakes. Back up and decide if you'll need to charge more for your service or product. The whole thing works like the pieces to a jigsaw puzzle. From your market research, you'll know what people are likely to spend for your product or service.

If you can't charge more—you are already at the top of what customers will pay—then you'll have to figure out if you can cut down on expenses. If that doesn't work, add something else to your product or service to make it worth more without costing you more. Worst-case scenario: You decide there's no way this particular business can earn a profit and go on to something else.

But—and this is at least half the point of the business plan—you'll know before you've invested heart and soul (as well as time and money). The income statement is a cool tool.

Polishing The Plan

You've finished that business plan. It's smart, savvy and chock-full of realistic information. But you're not quite ready to call it a day (or night). Now you need to give it a final, affectionate polish by tending to these tips:

▶ **Spell-check central:** There's nothing that makes a document look quite as amateurish and unprofessional as misspellings and poor grammar. For starters, you can use the spelling and grammar functions on your computer's word processing program. But these things can sometimes misinterpret what you are trying to say and make matters worse, so you should also have a live human who is a spelling/grammar guru look over your business plan.

▶ **Title time:** Make a title page to go at the front of your business plan. It should feature your company name, your logo and slogan if you have them, and contact information: your name, address, phone number and e-mail address.

▶ **Contents crazy:** After the title page, put in a table of contents that lists each section of your business plan and what page it's found on. (Don't forget to number your pages!)

> There's nothing that makes a document look quite as amateurish and unprofessional as misspellings and poor grammar.

▶ **Margin Matters:** Another mark of the amateur is skimpy margins and hard to read text. Make your margins at least 1 inch all the way around and print the text in 11 or 12 point size. (The print on this page is 11 points.) If you make your print squishy and small, it's hard to read, and a banker with dozens of business plans to go through is liable to give up on it as contributing to bad eyesight and toss it in the garbage can. Also, don't use a cutesy font that's hard to read. Stick to something that looks business-like. Times New Roman is preferable. Remember, financiers don't appreciate trendy, cutting-edge or strange.

Hot Tip

Business plans, like businesses themselves, can and should change. Since your business plan is the blueprint for your company, keep revising it as you go along. When you make changes to your company, change the plan.

▶ **Paper perfection:** This is not the place to use that lime green copy paper left over from your mom's yard sale fliers. Use only top-quality white paper and print your business plan with a strong, sharp printer, not that shaky-looking antique that's been sitting in the basement for years. If you don't have a good printer, you can take your work on disk to a copy center like Kinko's for printing. Or your community college or library might have a computer center you can use.

▶ **Show and tell:** It never hurts to add extra material to back up your business plan. You might add copies of magazine or newspaper articles that illustrate the timeliness of your idea, charts or graphs, or copies of pertinent research studies. Make sure, however, that everything is neat, tidy and clearly labeled.

▶ **Wind it up:** Don't forget to wind it all up with a snazzy—but professional looking—binder. The kind with a clear, see-through cover and a plastic slider for binding always makes a sharp impression, but you can shop around your local office supply center for ideas.

▶▶ Business Brainstormer

Business Plan Checklist

Use this handy checklist to mark off the elements of your business plan. Put a check mark next to each item as you complete it, then go back and put a star next to each numbered section when you're done with it. Use the lines next to the elements to make notes on what you still need to research, calculate or project.

1. Executive Summary _____

Have you included:

❑ Business description_____

_____

❑ Marketing strategies_____

_____

❑ Competitive analysis_____

_____

❑ Design and development plans_____

_____

❑ Operations and management plans_____

_____

❑ Legal structure_____

_____

❑ Business financials_____

_____

2. Business Description _____

Have you described:

❑ Your product or service and any unique features that set it apart

_____

❑ How your product or service will get to your customers_____

_____

Continued on next page

Continued from previous page

❑ Whether you'll go wholesale or retail_____

_____

❑ How you devised your business idea (if appropriate)_____

_____

❑ What you'll charge your customers_____

_____

❑ How much financing you need and what you'll do with the money_____

_____

3. Marketing Strategies _____

Have you covered:

❑ Your market's size and structure_____

_____

❑ Your market's growth prospects, trends and sales potential_____

_____

_____

❑ Where and how you got your market research information_____

_____

❑ The information you'll use to get paying customers_____

_____

4. Competitive Analysis _____

Have you explained:

❑ Who your competitors are_____

_____

❑ Their strengths and weaknesses_____

_____

❑ The strategies that give your company an advantage_____

_____

❑ Any special weakness among the competition that you can exploit

_____

Continued on next page

5. **Design and Development Plans** _____

Have you included:

❑ Your design and materials, plus diagrams or blueprints_____

_____

❑ How you'll develop or manufacture your product_____

_____

_____

6. **Operations and Management Plans** _____

Have you discussed:

❑ Your qualifications and those of any partners_____

_____

❑ Your management team's responsibilities_____

_____

_____

❑ Any support staff or employees and what they'll do_____

_____

_____

❑ How you, your partners, staff or employees will be paid_____

_____

❑ Your working capital_____

_____

7. **Financials** _____

Have you included:

❑ Your start-up costs_____

_____

❑ A projected income statement_____

_____

Chapter Five

A Capital Idea!

I t's been said that you need money to make money. But how much you need depends on what sort of business you're starting. In this chapter we go behind the veil of the mighty money mystery and discover everything you ever or never knew that you wanted to know about working capital. We'll explore equity investments vs. loan financing, seek out all options for finding people willing to front you the money and take a stroll along what many feel is the easiest road to finding start-up funds. Besides all this, we'll explore networking, which—when mastered—has an almost mystical power to get you what you need to get going.

Mysteries Of Money

Do you need money to make money? In most cases, the answer to that question is yes. It depends, of course, on what kind of business you're starting and what resources you already have on hand. An entrepreneur who's planning a child-care service—going to clients' homes to supervise their kids—needs a lot less start-up money than one who's going to manufacture a programmable solar-powered lawn mower.

The child-care service might not need much more than the inborn talents of the business owner. It can handle its management operations (like paying bills, designing advertising and answering phone calls) from the owner's home, so it doesn't need to rent space. It doesn't need any special equipment because it's going to customers' homes where they have their own baby bottles, cribs and toys. It doesn't need employees because the entrepreneur can do the job alone. It's basically a no start-up cost business.

> **When you know what you'll need up front, you have fewer unpleasant surprises down the line.**

The solar-powered lawn mower business, on the other hand, will need a manufacturing plant, manufacturing equipment, materials to build the mower, employees to put the mower together, and a management staff to oversee them. You'll also need computers, copiers and other business equipment to keep everything running.

So to go back to our initial question—you don't need start-up money for the child-care business, but in the case of the solar-powered lawn mower operation, you do.

While we're at it, let's rethink that child-care business. You might need a lot more than you first imagined. What about business cards? How about fliers or brochures? Will you want to bring special equipment like arts and crafts supplies or exercise mats? What if you decide to get special child-care training to give your business extra credibility? That could be another expense. And what about the cost of your business license? How about transportation costs? You might have to take the bus if your clients don't live within walking distance.

All these things quickly add up to make a seemingly low-cost business like child care a rather costly start-up. That's why it's so important to calculate everything you can think of in terms of costs and expenses while you're in the planning stages of your business. When you know what you'll need up front, you have fewer unpleasant surprises down the line. You look smart and well-prepared in the eyes of potential investors, bettering your chances of winning that money.

Going With The Pig

Once you've got an idea of how much money, or *capital*, you'll need to start your company, you can start the hunt for funding. There are several options to choose from, all with their own pluses and minuses. You may decide to go with a bank, a nonprofit organization, the federal government, your community, a private investor, or the first choice of many newbies—pig power.

Some start-up entrepreneurs go with what might be the easiest source of cash: their own piggy banks. If you won't need a huge infusion of capital, this might be the option for you. Do you have a savings account you can tap? Are you expecting a birthday check from Great-Aunt Mildred? Have you socked away several years' worth of allowance under your mattress?

"I didn't need business loans. My parents raised me to have savings, and it all came from my pocket."

If none of these scenarios fits, you might still have assets you can turn into cash. If your older brother, for instance, has been coveting your baseball card collection, you might consider selling it to him—or to the highest bidder on an auction Web site like eBay—for that start-up money. You might have a savings bond your parents purchased when you were born that you can cash in. Or you might hold a garage sale and try to *liquidate* (which means turn into cash) all that stuff stashed in the nooks and crannies of your room and the garage—those old comic books, the bike you outgrew two summers ago, the guitar you never learned to play, and the *Baby-Sitters Club* books you inherited from your sister. (Sorry, you can't sell your sister along with them.)

Robert Sek, whose dotcom business projects revenue of $500,000 this year, started off with pig power. "I didn't need business loans," Robert says. "My parents raised me to have savings, and it all came from my pocket."

Shawn Gollatz, the magician, also used pig power to fuel his business. "Over the past few summers, before I made any money doing magic, I mowed lawns for my neighbors and their friends," he says. "I got a little money that way and used it to buy more magic tricks."

◀ Pluses And Minuses ▶

Using your own funds can be a good way to start out, for fairly obvious reasons. You don't owe anybody money, so you don't have to worry about paying it back. You don't have to give anybody shares in your company, so you own the whole thing and you don't have to share management decisions. These are the pluses.

The minuses are that even if you liquidate everything you own, including your bedroom furniture and all your clothes, you might not have enough to fund your business. So you'll have to go for some sort of financing anyway.

> Lots of entrepreneurs use a combination of financing options because it keeps you from putting all your monetary eggs in one basket.

There's nothing wrong with this. Lots of entrepreneurs use a combination of financing options and, in fact, many experts recommend doing just that because it keeps you from putting all your monetary eggs in one basket.

But if you sell your baseball card collection for $2,000 and then discover two months later that it would now be worth $3,000, you may regret your decision for years to come. On the other hand, if the $2,000 you get for your cards starts you off on a business that ultimately makes you $20,000, it might not be such a bad decision. You need to think out your strategy.

You need to think out your strategy.

If you're planning on tapping into your savings account or cashing out that savings bond, you should consult your parents. If they—and you—have counted on that money to pay for your college education, they might not be too pleased to see you snap it up for your business.

But most parents are supportive of entrepreneurial efforts. When you discuss your plans with them, they just might come up with an alternative. Which brings us to what is perhaps the most popular method of financing for small-business newbies: family and friends.

Lend Me Your Dough

At this point we need to take a break and explore the two types of financing out there: *debt* and *equity*. No matter who you borrow from, you'll use one of these two methods.

◄ A Debt Of Gratitude ►

Debt financing is the one you're probably the most familiar with. It's the one used when you take out a loan from the bank, when you borrow against a credit card or even when somebody borrows money from the mob. (You know, pay us back on Friday or we break your kneecaps.)

With debt financing, you borrow a sum of money and you agree to pay it back—a certain amount at a time—over a specified period. You might, for instance, borrow $1,000 and make monthly payments of $50 each for 20 months, or you might arrange to pay back $500 in six months and the other $500 after a year.

subway to the stars

In 1965, Fred Deluca (below, left) was 17 and struggling to earn enough money for college by working for minimum wage at a local hardware store in Bridgeport, Connecticut. At a backyard barbecue, a family friend and nuclear physicist, Dr. Peter Buck (below, right), suggested that Fred open a sandwich shop and started him off with a loan of $1,000.

The new eatery was called Pete's Super Submarines after Dr. Buck, who also became Fred's partner. Unfortunately, it was in an off-the-beaten track part of town, so sales were poor. Undaunted, the partners forged ahead, opening a second off-the-path store, which also did poorly. Ever optimistic, Fred and Dr. Buck opened a third shop located in a high-visibility area.

The third time was the charm. The new store—still in operation today—was a success. The company changed names and adopted an eye-popping yellow logo. Today, that first tiny eatery has exploded into more than 14,000 Subway sandwich stores in 71 countries.

Photo Courtesy: Subway

But it's not quite that simple. If banks and other lenders operated as we've just explained, they wouldn't make any money. If you lend your brother $10 and he pays you back $10, you still only have the original $10—and until he pays it back, you don't even have that. So lenders charge you *interest* for the privilege of borrowing their money.

Let's say you ask Buddy First National Bank for a $1,000 loan. The bank decides you're a safe bet, so it gives you the $1,000 at 10 percent interest and asks you to pay it back in one year. This means that you actually owe the bank $1,000—plus $55.04, which is the interest on your loan.

That's one reason people don't like borrowing from banks. You have to pay them more than what you borrowed. Another negative to borrowing from the bank is that if you *default* on the loan—your company goes belly-up and you can't come up with the loan payments—the bank can take over your assets, like your business equipment. And if you own any major assets like a store, a manufacturing plant or even a home, the bank can take them, too.

That's another reason people don't like borrowing from banks. But rather than robbing a bank, it's a viable option.

◀ An Equitable Arrangement ▶

Equity financing, on the other hand, doesn't require that you pay back the loan. And it doesn't charge a penny of interest. Instead, when you borrow capital in an equity arrangement, you give your investor a share in your company.

> **When you borrow capital in an equity arrangement, you give your investor a share in your company.**

Let's say you borrow that same $1,000, but this time you borrow it from your Uncle Milton in an equity arrangement. Uncle Milt thinks you have a sound business idea and he believes you are a smart young whippersnapper who'll go far. So he gives you the money. In exchange, you give him 10 percent of your company (or 5 percent or 12 percent or whatever—you and your investor can decide on any percentage you choose).

Now, while the bank charges you interest for the privilege of borrowing money and earns a tidy sum if you pay it back, Uncle Milt is taking a different sort of gamble. He's betting that your business will succeed and that he'll make money when it does. If in, say five years, your company shows annual profits of $100,000, you'll pay Uncle Milt $10,000 (10 percent)—which is a lot more than the original $1,000 he invested.

The downside of equity financing is the same as selling stock. If you give up enough equity, you run the risk of also giving up control of your company.

Friends And Family

Now back to our original topic—borrowing from friends and family. These people can be excellent sources of capital. They know you, they believe in you and they trust you—or at least they usually do. Some may be harder sells than others. Your grandmother's best friend might think of you chiefly as the person who painted her dog pink when you were 4 and has never forgiven you (neither has her dog). Your Uncle Roy might be the type who thinks any new idea is a load of hogwash until he has absolute, rock-solid proof to the contrary.

But these are not necessarily major negatives. You should present your business idea to friends and family the same way you would to the bank, including your business plan. If you can convince your grandmother's friend Sadie and your Uncle Roy, you'll know you have the right stuff. And after them, that dour banker won't be nearly as scary.

Once you've found the friends or relations willing to pitch in funds, it's time to put pen to paper. Just because you've got family ties is no reason to treat them any different than you would any other lender or investor. First, you'll have to decide whether you want a debt or an equity situation.

If you go with debt financing, you'll need to consider—and discuss—several factors.

> **Hot Tip**
>
> When you present your business idea to friends and relations, remember that you're a businessperson and they are potential investors who have the option to turn you down if they're not mad about your plan. Don't get your feelings hurt if the answer is no.

◄ Assuming The Worst ►

One decision is whether your loan will be *secured* or *unsecured*. If a loan is *secured*, it means the lender holds *title*, or ownership, to the property. If you use the bank's money, for instance, to buy that lawn mower manufacturing plant, the bank goes on record as owning the plant along with you. When you buy a car from a dealer using bank financing, the bank holds title to the car until you pay off the loan. Until you do, you can't sell the plant or the car unless: a) the bank agrees to let the buyer take over payments (which is called *assuming the loan*) or b) the bank gets paid off with money from the sale. If you owe $20,000 on your manufacturing plant and sell it for $30,000, the bank takes $20,000 of those funds to pay off your loan and you keep the balance of $10,000.

So if you borrow $1,000 from your Aunt Bea to buy a computer for your company and it's a secured loan, technically she owns the computer until you pay off the loan. The reason for a secured loan is that if you default and fail to pay it off, the bank (or Aunt Bea) holds the title to your property and can sell it to pay off your debt.

> **In an unsecured loan, you don't sign away title to your property. Your lender trusts you to pay the money without tying up your assets as a backup plan.**

In an *unsecured* loan, you don't sign away title to your property. Your lender trusts you to pay the money without tying up your assets as a backup plan.

◀ An Interesting Proposition ▶

Next, you'll want to decide what the interest rate will be, what your payments will be and when they'll be due. Most loans are written so that you make a payment once a month, and you pay interest as part of that monthly payment. Let's say you're borrowing that $1,000 from your aunt—to be paid back in a year—at 10 percent interest. Remember that by the time you've finished paying off the loan, you will actually have paid $1,055.04. That means you will give Aunt Bea $87.92 per month for 12 months.

If you borrow the same amount of money at 15 percent interest, your payments will be $90.26 per month, and you'll end up having paid a grand total of $1,083.12. So it behooves you to get the interest rate as low as Aunt Bea will go for.

A Ripe Idea For Profits

Sisters and business partners, Los Angeles-based Anna and Sarah Levinson (l.-r.) brewed their first batch of trendy nail polish at home when they were 14 and 17. "When my sister was 5, she started mixing colors together," says Anna, the older of the two. "About five years ago, the idea of how to make nail polish just popped into my head. I went home and started mixing them. We were just having fun creating all these colors and wearing them. We didn't think about marketing them at the time.

"Everywhere we went, people were complimenting our colors," Anna, now 23, recalls. Sarah, then in ninth grade, began selling their creations at school. It cost about a dollar to buy the empty bottles from beauty supply stores, so the duo decided to charge $5 for their dynamic designer polishes.

"My sister was studying business at Santa Monica City College," says Sarah, now 21. "She had a little more knowledge about how to make it a more professional thing. She had a friend who mentioned a small boutique. We just brought in our homemade samples. They never saw them before, and they wanted to sell them. At the time we wholesaled them for $5, and they sold them for $10."

Fast-forward six years and Anna and Sarah are the bosses of Ripe, one of the coolest cosmetic companies around with 70 shades of polish, 50 lipstick colors and annual revenue of $200,000 in 1999. The sisters' creations have been worn by Hollywood celebs on everything from the Emmy awards to "Beverly Hills 90210", are used on MTV in-studio productions, and have been written up in *Marie Claire* and *Elle* magazines.

Where did they get the financing to go Hollywood and beyond? "When we started, our mother and grandmother gave us a couple hundred here and there to get going," Anna says. "Then, I cashed in my graduation money and bought our first bulk amount of raw materials. After that, we cashed in the Disney stock we got when we were born. Once we started getting into more stores and our production was larger, our grandmother helped out with some investments. So it's been just family so far."

"I cashed in my graduation money. After that, we cashed in the Disney stock we got when we were born. Once we started getting into more stores, our grandmother helped out. So it's been just family so far."

Photo Courtesy: Ripe

If you're wondering where we got the monthly payments of $87.92 and $90.26 (which aren't exactly nice round numbers), we looked it up in a little book called a *mortgage payment table* that banks or title insurance companies will often give you for free. You can easily calculate this information by plugging in your loan amount, interest rate and the length of your loan on various Web sites like www.FinAid.org or www.youngbiz. com or with computer software programs like Inuit's Quicken.

> **You can calculate monthly payments by plugging in your loan amount, interest rate and the length of your loan on various Web sites.**

Why not just figure out the payments on your own? It's difficult because of the way interest-bearing loans are calculated. Each monthly payment is divided into *principal*, which is the actual amount you borrowed, and *interest*, which you already understand.

Where it gets complicated is that the exact amounts of principal and interest change each month. The principal changes because you're paying down the loan. (It makes sense: If you owe $1,000 and you make your first payment of $87.92 ($79.59 in principal and $8.33 in interest), you now only owe $920.41.

But the interest changes, because you only pay on the current principal. So the first month you're paying 10 percent interest on $1,000, but the second month you're only paying 10 percent of $920.41.

Unless you're a major math-aholic, this can lead to a massive headache. Especially if you have a loan that lasts—like most home loans—for up to 30 years. And that's why you use a loan calculator, which takes all this into account, evens everything up and figures out a nice payment that's the same every month.

If you don't already have a headache, take a look at an interest calculation page from a real business loan on page 111. You'll see that although the loan amount—$456.68—is the same every month, the principal and interest change each month as the balance—the amount you still owe—decreases.

◄ Write It Up ►

Once you and Aunt Bea have made all these decisions and agreed to them, it's time to put the whole thing in writing. Buy an inexpensive form

Year-To-Date Account Activity

Payment Due Date	Amount	Interest	Principal	Account Balance
				7,662.97
12-23-99	456.68	57.47	399.21	7,263.76
1-23-00	456.68	54.48	402.20	6,861.56
2-23-00	456.68	51.46	405.22	6,456.34
3-23-00	456.68	48.42	408.26	6,048.08
4-23-00	456.68	45.36	411.32	5,636.77
5-23-00	456.68	42.28	414.40	5,222.36
6-23-00	456.68	39.17	417.51	4,804.85
7-23-00	456.68	36.04	420.64	4,384.21
8-23-00	456.68	32.88	423.80	3,960.41
9-23-00	456.68	29.70	426.98	3,533.43
10-23-00	456.68	26.50	430.18	3,103.25
11-23-00	456.68	23.27	433.41	2,669.84

···keep in touch···

OK, you've successfully negotiated a loan from Uncle Fred or Aunt Grace, filled out the paperwork and signed on the dotted line. But your job's not over. You need to establish a communications link with your lender and keep the lines open. When people lend you money—even if it's a debt and not an equity relationship—your business becomes their business. Let them share in all the excitement of a brand-new company that's going places.

This is not only fair, but it's also smart. When you stay in touch, keeping them informed of your progress and especially your successes, they'll be more inclined to fund another lend sometime in the future.

called an *Installment Loan Note* or *Promissory Note* (because you're *promising* to pay the loan in *installments* or periodic chunks) at your local office supply store. You just fill in the blanks, you and Aunt Bea sign and date it, and it's official. You can also take advantage of legal software like Family Lawyer by Parsons Technology, which lets you be your own attorney and design your own simple loan documents.

You Can Bank On It

Let's say you've exhausted the list of friends and family you can borrow money from. You may have negotiated debt or equity loans with several people, but you still need more capital. Or maybe nobody you know has a dime to spare. Or they're all backward-thinking sticks-in-the-mud who don't recognize your business brainstorm is worth investing in.

In any case, it's time to move on to a different sort of lender—the bank. Let's say right up front that bankers can be the biggest sticks-in-the-mud in the known world. Their first, second and last instinct is to act conservatively. They're trained to think this way. Also, unlike your Uncle Milt or Aunt Grace or your best friend or next-door neighbor, they have to report to a higher authority: the bank loan committee, which is also made up of crusty, ultra-conservative types. If your bank loan officer takes a chance and you default, his superiors will have an extremely unpleasant fit, which may include firing him. Unless he's particularly brave, he doesn't even dare suggest that the bank loan you money unless he's got your success written in blood.

This is not to say that a bank loan is impossible—just that as an entrepreneur, and particularly a teenage entrepreneur, you have to work five times as hard as an adult businessperson with a proven track record to win that loan. (Even when you *are* an adult business tycoon with proven skills, a bank loan can be difficult to get.)

Shawn Himmelberger, the landscaper, went to the bank for a loan on a new truck for his company. "I didn't have any credit." Shawn says. "I always paid for everything in cash, so they didn't want to give it to me." To solve the problem, the Pennsylvania teen asked his grandmother to co-sign on the loan. He also had to show the bank his income and expense records to assure them he could afford the truck.

Shawn won the loan, bought the truck—which brought in more business—and forged a good relationship with the bank. Because of his terrific payment history, the bank later gave him a loan for a snow plow for his business.

> **As a teenage entrepreneur, you have to work five times as hard as an adult businessperson with a proven track record to win that loan.**

Hot Tip

Because you're not legally an adult until you're 18, you must have your parents co-sign the bank loan, which means they agree to honor the loan if you default.

◀ Grading Applications ▶

What happens after you fill out the loan application? You turn it in to your banker. Then you go home and wait. Like teachers grading term papers, bankers don't give you an answer on the spot. They spend hours poring over every element of your application. And then, even if they think your business sounds profitable, they have to take it to a *loan committee*. This is a weekly (more or less) meeting of bank bigwigs who take your loan

Hot Tip

Include your banker in events like your grand opening party and Christmas open house. Keep him informed and excited about how your business is doing.

Choose the bank you want as your loan partner carefully. If you already have a checking or savings account with a local bank, that's a good place to start. If your parents have been dealing with a particular bank for many years, that could be a good place to start, too.

A small community bank, like the Bank of Spudville, is generally a better place to start than a mega-player that's got branches nationwide like the Bank of America or Chase Manhattan because it has more of an interest in its own town.

Talk to other entrepreneurs in your area who have businesses similar to yours. Find out who funded their loans—a bank that's lent money to another successful hot dog stand may be receptive to yours. You can also pump your attorney and accountant for tips on approachable banks. Since they deal with other entrepreneurs, they may be able to make recommendations—and they'll probably even put in a good word for you as well.

officer's recommendation and your application and then pore over it some more before giving you the OK.

Touched By An Angel

Who do you turn to if the bank decides that your potential relationship is not a match made in heaven and in fact is not destined to be a match at all? How about an angel?

Once upon a time, an *angel* was an investor who backed big Broadway shows—the kind of person willing to take a chance on an unknown venture with exciting possibilities. Nowadays, an angel is anybody who invests his or her own money in an entrepreneur—which means he's still an individual willing to take a chance on an unknown venture with thrilling possibilities. Except instead of backing a big-budget musical, he's backing a start-up company like yours.

◀ Knocking On Heaven's Door ▶

Finding your own personal angel is not necessarily as staggering a feat as you might imagine. Instead of presenting yourself at the pearly gates and requesting an audience with people in sandals and white robes, you search out angels in your community.

Start by making a list of everybody you know who might qualify for those angel wings. This means not friends and family, but people you're acquainted with because of their professions or businesses. Try thinking along these lines:

Hot Tip

If you'll need mega-bucks— $500,000 to $1 million or even more— then shop for a venture capital lender. A good place to start is with the Angel Capital Electronic Network (ACE-Net) at ace-net.sr.unh.edu/pub.

▶ **Professionals:** These might include your doctor, dentist, orthodontist and your dog's veterinarian. Professional people usually have a fair amount of discretionary income (which means money they can spend on fun stuff instead of on necessities like food and housing).

▶ **Other businesspeople:** Tap into other successful businesspeople you know—the owner of a restaurant where your family often eats, the real estate agent who sold your family the house you live in, or maybe even your karate or swimming teacher.

▶ **Potential customers:** Future customers make good angels because it's in their best interest to get your business up and running. An overworked professional woman, for instance, might be interested in funding your personal chef service so that you'll be able to come to her rescue with home-cooked dinners. Or the owner of a boutique who's sure she can sell your handcrafted jewelry might be willing to fund the money to buy materials.

Hot Tip

Don't get discouraged in the search for funding, advises Jason Ryan Dorsey of Golden Ladder Productions. "We talked to five venture capitalists. Four said we were nuts, but one said, 'Wow, that's a concept.' That's what it takes. It's numbers—just going out there and consistently hitting that market and letting people know why it's going to help them or the people around them. If you do it enough, somebody's going to say, 'That sounds good. I want that.'"

▶ **Potential suppliers:** The condiment company man who plans to sell you dozens of jars of mustard and pickle relish every month has a strong interest in seeing your hot dog stand get off the ground. So he might be angel material as well.

When you find your potential angels, the next step is to convince them that your business is the perfect investment. The hidden bonus here is that angels—unlike the bank—are more likely to be motivated by the excitement of a new business than by its potential profits. Since many angels are themselves entrepreneurs, they often get a kick from seeing you succeed and knowing they played a part.

···▶ castles in the air ·············

As the son of a prominent real estate developer in New York City, Donald Trump—according to some people—had it made.

Instead of starting a new company, he took over his father's business—his first "big" deal (with Dad's help) was in 1968 when he was 22. But Donald wasn't a lazy heir—with entrepreneurship in his bones, he set out to build his own real estate empire. By the end of the 1980s, he had bought or built more than a dozen glitzy properties (almost all named after himself) including the Trump Tower, Trump Palace, Trump Plaza and the Taj Mahal, a mega-palatial casino in Atlantic City, New Jersey, and his very own airline, the Trump Shuttle.

Although he had started out with his dad's money, it only went so far. Donald had to borrow—heavily—to build his castles. He could have sold stock in his enterprises to finance new ventures, but he didn't want to give up a single share of his kingdom. So he kept on borrowing and living the life of a glam celebrity. Getting lenders to make loans wasn't hard because of his golden reputation.

But when the economy took a nose dive going into the 1990s, Donald discovered he couldn't make all those loan payments. The banks forced him to sell his airline and some casinos, and he almost went bankrupt. His money problems were big news on TV, newspapers and magazines, and suddenly he didn't look quite so princely.

But there's a happy ending to the story. Like all true entrepreneurs, Donald Trump bounced back. He voluntarily sold off other properties to pay back debt, got his loans under control, and today is again a glamorous mega-millionaire celebrity businessman.

Helping Hands

As a teen, you might have a harder time getting a bank loan than some adults. But you've also got a big advantage no adult can tap into—teen organizations. There are several associations out there designed specifically to give teens (and some younger kids, too) financial help getting started in business. Even better, these groups provide all sorts of professional advice and support along with the money, which can be in the form of a loan or a *grant* (money given for a specific purpose that doesn't have to be repaid).

You really owe it to yourself to check into them. "A lot of people are not aware of how many youth groups there are in a city, especially a major one," advises Donna Sayer of DJ's Catering. "That's what they're funded for. They are there to help you. Once you've taken advantage of that, it's a really great experience."

One such organization is Youth Venture, which helped Jason Upshaw open Second Gear Bicycles. Youth Venture requires that your business benefit your community in some way. Then it helps you write a business plan, provides grants and/or loans and connects you with businesspeople in your community who are on-call to answer your questions. And, says Todd DeAngelis, a program director in Boston, once you become a Youth Venturer, you're a member forever—if you want to be.

NFTE, which is pronounced "nifty" and is short for the National Foundation for Teaching Entrepreneurship, is another terrific teen organization. NFTE provides not only business training but also offers business plan competitions that are well worth entering.

"Contact organizations like NFTE and ask when they're having their next competition," urges Donna Sayers. "Basically, all you need is a business plan. Be able to produce it, show that your business would work, how it would profit, how much money would go into it, and explain why you want to start the business. Just simply try."

Hot Tip

You can find teen organizations in lots of places. "Look in different entrepreneur magazines," advises Donna Sayers, who knows just where to find help—she received $500 from an entrepreneurship program at Columbia University and won another $500 from a teen entrepreneur competition sponsored by Fleet Bank.

Donna knows what she's talking about. She's entered—and won—business competitions. "Sometimes, the prize is a trip to New York or other cities, and you get money to put toward your business or toward college," she says. "NFTE has some great competitions; Kidsway has some competitions as well. Most are nationwide."

You'll find a list of teen organizations in the resource section of this book, along with all the information you need to contact them. So go for it!

The Power Of Networking

There's an incredibly powerful tool available to help you search out angels and other lenders, seek clients and customers, find suppliers and other vendors, and just about any other business-related person you might desire. What is this fantastic tool? It's called *networking*.

When you network, you get out into your community and actively work to meet people and tell them about your business. This is not standing on the street corner, tripping people as they pass by, and forcing your flier into their hands. It's making a habit of introducing yourself and your company in every possible appropriate situation.

> When you network, you get out into your community and actively work to meet people and tell them about your business.

When you pop into the hair salon for a trim, for instance, tell the stylist about your Parents Night Out child-care service and explain that you would be delighted to have her as a client if she's got kids. Ask her to pass the word to her customers and co-workers. Be sure to give her your business card—if you don't, how will she or the people she tells get in touch with you?

Also, make it a point to tell everybody you meet while walking your dog, shopping at the mall or supermarket, going out to eat, or doing research at your public library. That's also a terrific way to use networking to find customers.

···the club·········

Most communities have a variety of networking clubs or groups who meet weekly or monthly for the express purpose of exchanging contacts. Some are private organizations and others are city-sponsored like the local chamber of commerce. You usually pay dues to belong and you gather—frequently over breakfast—to tell the other members about your business, hand out your cards, and find out how you can help—or be helped—in matters like finding customers, financing or suppliers.

Plus, you get to practice networking. Groups often host guest speakers who provide information of interest to entrepreneurs (like insurance, taxes, computer innovations or motivational topics) and are good contacts themselves. And there are usually all sorts of newcomers floating around who can become good contacts and even good friends.

◄ Networking For Dollars ►

In this chapter, however, we're chiefly concerned with how networking helps you locate sources of capital rather than customers. It's not that difficult—you already practiced networking when you talked to professionals and other businesspeople in your search for an angel.

Now all you have to do is keep up the good work. Talk to people in businesses similar to yours to find out where they got financing. (An angel who's invested in an ice cream stand might be cool enough to invest in a hot dog stand—he's already shown an interest in food-related business.) Tell your parents' business associates about your financing hunt. If they're not interested, they may be able to refer you to someone who will be. And if the potential customers and suppliers you've already approached aren't financing fiends, they're certainly in the industry—and they probably have terrific contacts you might never find on your own.

Hot Tip

Take your business cards everywhere you go—to church or temple, the supermarket, to restaurants—even on walks with the dog.

▶▶ Business Brainstormer

Money Shopping

Use this work sheet to brainstorm possible financing sources:

1. How much money will you need? _____

2. What is your projected pay-back period? (Will you be able to pay back the money after your business takes on its first job, for instance, or will it take you several years?) _____

3. Do you prefer debt or equity financing? _____

4. Choose one or more of the following funding sources and answer the questions:

   ❑ Personal piggy bank

   a. Do you have enough savings to fund your start-up without dipping into don't-touch accounts like college? _____

   b. If not, do you have some of it? _____

   c. How much more do you need? _____ (People are often more apt to lend you money when you pitch in your own funds—they want to see that you believe in your company enough to invest your hard-earned dollars.)

   d. Can you—or do you want to—raise the capital on your own by mowing lawns or doing other odd jobs? _____

   ❑ Family and friends

   a. List everybody you can think of to approach with your business plan, from Aunt Jenny to Great-Uncle John to the people next door who've known you since you were 3—and don't forget your parents. _____

   _____

   _____

   _____

Continued on next page

❑ Romancing the bank

a. List banks in your area that work with teens. (You'll have to call or visit them first to check.)

_____

_____

_____

❑ Angel wings

a. List everybody you can think of who might make an angel for your business._____

_____

_____

_____

❑ Venture capitalists

a. Does your business need enough start-up money to interest a venture capitalist? (Remember this is the big stuff, like $500,000 more or less.)   ❑ Yes   ❑ No

b. If so, list potential venture capital firms you can approach.

_____

_____

_____

❑ Teen assistance

a. List the teen assistance organizations that might fit your business. Do your research to discover which ones operate in your area and which match you and your goals. Independent Means, for instance, focuses on girl power. (Sorry, guys.) Youth Venture looks for businesses that help their community.

_____

_____

_____

Chapter Six

Adventures In Advertising

The best business in the world isn't going to get very far if nobody knows about it. It doesn't matter whether you have a child-care service, a hot-dog stand, a personal chef business or the first programmable solar-powered lawn mower. If you don't attract customers to pay for your product or service, your business won't be successful.

You have to advertise. In this chapter we explore the many media you can use to achieve this goal, from newspapers to fliers to direct-mail to the Internet and beyond. We bypass radio and television because they're not the best places for SOHO businesses to advertise. Instead we uncover the secrets of publicity—which include starring on instead of advertising on radio and television—and we seek out the wonders of word-of-mouth.

Magic Media

Unless you've grown up in a hidden underground cave, far from the reaches of radio, TV, the Internet, newspapers, magazines, junk mail, advertising fliers left on doorsteps, billboards, posters or even those pieces of paper stapled to telephone poles with offers to trim your trees or help you lose weight, you probably know a fair amount about advertising.

Hot Tip

The first thing to do when you start your advertising campaign is to take a figurative step back. Revisit your market research and your business plan and evaluate—again—who your target market is and how you plan to attract them.

You know that it can be either entertaining or extremely annoying, that it can educate you about everything from the dangers of drunk driving to the delights of a new brand of chocolate bar, that it can motivate you to do something (like buy that pizza with 18 toppings) immediately, or leave you completely cold.

Obviously, you want your advertising to be entertaining, educational (about your product or service), and motivating. But how exactly do you accomplish these goals?

Taking A Flier

Fliers are probably the easiest and least expensive advertising tools you can use. Start off on a small scale by targeting the people in your immediate neighborhood. You can leave them on doorsteps, stick them on car windshields, tack them on bulletin boards, or hand them out as you *canvass*, or walk through, your area.

Even though fliers are short, sweet and cheap, they still require creativity and planning. The main goal is to get your message across— and you only have one page to do it in. Try these tips to make yours a winner:

▸ **Don't crowd me.** Keep it simple—as little information as you can put and still make your point. If you add too much type or too many graphics (like photos, drawings, designs and other doodads), it will look messy and unprofessional.

▸ **Bold is beautiful.** Use bold print and make it large, especially if you'll post your flier on a board where people will catch sight of it from a distance.

Hot Tip

Don't put fliers in mailboxes. The U.S. Postal Service gets very upset about this because mailboxes are legally supposed to be used only for stamped items.

▶ **Professional please.** Your flier should always look sharp and professional. Make sure it's computer-printed or very neatly hand-drawn and lettered.

▶ **Spell-check central revisited.** Remember to check and then have a trusted spelling and grammar guru recheck your work.

▶ **Contact!** Don't forget the bottom line—your contact information. Make sure to put your phone number, plus your address and e-mail address if these are pertinent, so customers can reach you.

Direct-Mail Dazzle

When you think of fliers, you usually think of using them in the way we just explored—leaving them on doorsteps or windshields or posting them on bulletin boards. But fliers can also be used in a direct-mail advertising campaign.

What exactly is direct mail? It's any sort of advertising that you send winging into the mailboxes of previous and potential clients, and it can take the form of sales letters, fliers, brochures, postcards or any other printed material you choose.

The best thing about direct-mail advertising is that it lets you reach people directly—the post office cheerfully delivers your message right into the mailbox of your potential customers.

You might send the same sort of simple flier we discussed earlier or a letter introducing yourself and describing your product or service, or a multipage brochure.

Which format should you use? Take a look at your market research and see what your competition uses and what's likely to appeal—as much or more—to your potential customers. Then experiment. We are going to talk here about brochures, but you can—and should—apply these same success secrets and tips to any other direct-mail piece you design.

> **The best thing about direct-mail advertising is that it lets you reach people directly.**

selling by the letter

A sales letter can be just as effective as a brochure. Some companies send one and not the other—some send both. Choose one based on your personal and company style as well as how many products or services you're offering. If you've got one or a few to offer, you can use either method effectively. But if you have lots of products, you can't effectively describe them all in a letter, so you'd go with a brochure—a sort of minicatalog.

When you write a sales letter, you use all the techniques you use for the brochure, but with a special twist. Write that letter as if you're writing directly to your potential customer and not as if you're mailing the same letter to a hundred or more people.

Take a look at the sample starting on page 127 for an idea of what a letter for a mail order sales product might look like. Yours, of course, should be tailored to your product or service and your target market. You might address it to parents of toddlers or to the presidents of million-dollar companies, to people who surf the Net or those who surf the big waves at Malibu.

◀ The Wow! Brochure ▶

A brochure is a sort of minicatalog. But while the typical glossy mail order catalog is packed with color photos (and is extremely expensive to produce), a brochure consists of a few simple pages. Use your brochure as a virtual display space for your products. You can also use your brochure to describe all the benefits of a service-oriented company, like your Parents Night Out child-care program.

When you design your brochure, use your imagination instead of your wallet. Choose a light-colored *card stock* (which is the weight of paper used for business cards) and one or two bold, professional colors for your text. Remember, a little bit of graphics goes a long way.

Design your brochure so that it's the tidy size of a No. 10 (business-sized) envelope when folded in thirds. Or try a hefty oversize that will make it stand out from all the other No. 10 envelopes in the mailbox.

A little bit of graphics goes a long way.

Chocoholic Central

Hi Susan!

I'd like to offer you a very special invitation. <u>And a free gift.</u>

I've chosen you to receive this offer because I know you value the little things that make life special for the ones you love—things like shiny red boxes tied with crisp organza ribbons and brimming with gifts you've made or purchased with care.

Imagine how special those gifts would be tucked inside a box handmade of the finest Belgian chocolate and embellished with marzipan flowers and edible gold leaf! Surprise them with that bauble from the jewelry counter in an eggplant, edible box that looks like a jewel itself. Tuck that practical handkerchief inside a magical chocolate confection. Or slip a heartfelt message inside that chocolate box.

Your family will swoon in delight. Your friends will wonder how you ever found these special gifts. And your business associates will remember you all year long.

Because I'm so anxious for you to try my chocolate boxes, I'm inviting you to choose any one from my selection of four chocolate boxes and receive it for 10% off! And when you order, I'll send you a rose-and-chocolate scented sachet to tuck into a drawer, in your car, or under your pillow for sweet dreams every night of the year!

I hope you'll take advantage of this special offer. <u>I can't offer it for long, but I can promise that you'll fall in love with these chocolate gems—and so will those cherished people you give them to.</u> (If you're not pleased for any reason, just send back the box in its special wrapping, and I'll cheerfully refund your money.)

Just fill out the enclosed reply form [see the sample on page 128] and pop it in the mail to me. Don't take too long! Because of the upcoming holidays, my offer must end December 1st.

Very best,

Arianna Arelson

Arianna Arelson

P.S. I've enclosed a page with some letters we've received from other customers like you who have given chocolate boxes in creative and heartwarming ways. Take a look!

123 Cocoa Court • Truffle Bay • FL • 30000 • (800) 555-4000 • www.chocoholic.com

Order Form/Reply Card

Yes! Send My Elegant Edible Chocolate Box Today!

Please mark the size you would like to receive:

		Quantity	Total Cost
❏ 4-inch by 4-inch square	$20.00	_____	_____
❏ 6-inch by 6-inch square	$28.00	_____	_____
❏ 8-inch by 8-inch square	$40.00	_____	_____
❏ 6-inch-diameter heart	$42.00	_____	_____
Florida Residents Add 6% Sales Tax			_____
Shipping & Handling			$3.95
Total			_____

Name_____

Address_____

City_____State_____ZIP_____

❏ Check   ❏ Visa   ❏ MasterCard   ❏ Discover   ❏ American Express

Card#_____Exp._____/_____

Signature_____
(as shown on card)

Remember, your order entitles you to a free decorative rose-and-chocolate-scented sachet!

Chocoholic Central

123 Cocoa Court • Truffle Bay • FL • 30000 • (800) 555-4000 • www.chocoholic.com

◀ The Hook ▶

If this sounds daunting, try reading all those direct-mail pieces that come to your mailbox. The best ones to study are the ones that pitch products or services similar to yours, but carefully examine all of them. What do they have in common? For one thing, they start off with something that immediately hooks your attention. Maybe it's a description of a product like chocolates "to die for." Maybe it's a description of the benefits of a service, like a winter trip to the sun and surf of the Bahamas.

Try the same approaches with your brochure. Experiment until you hit on something that sounds good and matches your niche.

If you've got testimonials, use them. These are short, positive comments from customers like "Our company sales tripled after Eight Legs Web Design put up our Internet site. –*Carl Smith, President, Dot-to-Dot Inc., Spudville.*" Or, "I get rave compliments every time I wear one of my Rosetta Stone bracelets. –*Lynette Jones, Potato City.*"

Testimonials lend credibility to your business, and they add another dimension to your brochure by showing that it's not just you who thinks your products or services are great—it's real people just like your potential customer.

◀ I Love Mailing Lists ▶

Hot Tip

If you use testimonials, they must be from real people who have given their permission. You can ask friends and customers for testimonials, but you can't invent them.

A winning brochure isn't all there is to a direct-mail campaign. There's also the mailing list—all those names and addresses you send your piece to. A mailing list can make or break a direct-mail campaign, and a good list can be worth more than double your ad budget.

You can target your audience more effectively with a mailing list than with any other advertising medium. You can choose Midwestern girls who've bought health and fitness magazines (if you're marketing aerobics

polo, anyone?

You've probably never heard of Ralph Lifshitz. But when you learn that Ralph changed his name in the mid-1950s and became Ralph Lauren, light dawns. Ralph's signature company, Polo Ralph Lauren, is known for its expensive, classy advertising as much as for its expensive, classy products.

And that's the genius of Ralph Lauren. As a designer, he founded Polo for men in 1968 and Ralph Lauren women's collection in 1971. Today, his brands include Chaps and Club Monaco, and the company designs and markets clothing, accessories, fragrances and home furnishings—and even has its own line of designer house paints. But what Ralph is selling as much as products is image—the soft-focus picture of elegant country house life.

Polo doesn't actually make any of its thousands of products itself—instead it watches over the work of scads of licensees (who pay for the privilege of sticking the Lauren name on their wares) as well as about 180 contract manufacturers in Asia and America.

Photo © Corbis Images/Mitchell Gerber

And although the company has gone public and sells stock on Wall Street, founder Ralph Lauren still controls 88.5 percent of the voting power—generating his own elegance.

clothing in the Midwest) or Northeastern families who buy marine equipment and make more than $50,000 per year (if you'll offer sailing classes in Maine).

The one-time rental fee for most lists runs from $100 to $150 per thousand names, and most list brokers insist you rent a minimum of 5,000 names. You'll also be charged extra fees for any *selects* or special qualifiers you might choose. (Instead of going with a broad band of teen musicians in the Pacific Northwest, for instance, you might choose teen *classical* musicians in the Pacific Northwest.)

Where exactly do you get your mailing lists?

▶ Rent them from any number of list brokers, which you'll find in your local Yellow Pages under "Advertising—Direct Mail" or within the pages of direct-marketing magazines like *Catalog Age* and *Target Marketing*.

▶ Rent or swap lists directly from your competition (yes! they'll often share).

▶ Rent directly from associations whose members fit your target market.

▶ Buy lists from a competitor who's gone out of business (doesn't happen too often but is worth keeping an eye out for).

▶ Build your own list from all the sources we explored in our market research chapter (and any more you can devise) and use it often.

Hot Tip

When you build your own list, you can use it as many times as you like for free. And you can rent it to other companies, earning you extra revenue without extra work.

The Golden Word

Although brochures and other direct-mail pieces can work wonders, they're not the only way to go. Some businesses don't use mailing lists at all, with the exception of their own in-house lists of present and previous clients. Instead, they rely on word-of-mouth referrals from other satisfied clients to win them new customers. In fact, most entrepreneurs will tell you that they get more business through word-of-mouth than through any other means.

Most entrepreneurs will tell you that they get more business through word-of-mouth than through any other means.

If this sounds simple, you are right. But with a catch. Like any other aspect of the business, you have to actively work at making those golden word-of-mouth contacts. Sitting home and hoping the phone will ring doesn't pay. Getting out in your community and letting people know about your business does.

"Word-of-mouth is the greatest asset young people have," says Jason Ryan Dorsey, who talks to thousands of kids per year during his speaking engagements. "We have a belief, a vision and a story. People want to support young people. If we let people know that, hey, we've got this product or service or idea, is there anyone you know who can help us or might be interested, then that word-of-mouth thing is huge.

"E-mail or fliers can work, but we find that getting face-to-face in front of a person works better. Let them see that you're 16 years old, and you've got this great idea."

Jason Upshaw agrees. "One of the most wonderful things about Second Gear," he says of his bike shop in Cambridge, Massachusetts, "is that we haven't done any advertising. Our word-of-mouth is very strong—we've got so much positive publicity

> "E-mail or fliers can work, but we find that getting face-to-face in front of a person works better. Let them see that you're 16 years old, and you've got this great idea."

thanks for the memories

Follow-up is a very important part of winning and keeping happy customers. "Do your best to provide long-lasting consumer relationships with letters and even birthday cards," advises magician Shawn Gollatz. "One of the things that helped me was following up after I did a show with a personal letter, making sure everything went OK and the customer was satisfied."

Kiera Kramer of Parties Perfect also follows up after gigs. "I like to send thank-you letters after big weddings for hiring us," the Southold, New York, teen says. "They usually give us good tips."

It's a smart way to let customers know you care about them—that you think of them as people rather than as paychecks—and it helps reinforce your image in their minds as somebody they would like to hire again.

through the years. We get mentioned here and there regularly, as if we've been around for 20 years."

Kiera Kramer also found that the golden word works like a charm. "Word-of-mouth was definitely the best advertising," she says. "I put cards at convenient places like the rental center where people get their catering things, at liquor stores, and at places where I thought people would buy food. I definitely got a lot of business from the rental place because people come back and tell them how wonderful we did and thank them for the recommendation. Then they take that to the next people and tell them this is a great business. They will talk it up—so it's really good."

Robo-Marketing

You don't need a company Web site any more than you have to develop a direct-mail campaign. But if you have a computer and you know how to design and update a Web site or you have a friend or relative who's a Web guru willing to help out, it's a smart move. An Internet site can act as your robotic (or maybe clone) marketing person, offering promotional materials to potential clients 24 hours per day, seven days per week. And you don't have to be anywhere near the office. People can read up on the products or services you have to offer, request brochures or other information and "converse" with you via e-mail even while you're out and about.

◄ No Spamming ►

People who shop the e-commerce way don't like hype. They expect to be informed and entertained, but they don't want to be electronically shouted at, patronized or pandered to. (Things you shouldn't do to your paper customers, either.) Sending requested e-mail updates is good business and fun interacting, but "spamming," or sending e-junk mail, is definitely poor Netiquette and will not win friends and influence cus-

Hot Tip

What's the best way to get hip on dotcom sites? Start visiting them all. Hang out where everyone hangs out. Then send e-mails to other dotcom entrepreneurs who share your market and ask if they want to swap advertising banners. Get listed with search engines, and get prepared for word-of-mouth to catch on like wildfire.

tomers. What will? The same elements that win you paper customers—honesty, integrity, fairness, service and respect. Show your Web customers they're important by how you treat them. Offer discounts, freebies and any other perks you can think up.

Try these tips for winning and keeping Internet mail order customers:

Show your Web customers they're important.

▶ **Give your customers easy access to you.** Don't force your customers to wade through page after page before finding your e-mail address and phone number.

▶ **Check and answer your e-mail on a daily basis.** Don't let virtual customers languish any more than you would phone or mail customers.

▶ **Update your site frequently.** If a product is sold out, let people know. This way they don't get frustrated drooling for something that's not available—and it shows them that your products are popular. They've got to move on these things!

▶ **Add new information frequently.** This helps you market new products as soon as you have them available and also keeps e-shoppers coming back for more. If your site stagnates with the same material, clients will get bored and stop visiting.

▶ **Don't frustrate customers** with a site that's slow or difficult to figure out. You'll quickly lose people this way. Keep your site user-friendly and easy to navigate.

▶ **Offer customers information and entertainment,** elements that will draw them in, hold their attention and make them feel you're a part of their world and they're a part of yours. Post articles of interest to your customers—the best landscaping plants for shady areas if you have a landscaping business or the new scoop on power beads if you're selling jewelry.

▶ **Go easy on the graphics.** Pictures add impact to your site, but if your customers have to wait endlessly to view your page because it's graphics-heavy, you're going to lose them. Make sure those photos are small enough to load quickly.

▶ **Check out competitors' sites,** just as you check out competitors' other advertising materials. Borrow the best of what they're doing, then do it better.

Read All Over

Newspaper and magazine ads—called *print ads* to distinguish them from TV and radio advertising—can be terrific vehicles for getting your message to your target market. Whether you use your local paper or a national magazine depends on your product or service and your target market.

If you'll have a lawn-care or personal-chef business targeted specifically to Spudville neighborhoods, for instance, it won't do you any good to advertise in *Seventeen* or *National Geographic*. The readership is way too broad—you can't aim just at Spudville residents. And advertising in national magazines is extremely expensive—as much as $1,750 for one ad to run one time—so you'd be wasting a lot of money. But an ad in the *Spudville Daily Record* newspaper could cost as little as $56, and you'd know your readership is in your target area.

> **Newspaper and magazine ads—called print ads—can be terrific vehicles for getting your message to your target market.**

But let's say you are selling a product like power bead bracelets and you plan to offer them on a mail order basis. In that case, you'd do better to advertise in a national magazine than in the local newspaper because you will have a much larger readership to draw from, which is what you need for mail order products.

Of course, magazine advertising isn't limited to mail order. You might use print ads to sell your solar-powered lawn mower or your child-care service or hot-dog stand if you've developed them into national chains.

Whether you choose magazines or newspapers, print ads come in one of two styles: *classified* and *display*. Let's start off with display ads, which usually feature some sort of graphics combined with the printed word and are found throughout a publication (as opposed to classifieds that consist solely of the printed word and are found only in the classified section). We'll concentrate on mail order ads since they're the easiest and least expensive for the newbie, but everything we'll explore applies to non-mail order ads as well.

◄ Vamp It Up ►

If you've done your homework and chosen a market niche you're familiar with and enjoy, you probably already know which publications will work for you—they're the ones your target audience reads and the ones you probably read, too. These are the best places to start because you already understand at least part of the demographics of their readers. If you're a vampire, and your target market is vampires, for instance, you probably know *Country Vampire*, *Vampire Today* and *Fashion Vamp* magazines.

Pick up those issues off your coffee table or night stand. Study them carefully. Will mail order do well here? Compare the number of "traditional" ads with the number of mail order ads. If mail order makes up a significant portion, you can figure that other mail order companies are experiencing success with the publication, which means it's a good place to be.

Hot Tip

While it's important to choose magazines (and mailing lists) geared toward your particular audience, it also pays to be creative. Sometimes you can do extremely well with an audience segment that doesn't at first appear to be the best choice. Men's colognes, for instance, sell well in women's magazines. Why? Women like to shop for their men.

Check for repeated ads featuring products similar to yours. If you're selling a carburetor tune-up kit, see who else is selling the same kind of kit or other auto maintenance merchandise. If all the other ads are for something entirely different, you probably don't want to advertise there, either. When you hit on a magazine with the "right" sorts of ads, head out to the library and skim through six months to a year of back issues. If you see that same ad repeated over and over again, it's because it's making money. And that's good—now you can give it some competition!

◄ Line Dancing ►

All direct-marketing ads follow one of two formats: the *one-step* or the *two-step*. (No, we're not talking about country-western line dancing.) The one-step ad encourages potential customers to order immediately, while the two-step ad introduces the product or catalog (step 1) and asks the prospect to contact you for more information, like a catalog or brochure (which you then send as step 2).

···dreaming of success ··········

If you were into beauty makeovers at the turn of the 20th century, you might well have been a fan of Madam CJ Walker, whose name meant health and beauty to a generation of African-American women. Madam Walker, the daughter of former slaves, was born Sarah Breedlove and orphaned at age 7, married at 14, and widowed with a daughter to support at 20. To make ends meet, she moved from the deep South to St. Louis and worked as a washerwoman.

In 1905, she moved to Denver, where she married Charles Joseph Walker, and the two went into business selling a scalp conditioner that Sarah invented, the formula for which she said was given to her by a big African man in a dream. Between the formula and her own genius for advertising and promotions, Sarah's dreams of entrepreneurial success came true.

Sarah traveled all over the South, selling her products door-to-door and giving lecture-demonstrations to promote her cosmetics, which grew so popular that she opened a school in Pittsburgh to train hair culturists. By 1910, Sarah had established a factory, hair and nail salon and another school in Indianapolis.

The hair culturists, known as "Walker Agents," were the forerunners of today's Avon ladies, selling the line of almost 20 hair and skin products and earning healthy revenues for themselves in the process. And Walker Agents weren't found just in the United States—they operated successfully in Central America and the Caribbean as well.

Sarah organized clubs and conventions for her agents, applauding and encouraging successful sales as well as political activism among African-Americans.

Today, Madam Walker's company is no longer in existence, but the theater center she built in Indianapolis is still operating, and her energetic advertising methods are still models of successful entrepreneurship.

Why would you want one type of ad instead of the other? Several reasons. You'd choose the one-step when:

▸ you're advertising one or a few products instead of an entire catalog.

▸ the product(s) can be easily described and understood.

▸ potential customers won't need further enticement or encouragement to purchase the product(s).

Take a look at the sample one-step display ad on page 139. Our hypothetical company, Chocoholic Central, isn't trying to cram every product in its catalog into one small ad—instead it's offering one product with simple variations, which are described with a few "brush strokes" of typescript. Part of the ad is an order form that the customer mails back to us with a check or credit card information. The middle of the order form says "Order Today In Time For The Holidays!" to further encourage that immediate order.

You should note that we've also encouraged telephone orders with a prominent toll-free number and given customers the option of ordering through the Internet with a Web site address.

◀ The Mail Order Two-Step ▶

So when do you use the two-step ad? When you want to:

▸ introduce a line of products or your catalog.

▸ sell products that can't be easily explained in a small ad.

▸ develop a list of interested prospects to send that expensive catalog to.

Check out the sample two-step display ad on page 140. Instead of advertising one particular product, it generates interest in Chocoholic Central's entire product line and entices the customer to order a catalog. And it's not free! We're asking customers to pay for the catalog. (We're also bribing them with a gift, but we'll talk about that in a minute.)

This method is particularly effective because you only send catalogs to people who have expressed an interest in your products. You know they are interested because: a) They've requested a catalog, and b) they've spent money to get that catalog. What a great way to develop your own mailing list!

Hot Tip

Most magazines work months ahead of the cover date, the date they appear on newsstands. So if you want an ad for Christmas goodies to come out in the December issue, you may have to submit your material as early as July.

One-Step Display Ad

Show Them How Really Special They Are!

**Why give them a gift in a plain cardboard box
when you can make the box a gift in itself?**

**Tuck that special something into one of our luscious Dark Belgian
chocolate boxes embellished with marzipan roses and edible gold leaf!**

Choose from one of four elegant, edible sizes:

		Quantity	Total Cost
4 inch x 4 inch square	$20.00	_____	_____
6 inch x 6 inch square	$28.00	_____	_____
8 inch x 8 inch square	$40.00	_____	_____
6 inch in diameter heart	$42.00	_____	_____
Florida Residents Add 6% Tax			_____
Shipping & Handling			$3.95
Total			_____

Order Today In Time For The Holidays!

Name_____

Address_____

City_____State_____ZIP_____

❑ Check   ❑ Visa   ❑ MasterCard   ❑ Discover   ❑ American Express

Card#_____Exp._____/_____

Signature_____

(as shown on card)

Or Call Us Toll-Free At (800) 555-4000 To Place Your Order!

And may all your dreams be sweet!

Chocoholic Central

123 Cocoa Court • Truffle Bay • FL • 30000 • (800) 555-4000 • www.chocoholic.com

Of course, you don't have to entice potential customers with a gift, as the sample ad does. You can give them a discount on their first purchase. Or you can advertise that your catalog is free. The choice is yours. Any way you go, it's still a two-step ad, and it still has the advantage of delivering built-in interest before you send off that expensive catalog or brochure.

The two-step ad is usually used in print media rather than electronic ones like radio, television and the Internet. And while it's traditionally used for high-ticket items that aren't easily described or won't sell without further encouragement (like swimming pools, sun rooms, furniture and fine art prints), it's also used for everything from antique roses to books, financial services and recipes.

Two-Step Display Ad

Show Them How Really Special They Are!

With elegant, edible gifts like our handmade boxes of luscious dark Belgian chocolate, our hazelnut chocolate hearts and more! All embellished with marzipan roses and edible gold leaf.

Order our 28-page catalog and we'll send you a free gift!

Just send $2.00 to:

Chocoholic Central

123 Cocoa Court
Truffle Bay, FL 30000
(800) 555-4000
www.chocoholic.com

And may all your dreams be sweet!

Anna and Sarah Levinson, the Ripe cosmetics team, don't have the budget for magazine advertising. But they've managed to get full-page magazine ads anyway. What's their secret?

One is bartering. If the magazine's doing a party, for instance, the sisters cheerfully hand over nail polish or lipstick to be used in the publication's promotional giveaway bags. In exchange, the magazine gives them advertising space.

Another technique the sisters use is developing a relationship with the magazine. If the publication has extra advertising space, it will occasionally pop in a Ripe ad for free. This works for the magazine as well as Anna and Sarah. A blank page looks bad but one with a slick ad shows other potential advertisers that the publication is in demand. These techniques work great with underground magazines, Anna cautions, but really large mainstream ones won't let you work the same deals.

Get Classified

The major appeal of classified ads is that they're far less expensive than display ads. Add to that the bonus of simplicity—there's no layout to design, no graphics to worry about, and no choice of fonts or type styles to obsess over. Add another bonus—defined interest. People who peck around in the classifieds are often there because they're looking for something in that particular section: lawn maintenance or child care or collectibles. So when they see your ad, they have an expressed interest in what you're selling. By contrast, people who see your display ad have generally just happened onto it; it was on the page they were reading, but they weren't specifically looking for what you're advertising.

Hot Tip

Local throwaway papers like the *Thrifty Nickel* or *Pennysaver*, which consist solely of ads, can be terrific places to advertise service businesses.

◄ Weed Out Words ►

You write a classified ad in basically the same way you write your direct-mail all in as few words as possible because you're charged by the word. Let's say you're advertising your house cleaning service in a throwaway paper. Here's what you do:

▶ **Your attention-getting headline:** "Let Us Do The Dirty Work!" This is more intriguing than "House-cleaning Service!" so people will read on to see what comes next. Magazines and newspapers will usually print your headline in bold at no extra charge, so remember to ask.

▶ **Your riveting copy:** Here's where you need to get your idea across in as few words as possible: "We clean house so you don't have to." We could say "We vacuum, dust, scrub bathrooms and wash floors," but this is a lot clunkier and uses a lot more words— and is therefore more expensive.

▶ **Your call to action:** This is where you tell your potential customer exactly what to do and when to take advantage of your offer: "Call today for our April-only Spring-Clean Special!" Notice that we've used the word "special" to tell customers they're getting a deal, and that we're motivating them by telling them if they don't act this month, they'll lose out.

▶ **Your phone number:** "The Squeaky Clean Team, 550-5555." This is one of the most important parts of the ad—don't leave it out!

Here's your ad in 27 simple words:

LET US DO THE DIRTY WORK!
We clean house so you don't have to.
Call today for our April-only
Spring-Clean Special!
The Squeak Clean Team, 550-5555.

Teen 'Zine Publisher

Sixteen-year-old Jasmine Jordan is the publisher of *Tools for Living* magazine, a bimonthly publication written by and for young people ages 13 to 19. "The basic themes are youth entrepreneurship and teen lifestyle," Jasmine says. "I created the magazine to publish young people's work. A lot of people love writing and they may not have adequate skills to send their work to a high-profile publisher and get published. I work with them so that no matter what their skills are, they can get published and feel good about themselves."

The Bronx, New York, teen started her business in 1996 at age 12. "I started with 50 magazines, and they sold out the first day. That cost about $300, an investment from my family. The magazine just started making money and growing on its own from there."

Tools for Living now has a circulation of 25,000, an impressive number for a small publication. Two thousand issues go to individual subscribers; the rest are bulk orders and donations from the publisher. Jasmine's first subscribers were members of her grandmother's church as well as people in her own and in her grandmother's neighborhoods. From there, the magazine took off on its own.

Jasmine also runs a clothing drive to collect and distribute business attire—everything from shoes to shirts to briefcases—to struggling inner-city entrepreneurs. Hand-in-hand with this venture, she operates the Working Teen Program. For a fee of $100 to $150 per person, she teaches newbie entrepreneurs the basics of business etiquette.

Jasmine promotes her programs through the best advertising source available to any entrepreneur—publicity. "I'm on television a lot," she says modestly. (She recently appeared on "The Montel Williams Show" as well as a local news station.) "A lot of people hear about me, so it's a lot of networking and word-of-mouth. That's great PR and free promotions."

Jasmine's advice for other teen entrepreneurs? "It's good to get involved with an entrepreneurship organization," she counsels. "They can help you and guide you. Don't let anyone get in your way or tell you that you can't do it because you can if you really want to. Just stay focused, and don't let anyone lead you astray."

> **"Don't** let anyone get in your way or tell you that you can't do it because you can if you really want to. Just stay focused, and don't let anyone lead you astray."

Public Relations Power

Public relations is another tool the smart entrepreneur takes advantage of whenever possible. It's like advertising in that it gets people to notice your company, but it works in a totally different way. When you advertise, you—in essence—brag. You tell customers and potential customers that your product or service is the best.

In public relations, however, you let other people tell your customers how terrific you are. This is even better than advertising when it's done properly. If you say that you have the best hot dogs in town, most people will respond with: "Of course you would say that. You're trying to sell them." But if people see a piece about your hot dogs on local television, and the reporter says your products are the hottest thing in Spudville, people think "Wow, it must be true!"

> **In public relations, you let other people tell your customers how terrific you are.**

Good public relations can accomplish two things:

1. It puts your company name out to people who may not otherwise have heard of you.

2. It keeps people who are already your customers thinking fondly of you and thus buying your product or service again and again.

In other words, PR is a terrific source of free advertising. Even better, there are all sorts of low-cost techniques you can use. Try some of the following:

▶ Local groups are always looking for guest speakers. Offer yourself on a free, or pro bono, basis to local associations or clubs that match your target audience. If you have a landscaping service, for instance, you can talk to women's clubs about flowers, men's clubs about the best way to keep your lawn green, the chamber of commerce and networking clubs about the ups and downs of being a young entrepreneur, and kids' clubs about keeping the Earth green. Just be sure to tailor your topic to your particular audience. When people hear your talk, they figure you must be an expert, and they're more likely to hire your company. Plus, you meet people—remember the power of networking and word-of-mouth.

- Join any organizations that match your target audience, and volunteer for things that will get you and your company recognized—and thought well of. Most people respect volunteers within an organization and consider them experts in the organization's area of interest. That heightens your credibility.

- How about going live on the air? Volunteer yourself for a local radio station's talk show. You can discuss your niche, for instance, local landscaping techniques or how to grow spring annuals. Listeners can call in with questions. When they talk to you—on the air!—they'll be interested in hiring your company. And remember word-of-mouth. They'll tell their friends and relatives.

- Contact local TV stations about covering your business on a news or talk show.

Volunteer for things that will get you and your company recognized.

publicity 90210

It never hurts to enlist other people to help publicize your product or service. Sarah and Anna Levinson, the cosmetics duo, developed a relationship with a makeup artist who fell in love with their line and now promotes it all over Hollywood. She totes Ripe cosmetics onto studio lots, shares them with the actors she works on and also carries out impromptu market research, reporting back on which colors get the hottest responses.

The makeup artist/publicity pal doesn't leave Anna and Sarah hidden behind the scenes, either. She got them onto the set of "Beverly Hills 90210" and introduced them to the cast. No star-struck amateurs, Anna and Sarah coolly distributed their nail polish—an excellent way to keep the promotional wheels rolling.

Photo Courtesy: Ripe

▶ Offer a free session of your service (like landscaping or meal cooking) or one of your products to a charitable organization as a prize for one of their fund-raisers (read more about this in Chapter 8).

Stop The Presses

You can get terrific free advertising by getting your products or services written up in magazines. What you need to do first is prepare a press release, a one- or two-page article about your products or company accompanied by a photo or two. Here's how you do it:

▶ **Do your homework.** Don't send your release to every magazine. Choose magazines that cater to your target audience—and don't forget trade publications. If you are selling clothing or jewelry, for instance, include fashion industry magazines on the list of places to send your press release.

▶ **Call each magazine to find out which editor to send your release to.** Be sure to get correct name spellings and titles. You can request details, such as if the editor has any special press release preferences.

▶ **Use the standard press release format.** Start your press release with a catchy lead, or opening, tailored to your target magazines and follow it up with a short but intriguing story. Double-space your material and keep it in an easy-to-read font and type size. Editors are incredibly busy people. If your release is too long, you'll lose their interest.

▶ **Send reprint-quality slides of your merchandise.** Many smaller magazines have very limited photo budgets, so any artwork they can use is a terrific bonus.

▶ **Personalize your mailing.** Send a cover letter with your press release, addressed to the proper editors, telling them who you are and that you think their readers will find your products of interest.

▶ **Follow up.** Wait a few weeks. Then call to make sure the editors have received your release and find out if they have any questions.

Hot Tip

As a teen entrepreneur, you have a built-in interest angle for a newspaper or magazine article. A successful kid biz is a novelty, so people almost automatically want to hear the details.

▶▶ Business Brainstormer

Planning For Publicity

Use this work sheet to brainstorm ways to grab publicity for your company.

1. What is your hook? What can you show or tell about your product or service that's new, exciting, interesting, important or fun?

_____

_____

_____

2. What groups will make the best targets for your publicity (e.g., garden clubs, chambers of commerce or networking groups, youth groups)?_____

_____

_____

3. How can you vary your focus to interest other groups? (If you're selling a personal chef service, for instance, you could first target working families and also talk to kids clubs about healthy eating.)

_____

_____

_____

_____

4. List local radio shows that might be interested in your story:

_____

_____

_____

5. Call and ask to talk to the show producers and discuss your idea. Note below their responses: _____

_____

_____

Continued on next page

6. List local TV shows that might be interested in your story:

_____

_____

7. Call and ask to talk to the show producers and discuss your idea. Note below their responses: _____

_____

_____

8. List local newspapers or magazines that might be interested in your story. (You'll have to determine by reading the publications what section or department to go after, like Lifestyle, which usually carries people-related stories, Business, Food or Local News.)_____

_____

_____

9. Call and ask to talk to the editors of the relevant departments and discuss your idea. Note below their responses: _____

_____

_____

10. What product or service can you donate to a local charity? (For some starter suggestions, check out Chapter 8.) _____

_____

_____

11. List the charities that might be good targets for your donation:

_____

_____

12. Call and tell the program director that you'd like to contribute to an upcoming event like an auction and find out when the next one will be. Note your results below:

_____

_____

a splashy start

A Grand Opening is a terrific way to kick off your new venture with a splash and let everyone know you're open for business. Invite friends, family, vendors and suppliers, people from your mailing list who live locally and local news media. If you'll be homebased, get creative with the site for your bash. If your new company will sell golf lessons, for instance, hold your party at a local golf course. That kid-care company might hold a picnic at the park. And a hand-crafted jewelry designer might hold a grand opening at a local jewelry store that will carry her products.

Be sure to have each well-wisher sign a guest book and leave his address—it's free names for your mailing list! Give out brochures or other sales pieces and perhaps a small freebie from your product line. Or, if you have a service business, a small notepad with your company name emblazoned on each page.

▶ **Be persistent.** If your first release doesn't get coverage, send another one, and then another in a regular publicity program. But don't send the same release over and over. You don't want to bore the editors to death. Vary your lead and the way you tell your story.

Sales Smarts

No matter how much advertising and publicity you do, there will still be times when you'll have to go out on sales calls. Even virtual businesses like Web site design that operate from the solitude of the owner's desktop occasionally have to go out to meet clients and convince them to buy their products or services. Some of us are born salespeople who love nothing so much as the challenge of persuading others to buy what we're selling. Other people would rather spend three hours in the dentist's chair than half an hour making a sales call.

> No matter how much advertising and publicity you do, there will still be times when you'll have to go out on sales calls.

◀ All-Star Sales ▶

Whichever type you are, you can morph into a sales all-star by following six simple steps:

1. **Establish rapport.** This means donning a relaxed, pleasant attitude. Smile, even when you're talking to your potential client on the phone. (People can hear a smile.) Use your customer's name, and when you meet in person, maintain eye contact. This shows that you're confident and honest.

2. **Get customers to tell you what they want.** Maybe it's nerves, but lots of salespeople plunge into blab-mode about their product or service before learning what the customer actually wants to buy. That doesn't work. Let your customer tell you what he wants before you start telling him you have it.

3. **Get the customer to commit to a purchase.** It seems simple, but countless salespeople miss the big picture—they don't get the customer to commit. They work hard to get that sale, but at the moment when the customer should be buying, she wriggles away, saying she needs to get somebody else's approval—her boss or her husband or her partner. So how do you get a commitment? Ask for it—tactfully. Respectfully say "Are you the one to talk to, or will someone else be making the buying decision?"

4. **Find the customer's hot button.** Customers can usually rattle off a list of needs, but there's usually one hot button that grabs their attention—and it's up to you to find it. If you're a personal chef, for instance, some clients may be swayed by the fact that your meals are healthier and lower-calorie than fast food while for others, the big draw might be your personal service, which will make them feel the glamour of having an "in-house" chef. You may not find the hot button right away, but keep

Hot Tip

Richard Williams, who went after corporate executives for his pager-repair service, won their business by telling them "I'm not trying to sell this. It's a value-added service [meaning it adds extra benefits to their products]." He drew charts to illustrate how his company could help them increase their own sales. And he was careful to dress the part of a professional. "I always showed up looking sharp."

asking, listening and observing, and sooner or later you'll figure it out.

5. Eliminate objections. Some customers know exactly what they need, but most want to be wooed. These are the ones who throw out all sorts of weak objections, like "Well I'd like to buy it, but it's just too expensive." Don't let them distract you. Figure out what the standard objections are likely to be; then figure out what to say to overcome them.

6. Close that sale. You can find all sorts of books and tapes on slick closing techniques, but you don't need them. If you've followed the five previous steps, all you usually have to do to close the sale is ask for the customer's order.

•••• rejection woes ••••••••••

Part of being an all-star is dealing with rejection. "No" is one of the most dreaded words in the English language because— unless it's the answer to a question like "Does this $100 bill belong to anybody?"— it means being rejected. For the entrepreneur, "no" can mean being turned down by a potential client, distributor or financier.

But as with everything else in business, the successful entrepreneur takes rejection as a learning experience. And the key to overcoming rejection is persistence. So what if that prospective client doesn't see the need for your services? Pick yourself up, dust yourself off, and go on to the next one.

A major sales secret is that it takes about 12 cold-calls to even get through to someone with decision-making power, and nine out of 10 of them will turn you down flat. But if you don't keep steaming ahead through those nine "nos," how will you ever get to that all-important 10th "yes"?

Don't be disappointed if you're not an overnight sales sensation. Selling is a skill, and like bike-riding, in-line skating or cooking, it takes practice. In this case, it means practicing on friends and family. If they or you notice rough spots, concentrate on how you can improve them. Review your performance after real-life sales experiences, and you'll soon be a sales all-star.

Chapter Seven

The Haul Of ReCord$

Even the most basic business has to keep records—if you don't, how do you know if you earned a profit? Sure, it's math, but it's fun because it's real—you're counting your own money. In this chapter, we hit the paper trail, tracking income and expenses and exploring the finer points of budgeting, paying bills and reinvesting in your business. We delve into the secrets of bank and savings accounts and tap into tips for making it in the stock market. And we discover how to have fun—or at least get funky with—filing.

The Keeper

As an entrepreneur, you're the keeper of all sorts of records—income and expense statements, tax filings, invoices, receipts, contracts and more. You keep some for the benefit of your customers, some to help your accountant and some to prevent the IRS from becoming unduly upset. And all these bits and pieces of paper help you, too.

At tax time, you can deduct many business expenses from your earnings. This makes your net revenues—the amount you pay taxes on—lower. Among legitimate deductions—as long as you keep receipts—are business equipment like computers and fax machines, mileage you burn on the road going to clients' homes or offices and entertainment expenses like the food for your grand opening.

> **Record-keeping doesn't have to be a drag. It's actually fun and exciting to see how well you did at the end of a day.**

Record-keeping doesn't have to be a drag. It's actually fun and exciting to see how well you did at the end of a day at the flea market or a month in the lawn-maintenance business.

Amy Beaver and her brother Keith use a record book to track earnings from their candles sales. "We kept track of how much we made for the day for each crafts show and then what our profits were on a weekly basis," Amy says. "We also keep track of inventory."

The book helped with more than just tracking revenues. When the duo planned to sell at crafts shows they'd already attended, they could look back over their records to see what styles of candles they'd sold and how many of each went home with customers, making ordering a snap. "We could order ahead of time because we knew we'd sell about the same," Amy explains.

Financial statements help you make the same sorts of snappy decisions. Whether you're a chronic number cruncher or finance-phobic, you'll want to give your company periodic financial checkups.

If there's a problem, you'll find out before it becomes critical. For instance, if you discover that your income barely covers your printing or operating expenses, you can change gears along with the number of direct-mail pieces you send out.

And if you are doing well, your financial statement will give you that warm, rosy glow

> **Whether you're a chronic number cruncher or finance-phobic, you'll want to give your company periodic financial checkups.**

by demonstrating how well you're doing—possibly even better than you expected. If you've been saving for a new printer or software upgrade, or if you're hoping to take on an employee, you can judge how close you are to achieving that goal.

Prepping For Profit And Loss

Let's start off with your income and expense statement, which can also be called a *profit and loss statement* or if you want to sound really businesslike, a *P&L statement*. We covered the bare bones of this statement in the business plan chapter, so now let's get intimate. You can use the sample income and expense statement on page 159 as a guide. Then make copies of the blank statement on page 166 to do your own.

◀ The Cost Of Goods ▶

The second item on the statement—and the first one we'll explore— is the cost of goods sold. Let's say you're selling beaded bracelets. You start off with one bracelet and figure out exactly how much it will cost you to produce, like this:

Crafts Item	Bulk Price	Amount Needed Per Bracelet	Cost For One Bracelet
Green Beads	$10.00 for package of 100 beads = 10.00/100 = .10 per bead	5	5 x .10 = .50
Blue Beads	$10.00 for package of 100 beads = 10.00/100 = .10 per bead	5	5 x .10 = .50
Silver Beads	$25.00 for package of 50 beads = 25.00/50 = .50 per bead	6	6 x .50 = 3.00
Green Ribbon	$4.99 per yard	1/2 yard	4.99/2 = 2.50
Total Cost Per Bracelet			**$6.50**

Now you know how much it will cost you to make one bracelet, which gives you a good starting point for how to price your product. You can't possibly sell it for less than $6.50 because you'll lose money. If you sell it for exactly $6.50, you break even—you don't make any money but you don't lose any, either. That's not the way to become a teenage (or any other kind of) millionaire.

This is where you go back to your market research and look at what similar bracelets sell for in your area. If most sell for $15, you can mark yours up 100 percent—which means you double your cost—and make a tidy profit. Priced at $13, your bracelet will cost less than your competitors', which is a good selling point.

◀ The Cost Of Services ▶

If you're selling a service instead of a product, you may still want to figure your cost of goods. Let's say you're going to do home tutoring, helping kids with reading skills. Take a look at your costs:

Study Aid	Bulk Price	Amount Needed Per Student	Cost Per Student
Reading Workbook	$10.00 each	1	$10.00
Gold Star Stickers	$2.50 for package of 100 = .03 per star	25	25 x .03 = .75
Happy Face Stickers	$2.50 for package of 100 = .03 per star	25	25 x .03 = .75
Bookmark	$3.50 each	1	$3.50
Total Cost Per Student			**$15.00**

In this case, you're not planning on making your profit from selling the workbook, stickers and bookmark, so you'll probably mark up your goods a small amount—just enough to cover your time and effort in buying your materials. You might tell parents that you have a one-time fee of $20 for materials.

Then you'll charge for your services. Some service businesses charge by the hour and others by the job. As a tutor, you might charge $15 per hour or $75 for a five-week program. If you do housecleaning, you could charge $10 per hour. Or if you know, for instance, that it takes you three hours to clean a three-bedroom house, you might charge $35 per job.

How do you know which method to use and how much to charge? Go back to your market research. How much do similar businesses in your area charge? What do you feel the job is worth to you?

Like the time it takes you to produce a beaded bracelet, your time is worth money as well. If you charge $15 to clean three-bedroom homes and it takes you an average of three hours each, you're working for $5 per hour. And you may get burned out in short order because you'll be working too hard for too little profit.

Hot Tip

Every service-oriented entrepreneur makes a few mistakes bidding jobs along the way. You might tell a homeowner you can paint her living room for $50 including materials and only realize later that the paint cost you almost that much. Count it as a valuable lesson you won't have to learn twice, and be gracious about it. If you call your price an estimate, you can come back later and tell her about the extra cost. But if you quote someone a firm price, you have to stand by it.

Incoming And Expenses

OK, now that you know your cost of goods and how much you'll charge for each product, we can go to work on Bead Babe Jewels' income and expense statement. You sold 100 bracelets at $13 each, which means your gross sales are $1,300. "Gross" in financial lingo doesn't mean "really disgusting" but instead refers to how much you make before you deduct your expenses.

Your cost of sales is $650, which is 100 bracelets that cost you $6.50

each to make. When we subtract the cost of sales from the gross sales, we get your gross monthly income of $650.

But this, of course, doesn't paint the entire picture. We have to deduct your expenses before we find out how much you really made.

◀ Expensing Around ▶

We put every ordinary expense on Bead Babe's statement so you can see all the items that might normally be covered, even though the company doesn't have to worry about some of them.

The first expense item, for instance, is rent. Because you're working from home, you don't have to pay rent. But if you had a commercial office space or a storefront at the mall, you'd plug in a figure here.

You have a separate phone line with voice mail that cost you $25 during the month of January but no utilities because you're homebased. You don't have any employees, so there's an empty space for that item. Postage—mailing off letters and bills like the one to the phone company—cost you $5 in January.

What's that $4.17 license? It's your $50 business license renewal. You really only pay it once a year in one lump sum. But for your P&L statement, we've amortized this cost, or shown as being paid out over the course of a year. We divided the $50 fee by 12 months, which gives us $4.17.

> Amortizing may seem like unnecessary extra arithmetic, but it allows you to spread that expense out over 12 months—and helps you save the money to pay for it.

Amortizing may seem like unnecessary extra arithmetic, but it's actually very clever. It allows you to spread that expense out over 12 months—and therefore helps you save the money to pay for it. When you add that $4.17 as an expense on your P&L statement each month, you're actually setting it aside—you don't spend it because you know it's a cost. When license payment time rolls around in June (or whenever), you have 12 months of $4.17—or $50—that you haven't touched all year sitting prettily in your bank account, ready to be used for your business license renewal. If, on the other hand, you hadn't amortized this fee, when June rolls around, you might have to scramble to come up with the money because you forgot all about it.

Bead Babe Jewels
Income & Expense Statement

For the Month of January 2000

Monthly Income

Gross Sales	$1,300.00
Cost of Goods	650.00
Gross Monthly Income	$650.00

Monthly Expenses

Rent	0
Phone	$25.84
Utilities	0
Advertising & Marketing	25.00
Employees	0
Postage	5.00
Licenses	4.17
Legal Services	30.00
Accounting Services	25.00
Office Supplies	10.70
Insurance	0
Subscriptions/Dues	20.00
Internet Service Provider	20.00
Loan Repayment	40.00
Total Monthly Expenses	**$180.71**
Net Monthly Profit	**$469.29**

We've also amortized your legal and accounting services. We've taken the amount of money you estimate you'll spend for your attorney and accountant over the course of a year ($360 and $300 each) and divided them by 12 to spread them over a whole year.

Bead Babe spent $10 on office supplies in January, so there's that expense. We left insurance blank because you don't have commercial premises like an office or storefront or equipment that needs to be insured—you're letting your computer and printer fall under your parents' homeowners policy.

The item called "Subscriptions/Dues" is for subscriptions to professional publications like *Giftware Business* magazine and for dues to professional organizations like the National Craft Association and your local

toy story

Mattel Inc. had already been in existence as a toy manufacturer for a decade when partner Ruth Handler came up with the idea that would make the company a toy story star. Ruth had noted that her daughter and her friends liked playing with adult-figured paper dolls and suggested designing a 3-D doll with the same curvaceous build.

So, despite the fact that the male ad executives at Mattel insisted the idea wouldn't fly, Ruth and her husband Elliot went ahead with production. In 1959, Barbie (named after the Handlers' daughter) was born as a teenage fashion model. Barbie's debut at the annual Toy Fair trade show in New York seemed more like fizzle than sizzle—buyers were not impressed.

But they didn't know girls. Once Barbie hit the stores, she was such a smash success, it took Mattel several years to manufacture enough dolls to meet demand. (Trivia tip: Ken, born in 1961, was named for the Handlers' son.)

Today the Handlers, whose company began as a garage workshop making picture frames and doll furniture, are no longer involved in Mattel. But their once-tiny business is an industry giant—a true toy story success.

Photo © Nathanson's Photography '99

chamber of commerce. Again, we've amortized your total annual $240 expenses over the course of 12 months.

You're paying $20 per month for your Internet service provider. And your last item is a $40 per month payment to Uncle Fred for the start-up funds he lent you. That brings your total expenses to $180.71 for the month of January 2000.

> "Net" doesn't have anything to do with fishing or hair but refers to the bottom line—what you actually made after expenses.

Now we subtract that from your gross monthly income of $650, and you have a net monthly profit of $469.29. "Net" doesn't have anything to do with fishing or hair but refers to the bottom line—what you actually made after expenses.

◄ April In Bead Land ►

Now let's check out the part of financial statements that gets the die-hard entrepreneur's blood pumping—comparing consecutive statements. We've done quarterly income and expense statements for Bead Babe Jewels, which means one for every three months of the year: January, April, July and October. When you match one against the other, you get a clear picture of your company's growth.

Take a look at Bead Babe's April income and expense statement on page 163. You can see that your gross monthly income has increased quite a bit. You designed a second bracelet that you're selling for more money but that you can still produce for $6.50 apiece.

Skimming through your expenses, your phone bill, postage and office supplies are up, but your other expenses—the ones we amortized—have remained the same. So your net income is now $1,315.46, which is a tidy increase from January's figure of $469.29. In three months, you've increased your monthly net earnings by more than $800.

◄ July Fireworks ►

Checking out Bead Babe's July statement, you can celebrate with fireworks. Your gross monthly income climbed to $1,915 from your previous quarter's $1,500. One reason is that you sold more products. The other is that you found a new supplier with outstandingly lower prices, which meant you paid very little more for your materials even though you made more bracelets.

Your phone, postage and office supplies are higher, which makes sense if you're doing more business. And your fixed expenses—the ones we amortized—are still the same. That leaves you with a net monthly profit for July of $1,683.45, which compared to your April second quarter figure of $1,315.46, means you're increased your profits by $367.99.

◄ October Anxiety ►

You thought you were doing pretty well in October—with $3,800 in sales, you sold $500 more worth of jewelry than in July. But when you do your financial statement, you see that you had a net profit of only $116.65—less than in January when you had sales of $1,300. You have three choices:

1. Have an anxiety attack.

2. Find something chocolate and inhale it.

3. Figure out what went wrong and then fix it.

As a millionaire-in-the-making, you go with choices two and three. (A little chocolate never hurts.) So what went wrong?

First, your cost of goods is higher than it's ever been—more than half your sales. (If you look back, you'll see that you've always paid 50 percent or less for your beads and other materials.) Your costs are higher because you decided to make and sell rings as well as bracelets. The supplier who was giving you the great deal doesn't carry ring materials, so you had to go with somebody else whose prices are higher. That's problem one.

Problem two is that you hired two friends as independent contractors to make and sell bracelets while you concentrated on the rings—a good idea, except that by the time you paid them $400 each, your expenses skyrocketed. Looked at another way, your sales increased by $500, but you paid your friends $800, meaning you paid them more than they brought in.

Fortunately, you kept your records and did your October statement so you can catch the problem before it continues or gets worse. So what do you do? You've got several choices:

Solution 1: Forget the rings, which are too expensive to produce.

Solution 2: Find a cheaper ring supplier.

Solution 3: If you think your market will support it, raise your prices.

Solution 4: Cut back on your help.

Bead Babe Jewels
Income & Expense Statement
For the Month of April 2000

Monthly Income

Gross Sales	$2,800.00
Cost of Goods	1,675.00
Gross Monthly Income:	$1,125.00

Monthly Expenses

Rent	0
Phone	$32.71
Utilities	0
Employees	0
Postage	6.75
Licenses	4.17
Legal Services	30.00
Accounting Services	25.00
Office Supplies	11.83
Insurance	0
Subscriptions/Dues	20.00
Internet Service Provider	20.00
Loan Repayment	0
Total Monthly Expenses:	**$190.46**
Net Monthly Profit:	**$1,315.46**

Bead Babe Jewels
Income & Expense Statement
For the Month of July 2000

Monthly Income

Gross Sales	$3,300.00
Cost of Goods	1,385.00
Gross Monthly Income	$1,915.00

Monthly Expenses

Rent	0
Phone	$47.13
Utilities	0
Employees	0
Postage	18.92
Licenses	4.17
Legal Services	30.00
Accounting Services	25.00
Office Supplies	26.33
Insurance	0
Subscriptions/Dues	20.00
Internet Service Provider	20.00
Loan Repayment	40.00
Total Monthly Expenses	**$231.55**
Net Monthly Profit	**$1,683.45**

▶▶ Business Brainstormer

Bead Babe Jewels
Income & Expense Statement
For the Month of October 2000

Monthly Income

Gross Sales	$3,800.00
Cost of Goods	2,000.00
Gross Monthly Income	$1,800.00

Monthly Expenses

Rent	0
Phone	$47.12
Utilities	0
Employees	0
Independent Contractors	800.00
Postage	19.92
Licenses	4.17
Legal Services	30.00
Accounting Services	25.00
Office Supplies	12.84
Insurance	0
Subscriptions/Dues	20.00
Internet Service Provider	20.00
Loan Repayment	40.00
Total Monthly Expenses	**$1,019.05**
Net Monthly Profit	**$116.65**

Do-It-Yourself
Income & Expense Statement

Your Company Name:_____

For the month of _____

Monthly Income

Gross Sales	$_____
Cost of Sales	$_____
Gross Monthly Income	$_____

Monthly Expenses

Rent	$_____
Phone/Utilities	$_____
Employees	$_____
Postage	$_____
Licenses	$_____
Attorney Services	$_____
Advertising/Promotions	$_____
Accounting Services	$_____
Office Supplies	$_____
Transportation & Travel	$_____
Insurance	$_____
Subscriptions/Dues	$_____
Loan Repayment	$_____
Total Monthly Expenses	$_____
Net Monthly Profit	$_____

On The Paper Trail

After all these facts and figures, you may be wondering how you keep track of all this stuff. The answer is that you hit the paper trail. First, you set up files for everything you need to keep track of—phone bills, office supply receipts, loan payments, etc.—then you log your income and expenses into your accounting records. If you have a computer and accounting software like Quicken, QuickBooks or Microsoft Money, this is easy. Every time you pay a bill, you enter it into the computer. When you pay that April phone bill, for instance, you tell the software program who you paid (BellSouth), how much ($32.71) and what it was for (phone service). Every time a customer pays you, you enter the payment into the computer. You might, for instance, log in your customer (Antique Rose), the money you're paid ($260.00) and what it's for (income).

> Is bookkeeping a nightmare on accounting street? Nope. "As long as you stay really organized, you'll be fine."

What's really fun about these programs is that at the end of the month or quarter or year—or whatever period you choose to examine—you ask the computer to generate a report and it puts together all your entries into an income and expense statement. Or you can choose from a dazzling array of other financial reports.

Richard Williams of EBS is all too familiar with the ins and outs of record-keeping. "I had to keep track of what people sent me and what I sent them," the Texas teen says of his pager-repair business. "I have a tax accountant who did everything at the end of the year, but, as far as day-to-day, I did everything on my computer through forms I developed myself." Is bookkeeping a nightmare on accounting street? Nope. "As long as you stay really organized, you'll be fine."

◄ Brain Power ►

If you don't have a computer, all is not lost. You still log in your payments to suppliers and checks from customers. But instead of the computer adding everything up, you do it yourself. You can buy inexpensive accounting books at your office supply center as Amy Beaver does. (A popular version is published by a company called Dome.)

Then you simply enter your expenses and income, just as you'd do with a computer, and add everything up. It takes more brain power than using the computer, but it works. When you're ready to do financial statements, you plug in the totals from your month (or whatever period) and tally everything up.

You Can Bank On It

One of the most exciting things about starting your own business is opening a company bank account. You get a rush of pride and accomplishment—your carefully planned baby has a real identity in the eyes of the business world. A bank account is proof that you're going places as an entrepreneur.

It's also a big responsibility. So much so that many banks won't let you open a bank account unless you're at least 18. Not even with your parents' permission. It doesn't say a lot for the bank's sense of trust or generosity. But not to panic. There are banks willing to work with you, although some won't do it unless your parents co-sign, which means they agree to be responsible for your account in the event you mismanage it. But they will give you checks and ATM cards and all the joys and obligations that go with them.

> **A bank account is proof that you're going places as an entrepreneur.**

◀ The New Account ▶

Go to the bank and ask to speak to the new accounts officer. She'll sit down with you at her desk and discuss how much money you plan to deposit to start off with, how much money on average you expect to keep in your account and how many checks you plan to write each month. You'll have a pretty good idea of the answers to these questions because you've done a business plan.

Your initial deposit will be the amount you've saved or borrowed (or some combination of the two). You can estimate the number of checks you'll write from the amount of creditors you'll have—the phone company, the jewelry wholesaler or the paint store.

Biz Whiz | Burning The Candle At Both Ends

Amy Beaver burns a lot of candles, especially on weekends. She and her brother Keith sell candles, potpourri and other scent-sational items at crafts shows, flea markets and home builders shows.

Amy, now 18, has been an entrepreneur since she was 9. Her parents set Amy and Keith on the road to business success. "They have a stand at the flea market," Amy says. "And they wanted to give us something to do so we wouldn't be bored out of our minds. So they set us up with a table, and we starting selling small children's toys.

"We didn't have much, just a few things," the Newport, Pennsylvania, teen explains. "It started to grow, and we started selling candles, potpourri and other scent-type things, until we got to mostly candles. We each got one-fifth of what we made that day, and the rest we set aside to buy more candles and for business expenses."

At first, Amy and Keith handled sales, but their parents ordered products and kept records. "As we grew older, we had to call in orders and do inventory and take care of the business side," Amy says. "We learned that way. And we had money now to do what we wanted to do, like hobbies. I ride horses, and that's really expensive.

"Being in business for yourself is a lot of hard work. You have to realize that you have to give up a lot of time, especially to start off. Once you get it going, it becomes a lot easier—it's still a lot of work, but it becomes much, much easier."

Being an entrepreneur, Amy says, taught her and Keith responsibility. "Suddenly, we were there in the adult world and we had to do mature things," she explains. "It really woke us up to a lot more." It also paid off in income—over the past three years, the business brought in $29,000. Amy has also won recognition—in 1999, Amy won a Young Entrepreneur of the Year award for her success as a teen biz whiz.

> **"Being** in business for yourself is a lot of hard work. You have to realize that you have to give up a lot of time, especially to start off. Once you get it going, it becomes a lot easier—it's still a lot of work, but it becomes much, much easier."

The amount of money you plan to keep in your account is a little tougher, but this is not a test with a fixed answer so just go with your best estimate. You might start with the net profit from your monthly income and expense statement. Then if you plan to take a certain amount for yourself each month, like $100 for flying lessons, deduct that amount. What's left is your estimated average monthly balance.

◀ The Plan ▶

Why does the bank want to know all this stuff? So they—and you—can decide which checking account plan to go with. Some plans require you to maintain a specific minimum balance, say $1,500 or $2,500 each month. If you dip below that, you get charged a fee of something like $12 or $15. In exchange for keeping that hefty balance in your account, however, the bank will pay you a higher interest rate or let you write as many checks as you like at no charge.

Hot Tip

Don't forget that the bank wants to see your fictitious business name statement to verify that you are a legitimate business. It might also require a copy of your partnership documents as well.

Other plans might require a smaller minimum balance but charge you a small fee for each check you write beyond a certain number (usually 10 to 15). Still other plans might allow you to have no set minimum balance and write an unlimited number of checks but not pay you any interest. These are all things to ask about and comparison shop.

Check-Writing Smarts

The big responsibility with a bank account—the reason banks are so leery of working with teens (and a lot of adults, too)—is that if you're not careful you can easily overdraw your account. When you write a check on your bank account, you're really writing a note promising the *payee*—the person you write the check to—that you have that money in your account, and the bank will give it to her when she presents her check.

If you don't have enough money in your account to cover your check, the check *bounces*, meaning the bank sends it back to the payee with a black rubber stamp on it that says "Non-Sufficient Funds." To add insult to injury, the bank then charges you a hefty sum—like $25—because your

··desperately desiring your dough··

The bank wants you to keep as much money in your account as possible. Why? It uses your money—along with the money deposited by its other checking and savings account holders—to make loans to businesses and individuals. It then collects interest on those loans. That's how banks profit.

To coax you to keep as much of your money as possible in your account where the bank can use it, the bank pays interest on that money. Now, when you borrow from the bank, you pay a high interest rate—anywhere from maybe 7 percent to 12 percent. When the bank pays you interest on the money in your checking account, it's low—usually less than 4 percent. But it is interest, and you earn it by doing nothing more than letting your money sit in the bank.

check bounced. If you still have $25 in your account, the bank will automatically deduct it; if you don't, it will collect it as soon it can.

The method for not bouncing checks is simple, yet an astonishing number of people fail. The reasons?

▶ They get sloppy and don't log checks they've written into their check register.

▶ They don't deduct check amounts from their balances.

▶ They don't bother to reconcile—or check their figures against—the statement the bank sends every month.

Take a look at the sample check register on page 172 to see how simple all this really is. For each transaction, simply enter your check number, the person or company you wrote the check to and the amount. Below that, write what the check was for. You enter income—checks customers write to you—in the same way. Then add or subtract as necessary. If you're working with a software program like Quicken, the program does all the adding and subtracting for you. Easy—as long as you enter each transaction!

Hot Tip

It's smart to have two separate bank accounts—one for your business and one for you personally. If you mix incomes and expenses, which in biz lingo is called "commingling funds," you (and the IRS) can easily get confused about what belongs to whom.

Check Register

Number	Date	Description Of Transaction	Payment/Debit	Deposit/Credit	Balance
	7/15/00	Antique Rose Sales Income		260.00	1,000.00 +260.00 1,260.00
1650	7/20/00	Ruby's Wholesale Jewelry Supplies Materials	663.40		-663.40 596.60
1651	7/20/00	Bell South Phone	47.13		-47.13 549.47
1652	8/1/00	U.S. Post Office Postage	18.92		-18.92 530.55
1653	8/1/00	Fred Andersen Loan Repayment	40.00		-40.00 490.55
	8/2/00	Melrose Avenue Sales Income		800.00	+800.00 1,290.55
	8/5/00	Bank Interest from July Statement		1.37	+1.37 1,291.92
	8/5/00	Bank Service Charge from July Statement	6.00		-6.00 1,285.92

Bank Statement Detective

The bank sends you a statement each month that shows:

▶ your balance at the end of the month

▶ the number of checks you wrote and your creditors cashed during that month

▶ the number and amount of deposits you made during that month

▶ any bank interest your account may have accrued, or gained

▶ any bank charges

You'll want to reconcile this statement as soon as possible after you receive it in the mail. What this means is that you go over the statement and check your register against the bank's statement. If you and the bank don't agree, you do some elementary detective work to figure out why and then fix it.

Some people find bank statements confusing because what the bank shows as your ending balance for the month is not usually the same as what your check register shows. The reason is that you know more than the bank does. If Uncle Fred doesn't cash or deposit that check you gave him, for instance, then the bank has no idea you even wrote it. So it doesn't appear on the statement. That could make it look like you had $40 more in your account than you actually do.

Hot Tip

Banks shudder at the thought, but technically you can write a check on anything—even a watermelon—so long as it's marked with the proper information and your signature.

Bank statement balances can also be different from yours if:

▶ You make an arithmetic error when calculating the balance in your check register

▶ The bank makes an arithmetic error (which very rarely happens but is possible)

▶ The bank deducts money for a monthly service charge because you ordered more checks or because a check bounced

▶ You forget to log in a check or deposit.

◀ Reconciliation Rewards ▶

Now that you know all this, you can reconcile a bank statement like the one on page 175. If you're working with a computer accounting program like Quicken, it's super easy. Just click on the reconcile tab. The software takes it from there, walking you through each step and rewarding you with a balloon-filled screen when you successfully complete the task.

If you're doing it on your own, the time-honored pencil-and-brain power way, you'll use the form on the back of the bank statement like the sample on page 176. Ask your parents to walk you through it. Once you've done one, it's simple.

Reinvestment Smarts

As a millionaire-in-the-making, you should reinvest as much money as possible into your company. What this means is that instead of taking all your earnings and buying personal stuff, you use the money to help your business grow.

> As a millionaire-in-the-making, you should reinvest as much money as possible into your company.

Shawn Himmelberger of Mud's Lawn Care did just that. He spent some of his profits to purchase a four-wheel-drive truck and a snow plow so that he could add snow removal to his list of customer services. The new equipment helped him expand his business and earn more money.

Shawn Gollatz of Jest Entertainment funneled some of his earnings back into his company by buying a computer, a fax machine, a sound system and more expensive props—equipment that helps him promote his business and allows him put on better shows, which in turn increases his bottom line.

◀ Opportunity Knocks ▶

Reinvesting in your company doesn't necessarily mean rushing out to buy new equipment. It can also mean buying advertising or marketing space in magazines, hiring a public relations specialist as Anna and Sarah Levinson of Ripe cosmetics did, or hiring employees to help you do more jobs like Kiera Kramer of Parties Perfect does. As your business grows, you might even want to open a storefront or start up in a second location.

If you don't need any of these things, keep that money in the bank.

Bank Statement

Bank Of Spudville
Statement Summary

Bead Babe Jewels
345 Entrepreneur Avenue
Spudville, FL 33333

Accout Type:	**Account Number:**	**Statement Period:**
Basic Business Checking	0788900022271	7/1/00 to 7/31/00

Beginning Balance	$1,000.00
Deposits/Credits	$261.37
Checks	$710.53
Withdrawals/Debits	$6.00
Ending Balance	$544.84

Deposits/Credits

Date	Amount	
7/15	$260.00	Deposit
7/31	$1.37	Interest

Checks

Check No.	Amount	Date Paid
1650	$663.40	7/25
1651	$47.13	7/28

Withdrawals/Debits

Date	Amount	
7/31	$6.00	Monthly Service Fee

Bank Statement (Reverse Side)

Complete this Section to Balance this Statement to your Transaction Register	Month _July_ Year _2000_		Your Transaction Register Balance $ _1390 55_
	Bank Balance Shown on Statement	$ _544 84_	
	Add (+) Deposits not shown on this statement (if any)	$ _800 00_	**Add (+)** Other credits shown on this statement but not in transaction register. $ _0_
	Total	$ (+) _1344 84_	**Add (+)** Interest paid (for use in balancing interest-bearing accounts only). $ _1 37_
	Subtract (-) Checks and other items outstanding but not paid on this statement (if any).		**Total** $ (+) _1 37_
	$	_1652_ $ _18 92_	
		_1653_ _40 00_	**Subtract (-)** Other debits shown on this statement but not in transaction register.
			Service Fees (if any) $ _6 00_
	Total	$ (-) _58 92_	**Total** $ (-) _6 00_
	Balance	$ _1285 92_	**Balance** $ _1285 92_
	These balances should agree	→	→

Then look for ways to put it to work. Lots of opportunities will come knocking on your door.

A supplier might call, for instance, and say something like "I've got 500 packages of beads I need to unload fast. I'll give them to you for half price if you can pick them up right away." This is good. If you can buy your materials for half price, your bottom line will soar. But you need to have the cash available to take advantage of this deal. That's why you left it in your account to use as a reinvestment when opportunity comes calling.

Hot Tip

Some teen entrepreneurs make a habit of dividing their monthly income into thirds: one-third goes back into the company, one-third goes for fun stuff like clothes or movies or saving for a car, and the final third goes into a college savings fund.

Here's another scenario: A customer calls your catering company and says she's throwing the major mega-party of the year and wants to hire you. You know you can make a terrific profit and also get unbelievable word-of-mouth publicity if you can do the job. But the party will be huge—you'll need to rent glassware, dishes, tents, a bandstand and subcontract with the most expensive florist in town. Can you afford to spend this much upfront? You bet. You've got money in your account, just waiting to be reinvested in an opportunity like this.

Whizard Of Wall Street

Reinvesting in your business is also reinvesting in your future. And another excellent way to turn your existing capital into more money is by investing in the stock market.

You already know that companies sell shares—or stock—to earn money for new projects or ventures. You know that one share usually equals one vote and one piece of ownership in the company. But up to this point, we've explored stocks from the standpoint of your own company.

Now let's look it from the other side of the Wall Street fence—you buying

Reinvesting in your business is also reinvesting in your future.

ownership in somebody else's company. This is a cool concept. Just by buying a share of stock, you can literally own a part of any company and watch it grow. Choose any firm you like, from McDonald's to Disney, Tommy Hilfiger to Nike, eBay to Martha Stewart. You can be a part of an old stalwart firm like Coca-Cola or a relative new kid on the Wall Street block like Amazon.com.

It's a real rush to look down the street after you've bought stock in, say FedEx, and see one of its purple, orange and white trucks parked at the curb. That's now your truck and your company!

The other rush about owning stock is, of course, watching your money grow along with the companies you've invested it in. As the stock price rises, the value of the shares you own rises, too.

You can leave your shares alone and watch them grow. Or you can sell them, take the money and use it to invest in your business, like Anna and Sarah Levinson of Ripe cosmetics did with their Disney stock. Or use it to start a new business or help pay your college tuition.

◀ Buying The Cutting Edge ▶

The first thing you need to do is decide what kind of stocks you want to purchase. "Buy something you understand," advises William Stevenson, vice president and branch manager at Salomon Smith Barney, a stock brokerage in Panama City, Florida. "Buy what you know that's on the cutting edge but that you feel comfortable with." If you're an Internet person, for instance, who really understands how e-commerce works as well as what's hot and what's not, you might want to start off with a dotcom company. If you're into fashion and you have a

> **Hot Tip**
>
> Track your own stocks and learn about others on Wall Street by going online at sites like The Motley Fool (www.fool.com), by flicking your TV remote to CNBC, a channel devoted exclusively to the stock market, or by reading all about it in stock-savvy publications like the Wall Street Journal.

> **Hot Tip**
>
> All stocks have their own symbols, which is what you use to get quotes, or what they're currently trading at. Some symbols are simple: America Online is AOL. Others are hard to guess, like YUM, which is the symbol for Tricon Global Restaurants.

Biz Whiz

Computer Whiz Kid

If you've got a question about computers, Daniel Davis is the person to answer it. Daniel, 15, is the owner of Chico, California-based Whizkid Computer Service. "I repair computers, build custom computers and do in-home service," he says. Besides all that, Daniel designs custom-order software for a structural engineering software developer, is the Webmaster of a dotcom giftware site and even makes "house calls" to clients in Sacramento, 80 miles to the south of home base.

A computer buff since age 8, Daniel bought his first machine when he was 10 and formally launched his company at age 13 in 1998. "People would pay me to work on their systems," he explains. "But when I attended a SIFE [Students In Free Enterprise] program that my mom's friend told us about, it really got me started and that's when I chose my business name and started doing a business-type thing."

Daniel counts about 50 steady customers and growing, most of whom he acquires through word-of-mouth and from fliers he distributes on the campus of a local college.

His start-up costs were minimal—paper, pens, pencils, office supplies and a tool kit. "I had almost all the stuff I needed," Daniel says. "It doesn't take too much to work on computers."

With revenue in 1999 of almost $2,000, Daniel is definitely whizzing along the computer fast track.

> "**People** would pay me to work on their systems. But when I attended a SIFE [Students in Free Enterprise] program that my mom's friend told us about, it really got me started—that's when I chose my business name and started doing a business-type thing."

flair and a feel for what's cool, you might go with a clothing designer.

Once you've chosen the stock you want to buy, it's time to lay your money on the line. The two main ways to go about this are to enlist the aid of a live and in-person human stockbroker like the folks at Salomon Smith Barney or Merrill Lynch or to go with an online brokerage firm like Ameritrade or E*Trade. Until you're 18, you have to have parental approval for each transaction, but that's OK—let them share in the excitement!

Hot Tip

Find folks in the know to help you learn the stock market, advises Jason Ryan Dorsey of Golden Ladder Productions. "I found that if you're a young person, you can go to stock brokers and say 'I don't where to start. How would you suggest I begin? What is something I can read?' They usually have a wealth of free resources they can provide so you can go out and learn."

Chapter Eight

The Distracto Factor

When you've got distractions like homework, athletics, band practice, skateboard rallies, set painting for the latest drama club production and those occasional TV specials, it's sometimes hard to stick to the business program. In this chapter, we focus on how to find a balance.

We will seek out the good and bad of holiday-only businesses and explore striking a balance between being an entrepreneur and the also all-important business of being a teen. And we'll uncover—and learn to cope with—the frustrations of being a teenage entrepreneur, from not being able to drive to jobs to customers not taking you seriously.

Warp Drive

You may feel at times that you need your own personal warp drive—light speed-plus—to be an entrepreneur. Yes, you've got discipline, perseverance and boundless enthusiasm. But when you factor school, sports, church, clubs and other extra-curricular diversions into the demands of running a business, you may feel overwhelmed.

This is normal. Every entrepreneur can relate. Sometimes you have to burn the candle at both ends—working at business, school and being a kid at the same time.

◄ Give Me Time! ►

"There's an old saying," explains Shawn Gollatz of Jest Entertainment. "If you want something done, give it to a busy man. I guess the busier you are, the more you can get done. I was lucky that I could get most of my schoolwork done at school. And that gave me time after school to handle shows, clients and contracts."

Even so, Shawn says he occasionally got overwhelmed. Now that he's away at college and moved his company, he's starting fresh with new clients and new challenges. While in high school, Shawn spent about four hours a day, or 28 hours a week, on the business—a lot of time, but he saw the rewards of doing a lot of shows and didn't want to cut down his hours. Some of the stress came from scheduling hassles, like getting caught in traffic while trying to make it to a gig on time—factors that affect adult professionals as well as teens, and ones that you can't do a whole lot about.

Shawn Himmelberger of Mud's Lawn Care in Port Clinton, Pennsylvania, also tried to get his schoolwork done on campus so he could spend more time on his business. "Sometimes it got hard," Himmelberger says. "I wished I had study halls every day. I did as much homework as I could in school and then when I came home I finished it.

"As soon as I was done, I went out and did my work. Sometimes I was up working until 10 or 11 at night. I did my business every day and on weekends—from 5 to 9 every day plus all day on weekends." Now that Shawn has graduated, he has devoted himself full time to his company.

Hot Tip

Finding the time for school, business and being a kid comes down to time management. "Set your priorities, and set your time around what's important to you," says Robert Sek of ID Enterprises. "What I found was that creating a company wasn't work for me because I enjoyed it. It comes back to a quote I always use: When you find something you enjoy, it's not work. Find a job you love, and you'll never have to work a day in your life."

Daniel Davis of Whizkid Computer Service cranks out a lot of business hours, too. "I usually get most of my homework done by 4," the Chico, California, teen says. "Every day from 4 until 8:30 at night I work on cgi [Internet] scripts. It's quite a few hours."

Richard Williams of EBS pager repair also spent mega-hours—from 30 to 60 per week—on his company, cramming in a lot of his entrepreneur time on weekends. "You have to keep in mind that I took care of everything from accounting and billing to shipping and receiving," Richard explains.

> "When you're that motivated, it doesn't faze you. . .we're all very motivated from the inside."

Now that Richard's in college and working hard to start a new business as well as negotiating the sale of EBS, he's being pulled in even more directions. "I don't think it was all that bad," he says of his tenure with EBS. "When you're that motivated, it doesn't faze you. I see that in a lot of entrepreneurs. We all love it, and we're all very motivated from the inside. I think all successful entrepreneurs are that way."

◀ Mind Crash ▶

Amy Beaver and her brother Keith are restructuring the time they spend on the business now that Amy's away at college. While she was in high school, Amy spent 10 to 12 hours per week on her company, most of it at the flea market.

"The flea market wasn't too bad because it was on Sundays," Amy says. But there were several times when we did home builders shows that were two weekends in a row. I would be there on a Friday night until 10 p.m. and all day Saturday. There were times when all my friends were at a football game, and I was sitting at a crafts show. Yes, that would crash your mind. But you have to do it. If I wanted to make this thing successful, I knew I had to give something up."

> "If I wanted to make this thing successful, I knew I had to give something up."

Jasmine Jordan of *Tools for Living* magazine crams in as much study work as possible while on campus at the School of Writing and Publishing in Manhattan, where she's an honor student. "I work a lot in school," she explains. "I don't really like to play around like the other kids do because I know I have things to do at home. So while the other kids are out having fun, I'll have to be working."

Amy and Jasmine have the right attitude. Part of being an entrepreneur is the ability—and the desire—to work harder than the next person. But you also have to learn to fall back on the life-saving trait of adaptability and sooner or later figure out how to compensate. If you don't, you'll either:

a. become a classic Type A personality—the type who works himself into an early heart attack if you're an adult or catches a bad case of galloping mononucleosis or pneumonia if you're a teen.

b. get so stressed out no one can stand to live with you, including yourself.

c. start making business mistakes that lead to disaster.

d. start making school mistakes that lead to disaster.

e. give up all your friends and activities, which in the end leads to all of the above.

And part of the fun of having your own business—the reason so many adults have turned to the SOHO way of life—is that you can have a life. Instead of an employer dictating when you come to work and when you go home, you get to be in charge—make your own rules and work around your own schedule. If you let your business run you ragged, you might do just as well—or better—to be a 9-to-5 person who's free to watch football or shop 'til you drop during nonworking hours.

Hot Tip

Shawn Gollatz says the joy of performing really helped him deal with the stress of school work and other daily activities. You may find that being in business helps you put the perils of teenhood in perspective, too.

◄ Get A Life ►

So what's the solution? The first of several solutions is to realize that no matter how exciting your business is, you have to leave time to have a life. Nobody expects you to do it all 25 hours per day, and you shouldn't expect it of yourself. Take time to romp around the yard with your dog, curl up with your cat, goof off with your friends or just relax with a good book.

You'll only be a teenager once, so don't waste it. If you like competing on the swim team, volunteering as a Big Brother or Sister, or designing decorations as part of the prom committee, go for it. Don't lock yourself in your office and forget to come up for air.

"I'm only one kid right now, and I don't want my company to grow that much," says Evan Macmillan of his Web design firm NetINVENT. "What I'm getting right now is on the upper edge of what I can handle. That's sort of where I want to keep it."

Employee Escalator

The trick is to work smarter instead of harder. One way to do this is by taking on assistance, possibly in the form of employees.

Employees, however, bring with them many pros and cons. When you hire help, you're not a swinging single anymore. You've got additional

▶▶ Business Brainstormer

The Time Bender

Use the work sheet on page 186 to plan time for school, business and activities. Block out the hours you're in school and participating in activities with specific time frames, like band practice, karate lessons, mowing the family lawn on Saturday mornings or baby-sitting your nephew every Tuesday night. Then block out the time you generally spend on homework.

What's left is the amount of time you should devote to your business. If you don't have as many hours available as you'd like, brainstorm what you can do to "create" time. Can you do some of your homework in study hall instead of waiting until you get home? Or during the hours you usually watch your favorite TV shows and tape them instead? Or catch a ride home from school with your brother instead of spending time on the bus?

Don't forget to leave some time for fun! All work and no play makes for stressed-out entrepreneurs.

Time Bender Scheduling Work Sheet

	Monday	Tuesday	Wednesday	Thursday	Friday	Saturday	Sunday
7:00 a.m.							
8:00 a.m.							
9:00 a.m.							
10:00 a.m.							
11:00 a.m.							
12:00 noon							
1:00 p.m.							
2:00 p.m.							
3:00 p.m.							
4:00 p.m.							
5:00 p.m.							
6:00 p.m.							
7:00 p.m.							
8:00 p.m.							
9:00 p.m.							
10:00 p.m.							
11:00 p.m.							

responsibilities. Suddenly, there's payroll to meet and state and federal employee taxes to pay.

It's not cheap, or simple. According to Mary Kwok-Chavez of Owl Payroll Service in Beverly Hills, California, you can expect to pay at least 7.65 percent in taxes on top of your employee's wages. Then you have to add in another 0.8 percent for federal unemployment tax until your employee has made more than $7,000 in a given year, and then another percentage for state unemployment tax—the amount varies with the state and how it views you as an employer.

> **Hot Tip**
>
> When you hire employees, you may need workers' compensation insurance, which pays for any injury or illness they may incur. Check with your insurance agent for details.

◀ Finding Mr. Or Ms. Right ▶

It's easy to think that hiring an employee will relieve all your headaches. If you're lucky—and wise—enough to hire the right person, you will indeed have a tremendous burden lifted off your shoulders. A stellar employee can be a sort of cloned you, doing anything from answering the phone to mowing lawns to packaging products to making sales calls.

But finding that gem of an employee can be tough. An awful lot of people simply are not motivated enough to show up on a consistent basis. Shawn Himmelberger tried several employees for his lawn-care service and is in the market for a steadfast assistant again. "The only employee I found who's good is my brother," Shawn says. "And he already has a full-time job."

> **Hot Tip**
>
> Younger siblings can make good assistants. Try paying them to help with projects like folding and stamping direct-mail pieces, packaging products or even—if they're old enough—entering routine data into the computer.

This is generally more of a problem if you have a labor-intensive business like landscaping or house painting or apartment cleaning, and less of a difficulty with a more glamorous-sounding company like Web site design or magazine publishing. But not always. Kiera Kramer of Parties Perfect has found the employee situation an easy one. "I've had up to eight people at a time working for me—mostly friends that I trust," she says.

If you hire friends or siblings, make sure they understand that this is a business arrangement. You can still be a buddy, but you're also the boss responsible for the company. If you think they'll get hurt feelings if you pull rank, think twice before hiring them.

◀ The Intern ▶

There are other ways to get help without hiring employees: one is to go the intern route. In medicine, an intern is a young doctor who's still learning his craft. In the business world, an intern plays a similar role— she's a high school or college student who takes a short-time job with a company (usually three to six months) to practice what she's studying. The cool part is that she often works for free. Why? To gain experience working in a real-world business environment and to be able to use that experience as a plus on her resume when she graduates and goes out job-hunting.

····contracting independence········

Instead of hiring an employee, you might go with an independent contractor—a person who differs from an employee because he works for more than one company. Let's say you need a bookkeeper. If you hire a bookkeeper as an employee, you pay him hourly wages or a monthly salary, you pay payroll taxes to the state and federal governments, and you pay workers' compensation insurance in case he gets injured in the line of duty.

If you hire an independent contractor to do your bookkeeping, you still pay her a set hourly or monthly rate, but you don't pay all those payroll taxes or workers' comp insurance fees, which is a considerable savings.

But there's a major catch here. The IRS casts a very beady eye on the practice of hiring independent contractors because it believes employers are trying to cheat their way out of paying taxes. For a person to be considered an independent contractor and not an employee, he must meet the following requirements:

▶ works for other companies besides yours

▶ sets his own hours instead of you telling him when to report

▶ comes ready-trained instead of you training him

▶ can't be fired (although you can choose not to use him again after he finishes his current project)

···employee hunt ····

High schools and colleges in your area may have a job placement service. Decide how much you plan to pay and by what method—hourly or salaried, which means by the week or month—and how much time you want your new gem to put in.

Specify that you want hopeful employees to send resumes or letters explaining why they'd be good for the job. This way you weed out a lot of nonstarters with no follow-through without even trying—they'll be the ones who don't bother to send anything in. And you can weed out a lot more who would like the job but aren't qualified.

If you need somebody to design your company graphics, write advertising copy, dream up killer menus, help you craft a business plan or sketch out a landscape, an intern can be just the ticket. But if you're looking for grunt assistance—pushing a lawn mower or washing dishes—an intern won't be interested, unless you can design your job description to sound like a "real hands-on learning experience." If you have a small eatery, for instance, and your culinary school intern helps wash up but also helps design menus and budgets and cooks innovative dishes, this could work.

The best way to find interns is by going to the source—the special school or college department that teaches the skills you want in your intern—and then asking them to recommend somebody or to post your advertisement.

Another way around the employee issue is to go with a partner, as Kiera Kramer does. "I find it a lot easier," says Kiera, who handles most customer calls and does the company's marketing. "That way, we can take on more parties, like if one person's busy, then the other one can take employees to the party—we wouldn't send out just anyone."

The Holiday Clause

A radical approach to the problem of finding time for business and school is to run your company only during nonschool chunks of time—in other words, have a holiday-only business.

Kevin Colleran's first business was a baseball card store that he ran the summer he was 11. As luck would have it, one of the shops in a building his father owned had no tenant for the summer, so Kevin persuaded his dad to let him take it over. When September and school rolled around, the Connecticut pre-teen closed up shop in the storefront and then brought the business back to a new virtual life as an online operation.

You might choose your own holiday-only business, like one of these:

▶ Summer day-camp for kids focusing on computer learning, cooking classes or arts and crafts

▶ Gift-wrapping service that operates during Christmas/Hanukkah holidays

···the amazon of e-commerce·······

In 1994, Jeff Bezos, founder of Amazon.com, began his meteoric rise to the top of the e-commerce world by packing up his car, his wife and his golden retriever and headed west. At the time, Jeff was 30 and the computer brain behind a New York City investment fund firm. But he wanted more—or at least something different.

He'd done his market research and discovered that: a) e-commerce was where the world was going and b) books were an ideal product to sell on the Net because the market wasn't overwhelmed with competition. So Jeff decided to become a Net bookseller and set up his business in Seattle because it's close to several large book distributors and has lots of computer techies.

Jeff raised several million dollars in capital and then he and his team spent a year designing the software to make Amazon.com do its stuff, opening their virtual doors for business in 1995. Since then, the company—which now sells music, videos, toys and more and also has its own auction site—is hotly traded on Wall Street and has a customer base of more than 10 million Web shoppers. Jeff himself is worth $6 billion (more or less), even though Amazon.com doesn't actually earn bottom-line profits and won't, says Bezos, for years to come.

Photo Courtesy: Amazon.com

▶ Desktop publishing company that designs, prints and mails greeting cards for customers only during major holidays

▶ Summer school for dogs teaching obedience and tricks

The drawbacks to this type of business are that: a) You only make money during certain segments of the year, and b) you risk losing customers during nonholiday periods because they forget about you or find somebody else to do the job. But if you really want to have your cake and eat it, too, you might consider this as an option.

You might try a sort of gene-splice cross between a year-round business and a holiday-only one with a weekend business like Kiera Kramer's party-assist company that operates mostly during party-popular Friday nights, Saturdays and Sundays. Or try something like one of these:

▶ Saturday cookie delivery

▶ Sunday morning bagel or donut and newspaper delivery

▶ Saturday afternoon story time for children

▶ Boutique or other shop open only on weekends

▶ Flea market sales

These types of ventures can be successful but when considering them, keep in mind that they might eat into your weekday time even if you're only officially open for business on Saturdays and Sundays.

Amy Beaver and her brother did as much of the nonsales work for their candle sales business—like taking inventory of their stock—as they could at the Sunday flea market. "We didn't waste time, so we still had time to ourselves," Amy says.

Hot Tip

A holiday or weekend business can be a good way to get your feet wet and see if entrepreneurship is for you.

But they still had to spend some weekday hours ordering new products from the wholesalers and shopping for products—things you can't do on weekends when the wholesale companies aren't open.

The Age Issue

Besides the distracto factor—trying to juggle school, business and having a life—you'll probably encounter other frustrations in your role as a teenage entrepreneur. One is that some adult businesspeople, from bankers to landlords to suppliers, won't take you seriously. They'll be polite but have the attitude that since you're "only a kid" you really don't know what you're doing.

The age issue was a definite problem for Robert Sek of ID Enterprises. "That was one of the biggest obstacles I faced," he says. "The majority of the time I was never taken seriously. I encountered a lot of discrimination because of my age. I liked to do things over the phone because age was never considered."

> **"I thought that being a teenager, my business wouldn't happen because people wouldn't take it seriously. But most people have been really nice."**

Jasmine Jordan devised her own strategy for the age issue. "When I first began the magazine, I was 12," she says. "I would call up all these businesspeople trying to get investments or sponsorships, and they wouldn't take me seriously. I couldn't get past the secretaries. 'You're 12.' Click. So I began reaching people through the mail, writing letters and asking that way. That's much better."

Kiera Kramer of Parties Perfect agrees. "I live in a really small town that's mostly older people," Kiera says. "I thought that being a teenager, my business wouldn't happen because people wouldn't take it seriously. And there are some people who say 'So who's this business you work for?' And I say 'It's mine.' But most people have been really nice."

◀ Next Generation Thinking ▶

"I've run into problems because of my age and people not believing in me," says Kevin Colleran. "It was difficult for businessmen, with their mind-sets, to think that I should be treated the same as a person with an MBA [a master's degree in business administration] or any elder. The words were coming from my mouth, but it was hard for them to look at me and say 'This is a kid who should be our partner or own a stake of the company I've put a million dollars in or raised capital for.'"

Kevin admits that when he approached company executives about handling their Internet marketing, he didn't have the same years of experience as people who were older and had already been out in the field. But he views this is an advantage instead of a handicap. Since he didn't have traditional rules of operation hammered into his head—operating methods that might not even work on the Net—he was free to go with fresh, new, Next Generation ideas that were hot.

One way to combat adult concerns about working with you is to point out that you're not fettered by outmoded ideas or methods. You've got energetic, innovative solutions to problems instead. This is a good approach, but be diplomatic about it. If you sound like a smart aleck, you won't get far. Instead, be understanding and reasonable.

If you sound like a smart aleck, you won't get far.

Teenager Richard Williams of Austin, Texas, also encountered problems because of his relative youth. "A lot of our sales and communications are via the Internet, e-mail and fax," Richard says. "So I somewhat escaped and avoided the age issue. There were several people who didn't like to take instruction from someone a whole lot younger than them and didn't know if they trusted someone a whole lot younger to do business with.

"I found that the easiest way to deal with the situation is when they bring it up, you let them know—just through talking with them—that you know your stuff. They'll be able to pick up on it. You go on strong and make sure they know that you know your stuff. Then if the age issue starts to come up, keep pushing through. Don't let it faze you."

Hot Tip

"When I first started, everyone was a naysayer," says Robert Sek, the ID card entrepreneur. "But I built [my business] out of that negative energy—I used to it fuel me even harder."

◄ **The Professional Touch** ►

Anna and Sarah Levinson of Ripe found that some shop owners were hesitant to carry their cosmetics, fearing the sisters were too young to stick to a program of keeping their products in stock. But the duo persuaded shopkeepers to give their goods a trial run and then set out to keep them as customers by earning their trust.

"They questioned our professionalism," Sarah says. "We didn't know exactly how to represent ourselves to show them how serious we were.

But we overcame this problem with persistence. If we were lucky enough for a store to give us a shot, we were very professional and made sure to keep their accounts serviced."

Kiera Kramer also found that being a professional sets customers' fears to rest. "When the first couple of customers called, they naturally assumed I was older and they'd start talking to my mom first and assume it was her," Kiera explains. "And she'd say 'No, that's my daughter.' Then when they talked to me, they'd say 'How old are you?'

"Most people thought that was wonderful. I haven't had anyone not hire me because of it. When they see us working and actually doing it, that's what proves to them that we can do it and we're true."

Hot Tip

Once you earn one customer or client, ask her permission to use her as a reference. Then when you make sales calls, you can suggest that a wary new potential customer call her. The mere fact that you have a reference person to vouch for your abilities can be a terrific way to overcome doubts. Then keep adding to your list of references as you add clients.

◄ Youthful Strategies ►

Every new entrepreneur has to work harder than the competition to earn those first customers. As a teen, you may find the going tougher than the average newbie because of your youth. But you've also got a strategy up your sleeve that an adult may not be able to use.

You can price yourself lower than your competition. Adults have to charge more because they have to make enough to pay the rent or mortgage on their homes, buy groceries and support their families. Thanks to your parents, however, you don't have all this overhead, so you can charge significantly less and still earn terrific revenues. "I could charge $50 per hour as a 16-year-old and be able to justify it because the alternatives were $100 to $150 per hour," Kevin Colleran says.

You've got a strategy up your sleeve that an adult may not be able to use.

Evan Macmillan, 14, agrees: "Since I'm still learning and I'm a kid, that all gets worked into my price. I'm pretty reasonable right now, a lot below what the average Web designer would charge for a well-designed site."

Donna Sayers of DJ's Catering Service in Brooklyn, New York, finds that people often expect to receive her services for less money. "Because I'm a youth and very new and don't have years of experience, I've found that people very rarely want to pay for the service they're getting. I know caterers charge a certain amount for a product, but when I have a party, people try to get something for nothing. That's been the hardest thing."

But Donna figured out how to overcome the problem. "For some customers, I've undercut my prices and lowered my profit for that first party to be able to show my product and what I can do. Usually by the second or third party, there's not a problem in paying the normal price because they notice the quality is great, the service is wonderful and very professional, and the food is really good. They understand they could have gone to an established caterer, but the food would not have been as good."

The Perks

Although you will face certain difficulties in being an entrepreneur as well as a teen—frustrations that most adults won't encounter—the kids we interviewed basically felt their youth was an asset rather than a hindrance.

Shawn Gollatz says he hasn't run into any serious barriers. "A lot of people in the magic and performing community are really helpful to young people interested in getting into magic," the Millersville, Pennsylvania, teen explains. "I think it's actually a benefit being young."

Amy Beaver says when she and her brother first started selling at the flea market at ages 7 and 9, their youth was a boon to sales. "I know it definitely helped," she says. "Customers would talk to us and kid around. They knew we were young and in charge of this. I think they sort of chuckled to themselves because we were like little businessmen running around trying to get a sale. They thought we were really cute."

> "I think it's actually a benefit being young."

Now that she's 18 and Keith is 16, their ages don't have the same impact. But Amy says it's not a problem. Like their customers, their wholesaler takes their youth for granted and treats them like anybody else. "Surprisingly, they were really good about it," Amy says. "There were no problems."

Jason Smith, the seed and grain dealer, discovered the same thing. "The people I worked with at Stein Seed Co. were very, very willing to work with me," the agriculture entrepreneur says. "I had phone numbers, and they said 'Any questions, just call, and we'll help you as much as we possibly can.'"

◀ Leveling The Field ▶

Kevin Colleran says the Internet gives teens in business equal opportunity along with adults. "I wouldn't be where I am if it wasn't for the Internet," he explains. "Not only because it was the medium I chose but because I couldn't drive anywhere. It definitely is true that the Internet levels the playing field."

> "I wouldn't be where I am if it wasn't for the Internet. It definitely is true that the Internet levels the playing field."

When you interact with customers via e-mail, it doesn't matter that you can't go anywhere by car unless somebody takes you, or that you look too young to have any idea of what you are doing. Potential customers don't know this stuff. They can't see you. If you conduct your e-mail interactions in a professional manner that includes good grammar and spelling, they assume you're an adult.

"It made me just as good as the marketing guy from New York or the marketing guy from L.A.," Kevin says. "Nobody cared."

Another reason the Internet levels the playing field—putting you on the same turf as older businesspeople—is that the Net is still a new game, and the rules are still being designed. Nobody has a corner on what works in terms of technology and marketing. New ideas are being explored every day. It's the perfect zone for young entrepreneurs.

"There are no laws written," Kevin says. "You can go out and do what you want. If something sounds like it makes sense to you, you can usually find some other Internet person who's willing to help you go out and go for it."

> "There are no laws written. You can go out and do what you want."

george strikes back

George Lucas didn't originally want to be a film director—he had his heart set on racing cars. But a few days before his high school graduation, he cracked up his Fiat in a crash that nearly killed him and changed his mind about racing as a career.

George turned his powerful mind from cars to cameras and enrolled in filmmaking school at the University of Southern California. He soon produced his first movie, a sci-fi flick called "THX-1138," which was released by Warner Bros. in 1971—and flopped in a big way.

George licked his wounds, picked himself up and started in again, this time directing and producing "American Graffiti," a box office smash that won Oscars for Best Picture, Best Screenplay and Best Director. Not only that, but in the mega-bucks world of Hollywood, the movie was made on a minimum budget of $780,000 but grossed $50 million.

Photo © Corbis Images/Kurt Krieger

At 29, Lucas was on a roll. "Star Wars" was made for $11 million and grossed $513 million—just during its original release. But George was more than a mega-movie maker; he was also an entrepreneur. He developed his own special effects company, Industrial Light & Magic; his own sound studio, Skywalker Sound; and eventually his own complete movie-making kingdom in a galaxy far, far away from Hollywood, Skywalker Ranch in Marin County, California.

◄ Staying Alive ►

Another asset you've got going for you—one that more than levels the playing field—is the freedom to take risks. You don't have to worry about feeding a family or keeping a roof over their heads, so you can jump feet-first into exciting projects. "I was willing to take risks," says Robert Sek of ID Enterprises. "I really didn't have anything to lose." With his parents providing room and board, he could spend his efforts on business instead of on staying alive. "In taking risks early, I learned how to take them and manage them effectively, which helped me to take more now."

Kevin Colleran agrees. "At our age, it's all about gaining experience. You've got free rent and barely any expenses so the only thing you're wasting is time. If you haven't made it to millionaire by the time you're 16, you'll hit it by 30 or 50."

Mentor Vision

A mentor is like a combination godfather (or godmother), teacher, confidante and advisor—sort of your own personal Obi-Wan Kenobe—and every entrepreneur should have at least one. He or she can give you advice on everything from the best way to conduct an advertising campaign in your particular industry to how to extricate yourself from a sticky employee situation to finding an angel—and more.

Hot Tip

Find at least one mentor who's not affiliated with the business community, advises Kevin Colleran. This will give you a different, broader perspective on what you are doing and where you are going.

Your mentors can be people you already know like relatives or family friends who are in business, teachers or youth leaders who've gone the business route or businesspeople in your area. As part of their entrepreneurship programs, organizations like Youth Venture provide mentors—adult businesspeople who volunteer to be on-call for you at all times during business hours or even when they're at home.

◀ Someone To Watch Over Me ▶

Robert Sek firmly believes in taking advantage of what mentors have to offer. "I think having a willingness to learn and listen is very important," he explains. "So many times I've seen people who think they know everything, whether it be a younger person or an older one. I always said I'm willing to learn from anybody and everybody because I don't know everything. If I can learn from someone who's been there and can help me not make the same mistake or learn that lesson a little bit faster, I will.

"I really learned from my network of mentors," Robert says. "I have mentors I network with and talk to about my personal and business life. It's nice having people you can turn to and talk to."

···the family factor···

Families are mentors, too, in their own way. Most of the teens we interviewed feel that their families played a big part in their successes, and they are very appreciative. "My family has always encouraged me and helped me in this profession," says Shawn Gollatz.

Whether they're chauffeuring you around town, helping you design partnership contracts as Kevin Colleran's dad does, helping shop for manufacturers like K-K Gregory's mom did, answering your business line like Shawn Himmelberger's mom does or just being there when you need them, your family is a part of your SOHO.

And like any entrepreneur with any other team, it's important not to take them for granted. Take the time to say thanks once in a while and to let them know you care. You'll feel good about it and so will they.

Robert found his mentors by simply asking them questions: "I would see successful entrepreneurs' names in the newspaper and write them a letter saying, 'Could I please have five minutes of your time? I'm a young entrepreneur, and I would just like to come and ask you a few questions about who you are and any advice you can give me.'

"I'd meet with them for five or 10 minutes and then ask if they'd be willing to be my mentors. The majority said yes. We set out our goals—what we wanted to accomplish and set the groundwork of what our relationship would be."

Robert meets with some of his mentors on a monthly basis and with others on a less-structured time frame. "I keep the lines of communication open and the relationship going," Robert explains. "Sometimes I need to ask them something important and I call them. But I also think it's important for each time I ask something that I call two to three times to say hello and see how they're doing, making it a two-way street instead of a one-way road."

Hot Tip

Finding mentors and building a strong support network is very important for the entrepreneur. Because you're putting everything you've got into the business, you need people who can offer that all-important morale. "Your network is everyone you know," counsels Robert Sek. "Not just professionals but your friends, your parents and your relatives."

Get out there and network.

Like Robert, Kevin Colleran actively hunts for mentors. "I track them down and ask them to give me some time," he says. "You'll find a lot of people would love to have a half hour slot to talk with a kid."

Why? For the same reason you want to talk with them—to gain fresh perspectives and new learning opportunities.

◄ Calling All Mentors ►

So how do you get your own personal magic mentor? Like Robert Sek, you can approach people you read about. You can also get out there and network. Keep your eyes and ears open when you attend business events: professional organization meetings, chamber of commerce meetings, trade shows and networking groups. You might find mentors among your suppliers or customers or in your lender, accountant or attorney.

This might sound like going around town trying to recognize a blind date and in a way it is. Listen to what people have to say and to the way they say it. When you identify somebody you think might make a good mentor, get to know them. Show an interest in their business and their ideas, and talk to them about yours. There is a certain chemistry involved, just like going on a date. A mentor will have a spark and be happy to be on your team.

But don't think that a mentor is at your beck and call. Although part of being a mentor is the honest desire to help an up-and-coming star (that's you), mentors are busy people. You won't have a monopoly on them. It's perfectly OK to call— or meet for a meal—and discuss a problem or share a triumph, but it's not OK to expect them to solve all your problems for you.

Hot Tip
Don't forget—what goes around comes around. When it's your turn to be a mentor, share the knowledge and be there for somebody else.

Hot Tip
By helping others, you help yourself—and have fun. "The greatest thing I've found is that you get to meet people," says Jason Ryan Dorsey of Golden Ladder Productions. "I made [a nice income] and got to speak with Miss America and Colin Powell. You never know when you're going to meet someone to take your idea to the next level and add a piece that you didn't see."

Giving Back

When you form relationships with mentors, you're operating in a give-and-take situation. They help you, and you help them. Many entrepreneurs—both start-ups and giant mega-corporations—believe in taking that idea one giant step further—in giving something back to their schools, their communities or even the world as a thank you for all they have gained.

McDonald's gives back with its Ronald McDonald House for families of critically ill kids. Mattel gave $25 million to UCLA Children's Hospital. Wal-Mart funds college scholarships for high school seniors, and Bill Gates and his wife, Melinda, have endowed a foundation with more than $17 billion to support global health and learning programs.

◀ Tossing Back Funds ▶

As a newbie, you probably won't be able to give billions back to your community like a bride tossing out a bouquet. But there are things you can do, and what's really excellent is that helping others helps your company at the same time. It's terrific publicity.

A landscaping company might plant flowers at a convalescent center or homeless shelter. A catering company might sponsor a Christmas party for seniors or for kids at an orphanage. A Web site designer might help young people come up with classy resumes and then put them on the Net so they can find good jobs. There are all kinds of fairly inexpensive things you can do to give back to your community.

And there are lots of absolutely free things you can do as well. Amy Beaver found the time in addition to school, choir, participating in the National Honor Society and her candle sales business to be a Big Sister to a needy child as well as volunteer at an elementary school six hours per week.

Hot Tip

Your time and effort are wonderful things to give. Shawn Himmelberger of Mud's Lawn Care plows snow and installs tombstones for his church for free. Shawn Gollatz of Jest Entertainment does balloon sculptures for charity—he gives most of the tips to the organization and just covers the cost of the balloons and travel. The magician says, "It's been a great opportunity to give something back to the community."

Mission: Possible

Jason Ryan Dorsey is on a mission—to help young people get excited about life and find direction—and he's moving ahead at warp speed. But finding himself founder of a nonprofit organization, professional speaker, author and member of President Clinton's National Campaign Against Youth Violence still comes as somewhat of a surprise. That wasn't where Jason originally thought he was going.

"When I was 18, I was a junior in college, a triple major," says Austin, Texas-based Jason. "I had really good grades, but I felt I was missing something. I was trying to get a good job so I could make all this money." But a mentor challenged that notion, asking what he planned to do with the fortune he intended to make besides retire young and become bored young.

That's when Jason, now 21, realized that what he really wanted to do with his life was help young people. He started by writing a book, *Graduate to Your Perfect Job*, to help kids prepare for the future and enjoy the present. When he couldn't find a publisher to take on the book in the time frame he had in mind, Jason raised $18,000 and formed his own publishing company, Golden Ladder Productions, to print the first run.

It wasn't easy. "I moved out of my fancy dorm into a garage and lived for a year on $4 a day," Jason says. "So I got really good at cooking Ramen noodles."

Fortunately, the book began to sell. Even more exciting, educators began lining up to ask Jason to speak to students as well as to teachers' organizations. In its second year, the company earned enough revenue to save the day. "I got all the debt paid off, put money in the bank, invested in materials," Jason recalls. "And I was able to move out of my garage—which was a big plus."

Golden Ladder has now grown into a full-fledged training organization with a staff and new offices. Jason is also the founder of the World Institute to End School Violence, formed after he wrote and published his second book, *Can Students End School Violence? Solutions From America's Youth.*

Photo Courtesy: Jason Dorsey

> **It wasn't easy.** "I moved out of my fancy dorm into a garage and lived for a year on $4 a day, so I got really good at cooking Ramen noodles."

"Donate your time and attention," advises Robert Sek of ID Enterprises, who conducts free Internet classes for underprivileged kids. "Someone helped you, so give back more than you receive."

When you come up with a philanthropic plan that involves your business, get the word out. Use all your public relations tools to put news of your program in the media. Sure, it's blowing your own horn, but people like to hear happy news. It makes the community a better place. And sometimes other, larger, companies or charitable organizations come to your aid with the funds to make your program bigger and even better.

"If you're sincere and open to input, both positive and critical, people will start to believe in you and your dream," says Jason Ryan Dorsey, founder of the World Institute to End School Violence. "They're willing to put their name on the line, invest their time, their money and their influence to make that vision happen."

Get 'Em While They're Hot!

21 Cool Businesses You Can Start Today

Table Of Contents

Introduction

ow that you know it all, it's time to focus on the specific business you want to star in. We chose 21 terrific businesses and arranged them in 10 different talent categories. So no matter where your interests lie, you should find something to light a spark. If you're a cat or dog person, for instance, check out the "Pet Parade" section. If you're a plant nurturer who loves to get those hands dirty with good old garden soil, dig into "Green Fingers." If you're a computer or Internet wizard, send yourself over to "Catch The e-Wave."

But don't confine yourself to the categories that leap out at you. Read, or at least skim through, all of them. Some businesses can cross boundaries—for instance, we've got computer tutor in "Catch The e-Wave" because it's an Internet business. But it could also fit in with "The Kid Biz" because you could specialize in tutoring young children on the computer. And remember that one business can ignite an idea for something similar—or for something totally different. And growing that idea is half the fun and excitement of being an entrepreneur.

◀ The Inside Scoop ▶

We've given you the inside scoop on each of these 21 businesses—from how to get started to what to charge to what you can expect to earn. Keep in mind, however, that these are estimates. Exactly how much you charge and how much you earn will depend on how hard you choose to work and what people are willing to pay in your area.

A cookie delivery service that operates only on weekends will naturally earn less revenue than one that operates seven days a week. And while customers in a sophisticated, urban area like New York City might cheerfully hand over $2.50 for a chocolate chip cookie, people in a small, rural community might consider $1 top range for the same product.

Keep in mind, too, that we've based the earnings for these businesses on the limited hours available to you as a school-attendee/entrepreneur. But when you graduate and have more time to devote to your company, you can increase your revenues substantially—and potentially become that teenage millionaire!

◀ Referral Service ▶

You can run most of these businesses in one of two ways:

1. You (and your partners if any) operate as a hands-on affair, going out to, say, interior landscape clients, taking charge of the greenery and taking home the payments. Or:

2. You (and your partners if any) act as a referral service, pairing up plant owners with reliable independent contractors you send out on assignments. You then either charge owners a fee for your service, or you have your contractors pay you a percentage of their earnings. With this option, you have the potential to earn more money. For a refresher course on independent contractors, go back to page 188.

Either choice can work well—it all depends on how you want to run your business, how much work is available in your area, and how easy (or hard) it is to find good contractors—which is the real key. If you go this route, you must be certain that the people you send out are honest, reliable and good at the job. Remember, they will be representing your company.

◀ Dress For Success ▶

The better impression you make on customers, the better your chance of making and retaining sales—and in most cases, the more you can charge for your products or services. Especially for service businesses, it's always a smart idea to design "uniforms" for yourself and any partners or employees. As Kiera Kramer of Parties Perfect did, choose a simple blouse—or polo shirt—and have it embroidered or silk-screened with your company name and

Hot Tip

If you are running a business that requires you to go to customers' homes, make sure your parents know exactly where you'll be, how to reach you through the client's phone number (or your own cellular phone if you have one) and when you expect to be home.

logo, maybe on the pocket or sleeve. This makes you look sharp and professional and shows customers that your business is definitely real.

If you will be selling or bidding your products or services on the spot, come prepared with sales receipts or contracts in a businesslike folder or notebook along with a supply of working pens. You should also have business cards at the ready at all times as well as a portfolio of your previous work like photos or samples of jobs you've done and a page of testimonials from satisfied customers.

OK, enough talk. Put yourself in high gear and get reading!

Hot Tip

If you're running a business where customers come to your home, make sure you first have your parents' approval.

Design
$cene

Photos © PhotoDisc Inc.

I f you are the artistic type—the one with paint splotches under your fingernails, dabs of dried hot glue on your clothes and bits of beads, feathers and glitter on your carpet—then this could be the category for you.

Clothing And Jewelry Design

You love making jewelry—you've got rings on your fingers, bells on your toes and dazzling dangles everyplace else on your body. Or you're an ace clothing designer who can whip up trendy duds on the sewing machine or turn ordinary T-shirts into painted originals. If either of these descriptions fits you, then you'll be in artistic heaven as clothing or jewelry designer (or both).

Fashion apparel is always hot, for everybody from infants to seniors, but especially among teens—which can give you a decidedly upper hand if you target the Next Generation market.

As a jewelry designer, you can work with beads; with traditional elements like gold and silver; with glass, fabrics, feathers, clays, even noodles and safety pins—whatever suits your talents and fancies. You can specialize in earrings, rings, pins or pendants or make matching sets.

If you go for clothing design, you can make garments from scratch, using your creativity to turn store-bought patterns and fabrics into original creations. Design your own fabrics with tie-dye or rubber-stamp techniques, or even sketch your own patterns for a totally designer experience. You can go with off-the-rack duds like jeans and T-shirts and personalize them with fabrics, paints, rubber stamps, beads or embroidery. But why stop at clothing? You can give customers a complete look with an entire line of designer tennies, hats and handbags, too.

> **Fashion apparel is always hot, but especially among teens—which can give you a decidedly upper hand if you target the Next Generation market.**

The advantages to this business are that you can let your creativity swing into high gear, you meet lots of interesting people while selling your art, and there's always the possibility that you'll be the next Donna Karan or Tommy Hilfiger.

The disadvantage is having to produce creative works on a schedule. It can turn a cool way to spend a weekend into hard work if you don't keep your creativity on high. And you can't be all artist—to earn money you've got to nurture those business skills along with your designer muse.

You'll need plenty of marketing creativity and drive.

◄ Starring Talents ►

You'll need the talent and skills to design and turn out jewelry, clothing or accessories other people will want to be seen in. In addition to all that artistic sensibility, you'll need plenty of marketing creativity and drive—you'll need to sell your products as well as make them.

◄ Necessities ►

What you'll need in the way of tools and supplies will depend on what you choose to design and in which medium you'll work. If you're going the jewelry route, your design studio will contain certain tools for hammering gold or silver and different ones if you'll string your creations from beads and shells. If you do clothing design starting from scratch, you'll want a sewing machine, but if you go with off-the-rack garments to customize, you may need nothing more than fabric paints and brushes or stamps.

If you're already working with jewelry or clothing, you probably have your tools at hand. But now that you'll be designing professionally, take inventory and decide if newer or additional equipment could make your work faster and easier—remember, the more pieces you turn out, the higher your income will be.

◄ Starter Costs ►

Your start-up costs should be relatively low, depending on what jewelry, clothing or accessories you'll be making, what tools and equipment you already have and what your costs for materials will be. If you plan to start with off-the-rack glad rags, remember that you must be able to buy them cheap enough to resell at a profit.

Look for items that are on sale or low-priced to begin with (like boys' T-shirts that come three in a package) instead of buying clothes that already carry designer price tags.

◄ Charge It! ►

How you price your products will vary with what you're selling—you wouldn't charge as much for a bracelet of glass beads as for one of amethysts or turquoise. And a cotton sun dress shouldn't be priced as high as a prom dress oozing with velvet and sequins. You can up the oomph of your goods—and therefore your prices—by dreaming up a trendy name for your company and then glamorizing your stuff with cool tags and labels.

> You can up the oomph of your goods—and therefore your prices—by dreaming up a trendy name for your company.

◄ Earn It! ►

You can expect to earn annual gross revenues of $5,000 to $20,000, based on how aggressively you market, how hard you choose to work and, of course, the popularity of your product line.

◄ Advertising Blitz ►

You've got a lot of ways to go to promote your products. You can sell directly to customers at flea markets and arts and crafts fairs or at home parties the Mary Kay cosmetics way. You can also sell wholesale to local merchants or through wholesale companies and sales representatives that can take your line all over the country. If you plan to go the wholesale route, hook up with sales reps at gift and clothing shows, which you can locate by calling local and regional chambers of commerce and convention centers, by reading trade publications or calling industry associations. Ask your local librarian for help.

Next Up

If you're a jewelry or clothing newbie, takes classes (offered by most crafts and fabric shops, community centers and local colleges), read books and magazines, watch crafts and sewing-oriented TV shows, and practice, practice, practice. Whether you're a novice or an old pro, you'll want to learn the business part of the industry. Go to trade shows—talk to designers who are already out there and get their advice.

Home And Garden Décor Design

Even though lava lamps and plastic furniture have returned from your parents' youth to become cool again, there has also been a major resurgence in handmade arts and crafts for every room in the house. But not everybody has the time or the talent to make crafted-with-care objects.

If you're the crafty type, this could be the business for you. Whether you excel at making trinket boxes or birdhouses, herbal soaps or scented candles, picture frames or ribboned pillows, you can be a pro as a home and garden décor designer.

You can go with just about any craft that appeals to you, as long as it appeals to a large target market, too. Cockroach homes, for instance, won't be a big seller no matter how cute you think they are. But birdhouses and butterfly abodes and even garden frog houses are big sellers. So are wreaths for front doors, hand-painted furniture, table runners and floor mats and anything else to grace homes and gardens.

> There has also been a major resurgence in handmade arts and crafts for every room in the house.

The advantages to this business are that you can earn money doing something you love, your start-up costs are low, and in time you might just become the next buzz name in home décor with a line of products in every department store in America.

The disadvantages are that having to produce crafts on a schedule can turn a beloved hobby into a stressful chore. Also, sooner or later, every successful crafter/businessperson discovers demand is outstripping supply. In other words, you reach a point where you can't do it all yourself, and you have to hire others to help you turn out in mass what you like to think of as one-of-a-kind items.

◄ Starring Talents ►

You don't have to be an art major for this business—all you really need is a genuine love for your craft and the talent and skills to turn out objects other people want to buy. It also helps to have a mastery of your techniques. If you've already successfully turned out candles, soaps or birdhouses, you have a pretty good idea how long each project takes, what materials you'll need and how much they cost—all of which is essential for pricing your wares.

> The trick to a successful business is to sell your products for enough money to justify your time and materials.

◄ Necessities ►

What you'll need in terms of supplies and equipment will depend on what you're going to make and sell. A woodworker who makes whimsical birdhouses will need entirely different tools than a candle maker. If you're already crafting, chances are you have the necessary tools. But take a good look at what you've got, and decide if there are other pieces of equipment that would make your work life faster and easier—remember, the more pieces you turn out, the higher your income will be.

◄ Starter Costs ►

Your start-up costs will be low, but again, this depends on what crafts you turn out, what tools and equipment you already have and what your materials costs will be. A crafter working with recycled bottles will have far lower overhead than one making boxes inlaid with sterling silver.

◄ Charge It! ►

How much you charge depends—again—on what you're selling. But keep in mind that the trick to a successful home and garden design business is to sell your products for enough money to justify your time and materials. People who attend arts and crafts fairs—where many craft designers sell—tend to be looky-loos who will only buy if your products are very inexpensive. A good way to solve this problem is by selling your wares to wholesalers or sales representatives who will turn around and market your products to retailers. You can also sell to retailers themselves, place your designs on consignment in retail shops, sell them yourself via mail order, or go the Tupperware-style home party route.

◀ Earn It! ▶

Your gross revenue can run from $5,000 to $20,000, based on the price and desirability of your line, how aggressively you market your designs and how hard you choose to work.

◀ Advertising Blitz ▶

Your customers can be friends and neighbors, people from your community who attend crafts fairs where you display your products, or the entire world if you use wholesalers and sales reps. If you plan to go the wholesale way, hook up with reps at gift shows, which you can locate by calling local and regional chambers of commerce and convention centers, reading gift-industry publications and by calling trade organizations. Don't forget to enlist the assistance of your local librarian.

Next Up

The course for this business is similar to that of clothing and jewelry design. If you're new to home and garden décor design, take classes (offered by most crafts and fabric stores, community centers and local colleges), read books and magazines, watch crafts-oriented TV programs and get in a lot of practice. Whether you're a novice or a seasoned expert, learn the business side of the industry. Talk to designers who are already out there selling and get their advice.

Because arts and crafts tend to follow fads, with angels and cherubs replacing the country cows that replaced those crocheted toilet tissue-cover dollies, be sure to keep up with current trends. Or, as a Next Generation designer, set your own new trends for others to follow—just make sure they're not too out there for your intended audience.

Catch The e-Wave

Photos © PhotoDisc Inc.

I f you're the computer wizard in your crowd, you can coax magic out of a keyboard and find absolutely anything online, this could be your category. Even if you're not Bill Gates, but you've got advertising, marketing and graphic design talents coupled with Web smarts, you can dive into the Internet surf and take advantage of the hot e-commerce industry.

Computer Tutor

Computers and software programs rank among the most fabulous tools available—as long as you know how to use them. And there are still a surprising number of people out there who don't know the first thing about computers—they're just now bringing them home from the store and into their lives. Plus, even computer-literate people often experience computer-learning disabilities—despite what it says on the back of the software box, most programs are not user-friendly. That leaves lots of would-be computer users floundering instead of working successfully.

But if you're a computer whiz, you can transform the computer-phobic into the computer-comfortable as a computer tutor. You can get customers up and running with a basic starter course that includes computer dos and don'ts, familiarization with pre-installed programs and how to navigate the Net. Or you can specialize in specific software programs like Microsoft Word, NetFusion or Lotus. You can work one-on-one with individual clients—from tots to SOHO owners to senior citizens—or train an entire room full of employees at a time for corporations.

> **There are still a surprising number of people out there who don't know the first thing about computers.**

The advantages to this business are that helping people become computer-savvy is always rewarding, giving you the same sort of glow as teaching them to read, and because you have to keep up with ever-changing technology and software updates, you've got the best excuse in the world for buying new computer goodies for yourself on a regular basis.

The disadvantages are that covering the same basics over and over with clients who seem dead-set on not learning can get boring, and although this is a hot field, the competition can be stiff.

◀ Starring Talents ▶

If you plan to tutor a particular software package, you'll need to know it inside and out. To teach computer basics, you should have a good grounding in everything a newbie needs to know, from how to prevent common crashes to weaving around the Web to how to get around in the usual assortment of pre-installed packages like Microsoft Word and Inuit's Quicken or Microsoft Money. Other must-haves are the patience to transfer your knowledge to your customers and the communication skills to transfer your enthusiasm and techniques without frustrating pupils as well as yourself.

> **You can transform the computer-phobic into the computer-comfortable as a computer tutor.**

◄ Necessities ►

For one-on-one tutoring, about all you'll need is your own computer and software so you can keep up to speed on industry innovations. If you go the corporate training route, you'll also want a desktop projector and a laser pointer so a classroom of clients can see what you're doing, and an inkjet or laser printer with desktop publishing software so you can print out training materials.

◄ Starter Costs ►

If you already have a computer, and you'll be doing individual training at client's homes or offices, your start-up costs can be as low as $350. If you go the corporate route and need to buy new software to train yourself on, make that $3,500. Add in another $2,000 if you buy a new computer.

◄ Charge It! ►

You can charge your clients by the hour, the day, or on a per-workshop basis—an average range would be $20 per hour for private instruction and $70 to $80 per hour for a full-day group session. Do your market research and comparison-shop prices in your area.

◄ Earn It! ►

As a computer tutor, you can earn annual revenues of $15,000 and up, depending on how many workshops or group sessions you do—these will net you more income than private sessions.

◀ Advertising Blitz ▶

Your clients can be private individuals, SOHO owners or corporate businesses who want to make their employees (and themselves) computer-literate. To get the business from private parties, establish relationships with computer retailers and ask them to refer customers to you. (Be sure to leave a stack of business cards for them to hand out.) Place ads in local newspapers and the Yellow Pages.

Go after companies and corporations through direct-mail campaigns and network at professional, civic and trade organizations. Another excellent technique is to get licensed or certified from software manufacturers or vendors who will then refer customers to you. (Sometimes there's a fee involved for getting certified; sometimes it's free.)

Next Up

Decide what programs you'll specialize in. Then make sure you're up to speed with the most recent versions and all their quirks. Start spreading the word among family, friends and neighbors.

Dotcom Mogul

◀ The Inside Story ▶

If you live for life on the Internet—you love nothing better than buzzing one site after another, learning all there is to know about how and why the Web works. Or if you've also got a flair for marketing the e-biz way, you can ride to the top as a dotcom mogul.

You can run your dotcom business several ways. You could choose the dotcom store route, selling products (but not necessarily books) like Amazon.com. You can opt for services like e-mail reminders of important dates or e-greeting cards—or any other service you can provide long distance, like genealogy searches, graphic design or term paper consultations. Or you can develop an online community—anything from entrepreneurial teens to kids for healthy living to vintage car buffs. As a dotcom mogul, you will be at the helm of a fast-forward company in a speed-demon industry. If you love the Net and the excitement of entrepreneurship, what more could you ask?

> As a dotcom mogul, you'll be at the helm of a fast-forward company in a speed-demon industry.

The advantages to this business are that it's super-creative, simmers with cutting-edge interest and is far less expensive to produce than any business that must sell its wares or services through paper catalogs. As a bonus advantage, with dynamite marketing, dotcom businesses can earn extra revenue by attracting advertisers to their sites.

The only disadvantage is that, while dotcom businesses are hot, the competition is growing hotter all the time, and you'll have to be clever to get to the top and stay there.

◀ Starring Talents ▶

As a dotcom mogul, you'll need to know not only e-commerce but the wants and needs of your niche market both inside and out. Whether it's supplying tips for term papers, empowering teen entrepreneurs or selling retro room décor, you'll have to be able to interpret your customers' whims to a T. You also must be able to build and maintain a Web site and update it on a daily basis.

◄ Necessities ►

You'll need a computer with a speedy 56K modem, a high-quality scanner and a digital camera for dropping in artwork and photos, and software—start with Web site creation programs like Microsoft's FrontPage or NetObjects Fusion, which you can buy at computer and office supply centers. Or download freeware like Netscape Composer. You'll also want a desktop publishing program and a good word processing package. You'll need to register your domain name, and you'll have to link to an Internet service provider that will get your site out there.

> You'll need to know not only e-commerce but the wants and needs of your niche market both inside and out.

If you plan to go with products or services, you'll also want to read up on mail order smarts. Internet sales are considered mail order by the federal government, and there are rules that must be obeyed. (You can start by going to the Federal Trade Commission's Web site at www.ftc.gov.)

◄ Starter Costs ►

How much you spend depends entirely on which route you take. If you go with an online community or a service like research that costs you little or nothing upfront, then your start-up expenses can be as low as $500 to $1,000 (assuming you already have the computer). But if you choose a "store" with products to be sold just as you'd sell through a retail shop or mail order catalog, then you'll have inventory to buy, which will drive up your costs.

◄ Charge It! ►

This is another variable element, dependent on what you sell, what you charge, who your niche market is, and what other e-businesses advertise on your site. If you've got a mega-audience like guys who like sports, you may be able to attract big-bucks advertisers. But if your site is small and intimate, you may be able to sign on only smaller advertisers with less dollars to spend. The best way to find all this out is to determine your market, and then do your research to find out what competitors charge for products, services and advertising.

◄ Earn It! ►

Again, your annual revenues will depend on a wide variety of factors, from what you're selling to who your advertisers are. You could earn zilch for several years until your site grows into itself and its market, or you could start off with a bang and revenue in the six figures after just a few years.

◄ Advertising Blitz ►

Start e-mail campaigns to alert customers to your site. Establish links to complementary sites around the Web, get listed with search engines, and send press releases to publications your target market reads. Chat up non-Net sponsors who may get excited about developing a Web advertising presence with your assistance.

Next Up

Learn everything there is to know about the e-biz, from banner advertising to getting listed with search engines to opt-in e-mail campaigns. If you plan to go with products or services, read up on mail order sales—Web sales come under the same category, and you'll learn lots about advertising as well as mail order laws. Make sure you're up to the nanosecond on Web hosting and Web page design. Then get out there and go for it.

E-zine Publisher

If you always thought it would be cool to be a high-powered magazine publisher, working with writers and editors setting trends for the nation (and even the world), here's your chance. As an e-zine or online magazine publisher, you can do all these things and more without ever paying a penny for printing or mailing. E-zines are very hot in today's humming Internet culture and are likely to get even hotter.

> **E-zines are very hot in today's humming Internet culture and are likely to get even hotter.**

Your choices for your publication's style and content are wide open. Teens' fads, focuses, issues and fun are terrific e-zine fodder—which puts you squarely in the know zone—but you can devote your 'zine to just about any lifestyle, sport, hobby or profession that appeals to you, so long as you can find a significant readership and the advertisers to sponsor your efforts.

You'll also be at the helm of an online community because e-zines are more than magazines—they're also interactive forums connecting readers to readers and readers to you. To encourage this sense of community, you'll host message boards, chat sessions and live interviews with experts in your audience's interest areas.

The advantages to this business are that it's creative, sounds glamorous and sizzling, and is far less expensive than a paper magazine because you bypass the enormous twin expenses of printing and postage. And with a successful e-zine, you can make a significant impact on your readers' lives.

The disadvantages are that, like traditional paper publications, it can

> **With a successful e-zine, you can make a significant impact on your readers' lives.**

take up to five years to find yourself making actual money, and—as with any publishing venture—you'll find yourself in a world where deadlines are a daily drama.

◀ Starring Talents ▶

As an e-zine publisher, you'll need to have your fingers on the pulse of your niche community. Whether it's teenage girls, surfing guys or poodle breeders, you must intimately understand what your audience wants, needs, thinks and feels—and then know how to deliver. You will need all the skills of a traditional magazine publisher, including top-notch writing and editing abilities, the ability to guide contributing or guest writers toward your particular vision, and the marketing smarts to attract advertisers and other sponsors.

> **You must intimately understand what your audience wants, needs, thinks and feels—and then know how to deliver.**

In addition to all this, you'll need to be able to build, maintain and update a Web site or else be able to farm out these tasks to some other trusted source. (If you can't get and keep your site up and running, you don't have a 'zine.)

◀ Necessities ▶

You need a computer with at least a 56K modem, a quality scanner and a digital camera for artwork and photos. For software, start with Web site creation programs like Microsoft's FrontPage or NetObjects Fusion, which you can buy at office supply or computer centers. Or download freeware like Netscape Composer. You also want a desktop publishing program and a good word processing package. You'll need to register your domain name and you have to link to an Internet service provider that will get your 'zine out to all your readers.

◀ Starter Costs ▶

While it's possible to get a small and intimate e-zine up and running for $500 to $1,000 (assuming you already have a computer), you'll need closer to $20,000 to develop one that's a major presence. The money will go toward writers, editors and other staff.

◄ Charge It! ►

You'll earn your revenue through advertising and how much you can charge will depend on how cool your 'zine is and what sort of advertisers you attract. If your audience is huge and made up of teenage girls, you can attract big-bucks advertisers like Guess and Mossimo. But if your 'zine is small and targeted toward a select audience of poodle breeders, you might be able to sign on only smaller advertisers like other poodle breeders or dog-bed manufacturers. On the other hand, you could try for mega-bucks advertisers like Purina Dog Chow. The best way to determine how much to charge is to determine your market and then do your research to find out what competitors charge.

◄ Earn It! ►

This is cutting edge publishing—so new that it's difficult to determine just what you can expect in the way of annual revenues. Of course, like any traditional magazine publisher, the more advertisers you attract, the higher your bottom line will be, but you can (and should) also go the budget route and develop revenues from advertising tie-ins with other Web sites. And remember that it's highly unlikely you'll see any profits for several years, so try for as much working capital as you can muster from angels or other sources.

◄ Advertising Blitz ►

Your market will be entirely dependent on what interest community you choose to serve. Once you decide on this, you can start direct-mail and direct e-mail campaigns to alert potential readers to your site. Establish links to complementary sites around the Web, send press releases to magazines with the same target readership, and start a Net ad campaign. You can also chat up non-Net sponsors who might be interested in developing a Web presence with your assistance—which will help you as well.

Next Up

Do your market research to make sure you'll have a significant readership in your area of interest. Scrutinize other e-zine communities of all sorts to see how they do it and how well it works. Then start devising your own style and format.

Web Site Design

◀ The Inside Story ▶

If you're in business today, a Web site is as important as an ad in the Yellow Pages—possibly even more so. With a Web presence, you've got access to millions of potential customers around the world. It's like rolling out a major advertising campaign, marketing brochure and mail order catalog in one easily updated package. And all without printing, postage or phone costs.

The problem is that for most people, designing a Web site is about like building your own TV set—a major mystery best left unexplored. They know they could benefit from a Web site but they haven't got even a foggy notion of how to go about it. If you can unlock the mysteries of Web page production (which is getting easier all the time) and scripting (which helps Web sites do fancy things like change colors when a surfer clicks on an icon), and you've got a flair for graphics and copywriting, then Web site design could be the business for you.

> For most people, designing a Web site is about like building your own TV set—a major mystery best left unexplored.

The advantages to this business are that it's creative, you can start on a minimum budget, and you don't even have to know hard-coding anymore to put up a site. And you can work with clients anywhere in the country or even the world without ever leaving your desk.

The only disadvantage is that this is one of those lone-wolf businesses, with no one around but you and your computer. If you need the stimulation of other people and activity, you can easily get distracted, bogged down or lose your edge.

◀ Starring Talents ▶

You don't have to be a computer geek, but you should be able to get along with your computer and have mastered the skills to get around in cyberspace. You'll also need a talent for graphics and copywriting because your goal for each client will be not only to put up the Web site but to design one that's easy to navigate through, visually appealing and cleverly worded.

◀ Necessities ▶

As a Web site designer, your most important tool will, of course, be your computer. Make sure it has a 56K connection speed or go with cable connection. You'll also need a scanner, Web page creation software and a desktop publishing package. If your Web page doesn't have the muscle to upload files to your Internet service provider, you'll want a separate program to carry out this task.

> Put up your own Web site to attract customers and to serve as an example of what you can do, and establish links with other Internet sites.

◀ Starter Costs ▶

If you already have a computer that's up to the job, you can get started for less than $1,000—if you don't, pencil in another $1,500 to $2,000.

◀ Charge It! ▶

You can charge customers anywhere from $20 to $50 per hour, depending on whether you're doing a simple home page for a very small company or a major online catalog with shopping cart technology for a big spender company.

◀ Earn It! ▶

You can expect to earn $20,000 and up, depending on the size of your clients' budgets and how many hours you devote to your work.

◀ Advertising Blitz ▶

Your clients will be businesses—you can target everything from SOHOs to nonprofit organizations to professional associations to government agencies. Choose a geographic or specialty area to start with—say, small businesses in your community or real estate agencies—then send direct-mail pieces explaining the values of a Web site and your services.

Biz Whiz | Baseball Cards To Big Business

When it comes to e-commerce, Kevin Colleran's done it all. The 19-year-old college business major from North Haven, Connecticut, led off with his first e-biz when he was 11, selling baseball cards on AOL after school was out for the day. That led to posting classified ads on AOL for customers for $3 to $4 a day each.

Surfing the Web, Kevin discovered search engines—and a way to earn more revenue. "I started getting clients who wanted me to submit their sites to search engines to increase their positioning," he explains. Soon, his company had morphed into a thriving enterprise that handled all aspects of Internet training, consulting and design for clients all over the world.

Kevin also became a player with other Web firms—including Neato.com, which does CD labeling—as director of special projects. But he wanted more.

"I've always gotten press because I've had companies so young," Kevin says. "I started getting little business plans maybe once a month from companies that wanted me to take part with them. I decided each year I would choose my favorite plan, run with it and see how it worked out."

Kevin's instincts were hot. He went with two e-businesses that developed new technology and marketing and came comet-crash close to becoming major players. Unfortunately, both efforts failed. "My first million-dollar deal fell through because of inexperience," Kevin says. "And the second fell through because of bad luck."

Bad luck? No. Through contacts made with Playboy on that second fall-out deal, Kevin now writes for Playboy online, covering concerts and travel adventures and parties with celebs including Jerry Springer, Michael Jordan and the MTV gang. And thanks to his detour into journalism, Kevin is now negotiating with Collegiate Monthly, the largest college newspaper in the country, for a lead position with equity shares. "My goal was to get on the boards of multimillion-dollar companies," says Kevin who still operates CyberMarketing Solutions. "And that's what's happening. It started with after-school baseball cards and leads to this."

> "My goal was to get on the boards of multimillion-dollar companies. And that's what's happening. It started with after-school baseball cards and leads to this."

Put up your own Web site to attract customers and to serve as an example of what you can do, and establish links with other Internet sites so potential clients can find you through as many paths as possible.

Next Up

If you don't already know how to build a Web site, learn. Surf the Web and study all sorts of sites, analyzing them for what works and what doesn't. Then design your own.

Entertainment Today

Photos © PhotoDisc Inc.

f you're a party person and you're blessed with a major helping of organizational skills, then this is your category.

Specialty Gift Wrapper

◀ The Inside Story ▶

We all like to receive gifts—and just about everybody likes to give them. It helps express your feelings for the recipient and gives you a delightful sense of the warm fuzzies. And the classier or more customized the gift looks in its wrappings, the more fun it is to give and to receive.

The problem is that most people don't know how to tie up a present with elegant ribbons and bows or personalize it with cut-outs, tags or other snazzy specialties—they think anything more complicated than sticking the paper together with cellophane and globbing on a bow from Wal-Mart is beyond their artistic capabilities. Most adults work full time, so they don't have time to sit down and doll up their offerings, especially not at major gift-giving seasons like Christmas or Hanukkah.

But if you're a gift-wrapping genius with a sense of style and fun, you can save the season or the day with a specialty gift-wrapping service. Your services will be most in demand at Christmas-time, but you can offer "packages" for every holiday on the calendar and birthdays, too. Customers can drop wrapables at your home, you can offer pick-up and delivery, or you can arrange with a retail store or mall to offer on-site wrapping.

> **Your services will be most in demand at Christmas-time, but you can offer "packages" for every holiday on the calendar and birthdays, too.**

The advantages to this business are that it's creative, you can get started on a shoestring, and you can easily make it either a holiday-only or a full-time affair.

The disadvantage is that while you'll tie up a nice income, you're not likely to get rich.

◀ Starring Talents ▶

All you need is a talent for designing fancy, fun or simply elegant wrappings and the skills to make them look sharp and professional. You'll also want to be able to work fast—the more quickly you can turn out a package, the more money you can earn.

◄ Necessities ►

You'll want a supply of holiday and special event-themed wrapping papers, ribbons, tape, a hot glue gun and some of the more commonly sized boxes, like the kind designed for shirts or jewelry. You should also stock up on accessories like silk flowers, gift tags or other tiny tie-ons.

◄ Starter Costs ►

You can get started for $150. Try shopping for holiday wrappings after the season's over—you can buy "leftovers" for as much as 75 percent off and then keep them on hand for next season. You can also keep starter supply costs down by using your imagination—purchase simply elegant brown or white paper used for mailing packages that costs far less than gift wrap, use found objects like shells or leaves and paint them gold, or snip designs from old greeting cards.

◄ Charge It! ►

Charge your customers by the size and design of each gift—you can wrap empty boxes to use as samples. You'll have to do research to find out what going prices are in your area (department stores and malls are good places to comparison shop), but shoot for $3.50 to $7.50 per gift. Charge an additional $5 for pick-up and delivery, and be sure to specify a dollar minimum or distance limit—say, within 5 miles of your home or "within the Country Oaks community" or with a minimum $25 order. Otherwise you could end up riding half an hour to pick up a $3.50 job—which would not be cost-effective.

◄ Earn It! ►

Wrap up tidy profits of up to $10,000 per year, depending on whether your business is strictly seasonal or a year-round affair.

◀ Advertising Blitz ▶

Distribute fliers to homes and businesses in your neighborhood and at local shops that can refer customers to you. Be sure to leave plenty of business cards for shop owners to hand out. Renew your ad campaign at holiday times of the year—and don't leave out special days like Valentine's Day, June graduations and weddings and Easter.

Next Up

Start shopping for supplies. Make up sample gift boxes and take pictures to put in your portfolio to show businesspeople and shop-keepers.

Party Planner

◀ **The Inside Story** ▶

Everybody loves parties—it's a chance to dress up or let your hair down, get together with friends and family, eat a lot of terrific tidbits that you don't usually get at home, show up, show off and have fun. But lots of people, especially adults, panic at the thought of inviting people to their homes and having to provide food, decorations and entertainment. Plus, in today's world, nobody has the time to plan a cool party.

If you're the premier party-giver in your crowd—friends and family can't wait for an invitation to your house because you always have something new and exciting on tap—then you can save the day and have fun as a party planner.

You'll create, plan and organize everything from bar mitzvahs to birthdays to murder mystery dinners. You can also specialize in children's parties—not the old pin-the-tail-on-the-donkey thing but princess, pirate or prehistoric-themed gigs where the guests get to dress in costumes provided by you.

> The advantages to this business are that it's creative, challenging, and you get to go to parties all the time.

Whichever you choose, you will do it all, from designing the theme to sending the invitations to arranging the site, the entertainment and the caterer. And you will negotiate with them all to make sure your client gets the most for her money.

The advantages to this business are that it's creative, challenging, and you get to go to parties all the time. If you are a people person, what more could you ask?

The disadvantage is that you'll end up working most weekends because that's when people like to party.

◀ **Starring Talents** ▶

As a party planner, you must be organized and detail-oriented to a fault. You've got to have a major creative streak to come up with new ideas and the planning skills to be able to put them into action. And you'll need to be a people person, capable of dealing with everyone from that cranky

5-year-old's overwhelmed mom to the morning-sick mom-to-be at a baby shower.

◄ Necessities ►

All you really need to get started for adult parties is a phone, a calendar, and a planning book for writing in your first events. For kids' events, you'll want to stock up on dress-up clothes or costumes like pirate, cowboy or even dinosaur duds.

◄ Starter Costs ►

Plan on start-up costs of $500 to $1,000, depending on how much initial advertising you choose to do.

◄ Charge It! ►

You have two ways to go here—you can charge your customers 10 percent of the party's budget, or for package parties like kid's birthdays, you can charge a flat fee of $50 to $75, depending on the size and complexity of the gig. Be sure your customers understand that they pay for food, decorations and entertainment—you're the planner, not the pocketbook.

◄ Earn It! ►

You can expect to earn annual revenue of $3,500 and up, depending on how many parties you do and how much you charge.

◄ Advertising Blitz ►

Your customers will be adults and kids who just wanna have fun. Distribute fliers or brochures around your neighborhood. Write fun and kicky articles about your business for local newspapers. Donate a party to the lucky winner of a charity auction—always good publicity—and give free parties for family and friends who'll spread the word.

Next Up

Start brainstorming party ideas. Read party-planning books and tour party-supply warehouses to see what's in store. Make a portfolio for prospective clients from a scrapbook with pictures from your parties.

The Perfect Party Girl

Kiera Kramer is a real party girl. As the owner of Parties Perfect in Southold, New York, Kiera, a high school senior, often finds herself with dos to attend on Fridays, Saturdays and Sundays, too—two or three a month. Her company does catering without the cooking—she and partner Jaclyn set tables, heat and serve food and wash up afterward. Their motto: Spend time with your guests, not with your kitchen.

Kiera came up with the idea at age 15 after noticing that her parents threw parties so they could spend quality time with friends, but ended up in the kitchen rather than where the action was. To test her idea, Kiera volunteered to do a party for one of her parents' pals for free. "They liked it so much and found it so useful that they insisted on paying us," Kiera says.

Parties Perfect bloomed from there and now handles everything from intimate dinner parties to large weddings, charging $10 to $15 per hour for regular parties and more for the bride-and-groom thing. "Everything depends on the dishware, whether it's hand wash or anything like that, as well as the number of guests," Kiera says.

Kiera, now 17, and partner Jaclyn hire trusted friends to help with the serving duties, but one or the other is always on site to supervise. Everybody wears a white blouse embroidered with the company name and black pants.

"One of the best things about this business," Kiera says, "is that the start-up costs were nothing—about $100. All I needed was some paper, envelopes and stamps to send business cards and thank-you letters. I made up business cards on my computer and used the money from the first party to buy the blouses."

For Kiera, who transformed herself from under-confident sophomore to super-assured business owner as well president of the student council, Parties are definitely Perfect.

> **"One** of the best things about this business is that the start-up costs were nothing—about $100. All I needed was some paper, envelopes and stamps to send business cards and thank-you letters."

Photo Courtesy: Parties Perfect

Green Finger$

Photos © PhotoDisc Inc.

f you're a plant person—everything you touch blooms magnificently, your house plants are the envy of friends and family, your garden earns raves, and you love digging around in the dirt—this could be the category for you.

Interior Landscaper

◄ The Inside Story ►

If you've got green fingers—sweet potato vines trailing over your kitchen counters, pots of geraniums on your windowsill and baskets of ferns dangling from your ceiling, and you have to be dragged away from the garden department of any store—then you can shine with an interior landscape business (which can also be called interior plant maintenance).

Everybody likes the beauty and psychological lift of house or office plants, but lots of people are convinced they're greenery Typhoid Marys—one touch from them and plants keel over. That's where you come in.

You'll feed, water, prune and doctor indoor plants on a weekly basis for residential and commercial customers—from offices to restaurants. You can go two ways with this business: caring for clients' existing plants or extending your service—and your earnings—by leasing plants as well. You provide the greenery, replacing them at no cost if they become unhealthy and provide seasonal plant décor from winter holiday poinsettias to spring tulips.

> **The advantages to this business are that your start-up costs are low, and if you like helping growing things thrive, you'll be in plant heaven every working day.**

This can be a growing field, especially if you educate clients about one of the newest health trends around, indoor air quality, or IAQ. Plants—some varieties especially—clean the air of environmental pollutants, from formaldehyde in carpet fibers to smoke and smog in our air.

The advantages to this business are that your start-up costs are low, and if you like helping growing things thrive, you'll be in plant heaven every working day.

The only disadvantage is that customers may see your service as a luxury instead of a necessity—if they decide to tighten their purse strings, you may fall by the wayside.

◄ Starring Talents ►

Besides those green fingers, you'll need a working knowledge of indoor plants, their care and feeding, including what blooms in what season and which plants grow best under which light and humidity conditions. If you plan to lease plants, you'll also need to know where to go to get the best wholesale prices.

◄ Necessities ►

All you really need are soil probes to test moisture levels, watering cans, a pair of plant snippers, plant foods, and chemical or organic insect controls. You might also want to invest in a good houseplant encyclopedia.

◄ Starter Costs ►

This is a nice shoestring operation. You can plant yourself in the business with start-up costs of less than $500.

◄ Charge It! ►

Charge your clients $7 to $10 per hour, based on the number of plants and the amount of work you'll do (whether you're merely watering and trimming or changing seasonal blooms, for instance). Be sure to figure in your transportation time, too. If you have four jobs on the same block and one across town, you'll want to make your hourly rate higher for the one that's farther away because you're spending extra time in transit. Don't forget to charge a leasing fee for your plants based on your costs plus a fair markup.

◄ Earn It! ►

Expect annual gross revenue of $6,000 and up, depending on how many clients you have, whether you're doing strictly maintenance or also leasing, and how hard you want to work.

◄ Advertising Blitz ►

Your customers can be homeowners or businesses, but businesses provide a greater income with less drive time, especially if you sign up large corporations or office parks with lots of small offices in one location. You can also target restaurants and hotels (which always like greenery for their customers) as well as hospitals, schools, or city and county offices.

Hand-deliver brochures to prospective business customers. Place ads in local publications. Build a referral network at garden centers and nurseries.

Next Up

Unless you're already an indoor plant expert, study up on plant care. If you plan to stress IAQ, get familiar with the best plants for healthy indoor air. Find or design a handy carrying caddy for your tools and materials. Design a proposal for your services, pointing out the benefits of plants in an indoor environment. Contact the Associated Landscape Contractors of America, which will provide you with a contract for your clients.

Exterior Landscaper

◄ The Inside Story ►

We all feel good when our world is green with trees, shrubs and grass. Landscaping increases the value of homes, encourages business at retail locations and enhances productivity at corporations and schools. But most people are intimidated by the very thought of greening their grounds and don't have the time to devote to it even if they have the talent.

If you like planting and maintaining trees and flowers, and you're not afraid to get your hands dirty and put forth physical effort, then landscaping might be just the business for you.

You can go three ways with this business—taking care of customers' existing gardens and replacing blooms on a seasonal basis; designing brand-new landscapes, planting them and then maintaining them; or working with landscape architects to install and maintain their designs. You'll do watering, weeding, pruning, fertilizing and pest control on a weekly basis. And you can carry out seasonal projects as well—everything from winter holiday lighting and decorating to snow removal.

> **If you like making things grow and enjoy physical labor, then this can be a very rewarding field.**

The advantages to this business are that your start-up costs are relatively low and you're outdoors every day. If you like making things grow and enjoy physical labor, then this can be a very rewarding field.

The disadvantages are that you're at the mercy of the elements—when customers are counting on you, you have to be on the job whether it's 110 degrees in the shade or 20 below and freezing.

◄ Starring Talents ►

You'll need a solid knowledge of planting and maintaining a wide variety of trees, shrubs and flowers. If you plan to do garden design—and especially if you plan to work with landscape architects—you should also be familiar with sprinkler systems and nonplant, or hardscape, materials like gravel, boulders and paving stones. A sense of logistics will also be valuable—the better route you map of customer sites, the less time you'll spend on the road between jobs and the more efficiently and cost-effectively you'll operate.

> The better route you map of customer sites, the less time you'll spend on the road between jobs and the more efficiently and cost-effectively you'll operate.

◄ Necessities ►

You'll need a power mower, edger, leaf blower, seed and fertilizer spreader and sprayer, an assortment of shovels and rakes and a gasoline can for on-the-job refills (take care to use an approved container and follow safe storage and usage practices). You'll also want a pickup truck and perhaps a small trailer to carry it all in.

◄ Starter Costs ►

Assuming you already have the truck, you can get in the green with start-up costs of $500 to $1,000, depending on how many tools you already have and what you'll need to buy.

◄ Charge It! ►

Charge your customers $10 to $15 per hour or a flat fee per project or per month—you'll base this on the number of hours you expect to spend on each visit or on the project. Don't forget to figure in your travel time and your materials—most landscapers mark up materials 50 percent to 100 percent.

◄ Earn It! ►

Expect annual gross revenue of $10,000 and up or more, depending on how hard you want to work and how far you ultimately expand your services.

Follow safe storage and usage practices.

Cleaning Up With Mud

Shawn Himmelberger is in the business of keeping his town green. As the owner of Mud's Lawn Care in Port Clinton, Pennsylvania, Shawn mows grass, plants trees and flowers, and does landscaping for more than 40 satisfied customers. He also takes on snow removal duties for another 25 clients.

Shawn, 19, has operated his company full time since 1998. But he's been in the biz far longer. "I got started mowing our grass when I was about 12," the green machine says. "My neighbors eventually started calling up and wanting their yards mowed. Once I started mowing their yards, I kept getting more and more people. I decided I liked it and it was good money so I kept on doing it."

Word-of-mouth is the fuel that keeps Shawn's business growing—he hasn't done any advertising. But he also listens to his customers' needs and sets out to answer them. When he realized that customers wanted snow removal service, Shawn purchased a new truck with four-wheel drive to help him navigate winter roads. Then he bought a snowplow—just one week before the first mega-snowstorm of the new millennium. His strategy worked: With the new equipment, he had as much work as he could handle.

Mud's Lawn Care earned almost $20,000 in revenue in 1999. "And that's while I was still in high school," says Shawn, who also earned a Young Entrepreneur of the Year award from a competition sponsored by a local business.

Shawn's advice for teens planning to start their own businesses? "I think they should go ahead and do it," he says. "It's scary in the beginning trying to make sure you're going to make it. But all you have to do is keep telling yourself you can."

"It's scary in the beginning trying to make sure you're going to make it. But all you have to do is keep telling yourself you can."

Photos Courtesy: Mud's Lawn Care

◀ Advertising Blitz ▶

Your customers will be homeowners and businesses that want their properties beautified and kept looking good. Target commercial accounts like apartment and condominium projects, hotels and motels, hospitals, businesses and office parks and government institutions. Architects, real estate developers and contractors building new homes or small tracts also make good customers.

Nab residential customers by going door-to-door with fliers or door hangers. Place ads in your local newspaper and in your neighborhood Yellow Pages.

For small-business customers and architects, developers and contractors, go on-site to hand-deliver fliers or brochures and explain your services. You may not get any takers the first time you visit, but don't get discouraged. A repeat visit or two can often seal a deal.

You can also target real estate agents whose sale or rental properties lack curb appeal (in other words, the house or business looks drab, boring or neglected from the street). Take a Polaroid of the place, then give it to the realtor with suggestions of how you can spruce it up.

Next Up

Learn everything you can about your new business. Garden centers and home improvements stores often give free clinics on planting trees and shrubs, sprinkler installation and the like. Watch garden design and landscape shows on television—you'll pick up lots of tips. Practice on your own home, or better yet, offer your services for free to a charitable organization if they can pay for the materials—it's terrific free advertising. Get a resale license so you can purchase wholesale materials. Establish relationships with wholesale nurseries in your area. They can help with questions or problems and can also refer you to new customers.

Have Pan, Will Travel

Photos© PhotoDisc Inc.

I f you love cooking or anything to do with food—if you're always experimenting with new dishes, and your friends like to pop in because your kitchen smells like a Keebler Elf cookie factory, then this is the category for you.

Cookie Delivery Service

◀ The Inside Story ▶

Who dosen't like getting flowers? Or cookies? If you are a cookie magician, conjure up smiles with a cookie delivery service.

You can sell a single giant cookie on a "stem" like a sweet-tasting rose or a huge bouquet of tasty morsels in one of several varieties: macadamia nut, oatmeal raisin, the ever-popular chocolate chip—whatever suits your fancy and your imagination. You can make up cookie bouquets tailored to specific events: wedding, anniversary or senior prom arrangements of meringue kisses, a devil's food just-got-dumped posy to cheer someone up, a new baby bouquet of chocolate-chip-off-the-old-block cookies, or a congrats-on-acing-that-exam arrangement of cinnamon stars.

The advantages to this business are that it's fun, creative and gratifying—you'd be hard-pressed to find anyone who doesn't adore cookies. The main disadvantage is that the business can be seasonal, with Valentine's Day being the single biggest holiday on the cookie calendar. (You can overcome this difficulty by encouraging customers to give cookies for every special occasion you can imagine, including Bad Hair Day, Ace Achievement Day, End of School, Back to School, Halloween, the Fourth of July, Secretaries Day, Bosses Day and Grandparents Day.) You'll also need to consider that the fresher your products, the better they'll taste and smell, which means you'll have to be on the hop to take orders, keep cooking and deliver all at the same time.

> Give cookies for every special occasion you can imagine, including Bad Hair Day, Ace Achievement Day, End of School, Back to School, Halloween...

◀ Starring Talents ▶

You'll need to be a mean cookie chef—no burnt bottoms allowed—as well as possess a good working knowledge of safe food-handling practices and health regulations, sales and marketing techniques and, of course, a major dollop of creativity.

◀ Necessities ▶

In most states, it's illegal to make foods for commercial consumption in your home kitchen, so you'll have to rent or make other arrangements to use commercial facilities. You might use a school or church kitchen after-hours, find a food co-op or business incubator (a facility that helps small businesses get rolling), or you may be able to get your mom's kitchen inspected and pepped up to comply with Health Department regulations.

> Your clients can be just about anybody or any business you desire to target, from corporate clients out to impress customers to restaurants and gift boutiques.

◀ Starter Costs ▶

Start-up costs, including your initial inventory of supplies, can run as low as $5,000, which does not include converting your own kitchen or renting somebody else's.

◀ Charge It! ▶

You can charge $20 and up for a cookie arrangement, depending on how elaborate it is. A single long-stemmed cookie—which may smell sweeter than a rose—can go for $2 to $4.

◀ Earn It! ▶

You can expect annual gross earnings of $10,000 and up if you have a strong corporate clientele.

◀ Advertising Blitz ▶

Your clients can be just about anybody or any business you desire to target, from corporate clients out to impress customers to restaurants and gift boutiques. Hotels, inns and boat charters—any business that wants to surprise and pamper its guests—also make good cookie arrangement clients. Don't forget friends and neighbors who may want cookie deliveries for their own families and friends.

Have those business clients eating out of your hand by delivering arrangements, along with a brochure, to the people who make buying decisions. Offer bouquet-giving suggestions. For example, tell salespeople they can give potential customers a long-stemmed cookie tied up with a business card, or suggest to bed-and-breakfast owners that they place a small bouquet in their guests' rooms.

Donate a cookie bouquet to be sold at a charity auction, or give a batch of single-stemmed cookies to attendees of a charity lunch or dinner. Get your business—and your donations—written up in local publications. Place ads in local papers.

Next Up

Develop cookie recipes that you can bake in large quantities. (You won't have any trouble finding taste-testers.) Check with local health authorities to find out if you can bake at home; if not, investigate alternatives.

Down On The Chocolate Farm

If you're a chocoholic, you need to talk to Elise Macmillan, 12, owner of The Chocolate Farm, which makes and sells fine candies. Elise got the chocolate biz bug in 1998 when she was 10.

"Young American Bank in Denver had a business day where young people could send in their business plans and sell things to customers," Elise explains. "At first, I really didn't know what I was going to do. But then I thought 'It's chocolates because lots of people like chocolate and I love to make it.' I chose an animal theme because I love animals and always have. It's nice that the chocolates have a theme because people can connect with it.

"That was when I really got started," the Denver-based choco-chef says. "The bank helped me grow a lot, and then we got a Web site and it really blasted off from there." Elise's brother Evan (who has his own Web design business—see page 7) is her webmaster.

Elise's family and part-time employees help with production, and she puts in hands-on chocolate-making time every weekend at an incubator, a facility that helps entrepreneurs launch their businesses. "We learned that the health department didn't allow food products to be made in an uncertified kitchen like at our home," Elise explains. "So we looked around for awhile and then somebody told us about the Denver Enterprise Center. It was a pilot project because they'd never worked with kids before. We tried it out, and it worked very well—and we're here now." The Chocolate Farm pays the center's going rates to use its kitchen—$14 per hour on weekends and $20 per hour on weekdays.

Elise sells her gourmet goodies on the company Web site, at corporate and special events and wholesale to retail stores, and sales have more than doubled each month. The Chocolate Farm received mega-accounting firm Ernst & Young's 1999 Young Entrepreneur Award in the youth category (age 30 and under) for the Rocky Mountain region and was featured in *People* magazine. And Elise and Evan have appeared on Fox National News and CNN as well as a variety of other media outlets. Elise's business really has blasted off and is heading for the (chocolate-dipped) stars.

Photo Courtesy: The Chocolate Farm

"The bank helped me grow a lot, and then we got a Web site and it really blasted off from there."

Personal Chef

◀ The Inside Story ▶

The dream of just about everybody these days is to throw open the door after a long day at the office and be greeted by the aroma of dinner in the oven. But the reality is that supper is generally a TV dinner or drive-thru burger.

If you love cooking and the feeling of nourishing hungry bodies and weary spirits, you can save the day (or more properly, the dinner hour) with a personal chef service.

You'll meet with clients to check out their food likes, dislikes and diet preferences, then plan meals, shop for groceries, and cook a week's worth to a month's worth of suppers to stash in clients' kitchen freezers.

The advantages to this business are that it's creative and gratifying, and your start-up costs are low. The only disadvantage is that this is a labor-intensive business—you can only service so many clients. So unless you hire independent contractors or employees, you can make respectable earnings, but you're not likely to get rich.

> In addition to cooking and meal-planning skills, you'll need a solid working knowledge of nutrition and a big helping of organizational smarts.

◀ Starring Talents ▶

In addition to cooking and meal-planning skills, you'll need a solid working knowledge of nutrition and a big helping of organizational smarts. It's hard to efficiently whip up dinners if you're constantly running back to the market for forgotten ingredients or hunting for misplaced recipes. You'll also need to be aware of safe food-handling practices and health regulations.

◀ Necessities ▶

Since you cook meals in clients' kitchens, you won't need to worry about finding a commercial facility. A computer and printer are handy—

but not a necessity—for keeping track of clients' food preferences, printing up menus, and printing out frozen-meal labels and reheating instructions.

Some clients will have good, workable pots, pans and utensils; others won't. For those nightmare kitchens, you'll want to invest in a travel set of cookware—not being able to find a measuring cup, for instance, can wreak havoc on a cooking session. Some personal chefs also provide their clients with disposable microwave oven-safe containers for reheating meals.

> *Your clients can be just about anybody who doesn't have live-in servants—which means just about everybody.*

◄ Starter Costs ►

Whip up a business with start-up costs of as little as $500—if you'll be purchasing a computer, printer and software, add in another $1,200 to $1,500.

◄ Charge It! ►

Charge your clients about the same as they'd pay at a middle-of-the-road restaurant, or $7 to $15 per meal, per person, or you can charge by the month at rates of about $200 to $250 for a family of four. (Most clients will want a month of meals at a session.)

◄ Earn It! ►

You can expect annual gross revenues of $7,500 or more if you contract out your services.

◄ Advertising Blitz ►

Your clients can be just about anybody who doesn't have live-in servants—which means just about everybody. Single parents, two-income families, older people who may have difficulty getting around, young professionals who may have trouble *not* running around—you can target them all.

Since this business is still new and exciting, publicity is an excellent way to go. Write up a press release, and get your story in local publications. Donate two weeks' worth of meals to the lucky winner of a charity auction. Place ads in local papers. Make up a brochure, and send it to a mailing list of middle- and upper-income families, retirees and young professionals.

Next Up

Don your chef's hat and develop a series of recipes you can make up in large quantities. Aim for healthy meals (don't forget desserts!) for a family of four with some recipes targeted toward low-fat and other special diet considerations like vegetarian or sugar-free.

Cooking Up A Catering Business

As the owner of DJ's Catering Service in Brooklyn, New York, 18-year-old Donna Sayers is living her dream. "Culinary arts was my life dream and all my ambition," Donna says.

But it didn't come without a lot of preparation. "Culinary arts is my major," Donna explains. "I studied it in high school from my freshman year to now. I interned at a lot of restaurants. A good friend's aunt had a catering business, so I worked there."

Two years ago, at age 16, Donna decided to cook up her own catering company, which offers ethnic variety for every palate. "It's multicultural," she says. "So there's diversity in the types of food as well as in the servers."

Donna's start-up costs rang up at about $2,000, half of which she won in youth entrepreneurship competitions. She already had pots and pans, so most of the money went toward paper supplies and advertising.

As it turned out, however, word-of-mouth did the trick. "My first set of customers was people I already knew," Donna says. "It kind of snowballed. Friends and family would have gatherings and holiday events, the pot-luck kind where everybody brings a dish. I'd bring something, and everyone would love it. The next function, they would request that I bring something.

"Before you knew it, it was 'I'm having this party at work. Can you make this for me and I'll pick it up and pay you so much?'" And things kept on cooking—Donna soon found herself catering for youth and business organizations as well as office parties. "People who attended the office parties hired me to do private functions for their families or friends," she says. "And I was making money for something I absolutely loved to do. And people are definitely enjoying it."

> "**People** who attended the office parties hired me to do private functions for their families or friends. And I was making money for something I absolutely loved to do. And people are definitely enjoying it."

Helping Hand$

f you're a natural pitch-in person—the one who loves to plan, organize, and roll up your sleeves for everything from putting the house in order to shampooing the car to running errands for senior neighbors, then this could be the category for you.

Auto Detailer

◀ The Inside Story ▶

America is a commuter country. Everybody has a car or truck, and most people consider their vehicle an extension of their personality. Keeping it looking and smelling clean makes the owner feel good. And for businesspeople like real estate agents who spend a lot of time driving clients around, a clean car is a necessity. The problem is that in our hectic, workaholic society, nobody has the time to keep ol' Betsy looking her best.

But if you love keeping cars looking sharp, you can provide the solution as an auto detailer. You'll travel to clients' homes or offices to wash, wax and pamper the family vehicle. Besides the usual bath and wax, you'll shampoo carpets, clean upholstery, polish chrome and shine tires.

The advantages to this business are that you can start on a shoestring, and you're out in the fresh air.

The disadvantage is that you're at the mercy of the weather. If it rains or snows you can't work at all, which wreaks havoc with your cash flow. (You can compensate at least in part by taking on at-home clients with garages during inclement weather or by having customers bring cars to your garage if it's OK with your parents.)

> **Everybody has a car or truck, and most people consider their vehicle an extension of their personality. Keeping it looking and smelling clean makes the owner feel good.**

◀ Starring Talents ▶

You will need some experience with washing, waxing and detailing vehicles. You must know what products are safe for which finishes and which give the best results. You'll also need the physical stamina to be outdoors all day on nonschool days doing fairly intensive labor and the drive to keep at it even when the temperature turns hot and sticky.

◀ Necessities ▶

Assuming you already have your own wheels to carry you to jobs, here's what you'll need: a wet/dry vacuum, mini-carpet shampooer, buffer/polisher, brushes, rags, soap, window cleaner, wax, leather upholstery and tire cleaners, a bucket, a hose, and a truck or van to cart them around in, plus access to an electric outlet and an outdoor water spigot. Since you'll be dealing with people's automotive babies, you may want to carry liability insurance—check with an agent for prices and terms.

> Introducing yourself to people in small companies and the human resources or personnel staff of larger companies can go a long way toward gaining business.

◀ Starter Costs ▶

If you've already got those wheels, you can lather up start-up costs of less than $500.

◀ Charge It! ▶

Charge your clients $10 per hour or by the job—making sure to take the kind of car, owner and economic area into consideration. It will take you more time and supplies to pamper a sleek sports car decked out in leather, chrome and other goodies than to give a good shampoo to a basic model that doesn't have a lot to work on.

◀ Earn It! ▶

Expect annual gross revenue of $6,000 and up, depending on what types of cars you're detailing and how hard you want to work.

◀ Advertising Blitz ▶

Your clients are anybody with a vehicle and the income to pay for your services. Place fliers on car windshields in office complex parking lots and distribute them inside the offices, too. Introducing yourself to people in small companies and the human resources or personnel staff of larger companies can go a long way toward gaining business.

You can also solicit business from car dealers by selling them "free" coupons to give to people who buy their vehicles. Go after homeowners and SOHO business owners by placing your fliers on front porches, or by running ads in direct-mail coupon books.

Next Up

Make sure your own vehicle sparkles—it doesn't need to be new, but it should have a good paint job and look clean and shiny. Obviously, no one's going to trust you with their car if yours is a mobile disaster area. Your vehicle can be the source of on-the-road advertising, so have your company name and phone number painted on the sides or get a vinyl/magnetic-backed sign.

Right-Hand Man Or Woman

◀ The Inside Story ▶

There are all sorts of odd jobs around the house that people have a hard time getting done either because they don't have the time or energy—or in the case of older people, the strength or dexterity. Everything from setting up the Christmas tree to shopping for groceries to cleaning out the garage to reorganizing the linen closet can seem like overwhelming tasks.

But if you like being on the go all the time, always doing something different and accomplishing a variety of tasks for a range of different people, this could be the business for you. As a right-hand man or woman, you'll respond to any reasonable request from homeowners or apartment dwellers. You might help pack or unpack during a move, line up a gig shopping for groceries every Wednesday afternoon, arrange to set the trash cans at the curb on Friday mornings, pick up dry cleaning for a client one day, and store all that lawn furniture for the winter for another the next.

> If you like being on the go all the time, always doing something different and accomplishing a variety of tasks, this could be the business for you.

Personal service businesses are thriving these days, and yours can be among them. Depending on your neighborhood and its residents, you could specialize in helping seniors, who often appreciate assistance with things you take for granted like putting away or taking down groceries from high shelves or doing hard-on-the-knees stuff like cleaning out low cupboards. Or you could target double-income families where no one's home to do a lot of odd jobs or single parent families with the same problem.

The advantages to this business are that you can start on a shoestring, you're always out doing something different, and it's rewarding to know you're helping people's lives run more smoothly.

The disadvantages are that you might sometimes feel like you are running in all directions, and that some people can be cranky until they learn to trust you.

◀ Starring Talents ▶

All you need for this business is a genuine desire to help people and the ability to get along with all sorts of personalities.

◀ Necessities ▶

This is a real shoestring operation. If you'll include grocery shopping in your operations, you'll need either a set of wheels or a conveniently located market and a shopping cart or wagon to transport buys back to clients. Other than that, all you need is a phone, a calendar and a planning book.

◀ Starter Costs ▶

If you already have a vehicle or other shopping carrier—or if you won't include grocery buying—you can get up to speed for about $150.

◀ Charge It! ▶

> All you need for this business is a genuine desire to help people and the ability to get along with all sorts of personalities.

Charge your clients by the hour. You'll have to do market research to determine the right rate in your area, but as a ballpark figure, you might consider $6 to $10. If you shop for more than one client at a time, be sure to have each order rung up separately so you can bring back receipts. And remember that clients pay for the goods—not you.

◀ Earn It! ▶

You can expect to earn annual gross revenues of $6,500 to $10,000, depending on how many customers you have, how much you charge and how hard you choose to work.

◀ Advertising Blitz ▶

Distribute fliers around your neighborhood, at apartment complexes and senior centers. Introduce yourself to the directors of senior centers and ask them to refer clients to you—don't forget to leave a stack of business cards. Post fliers at supermarkets and garden centers. Send press releases to local publications. Sell your services to real estate agents who can give "free" coupons to new home buyers or renters.

Next Up

Design a flier that explains your services, and get busy networking!

House Cleaning Service

◄ The Inside Story ►

House cleaning is one of those jobs that has to get done sooner or later. And you can't put it off too long or your home becomes a showcase for dust bunnies. The problem is that—again—with so many homes where both parents work (and so many working single-parents), there's nobody at home to do the sparkle thing anymore.

But if you get a charge out of making things gleam, you love the unmistakable scent of a freshly cleaned house and the glow of accomplishment from a good day's work, then you can save the day with a house cleaning service.

You'll clean homes, apartments and condominiums, either with the usual assortment of supplies or with environmentally healthy "green" products. You'll treat your clients to routine weekly cleaning services that include dusting, bathroom-cleaning and floor-mopping. And you can earn lots of extra income by offering add-on services like oiling wood cabinets in the kitchen, stripping and waxing floors, and cleaning and contact-papering pantries and linen closets.

> **If you like the kind of work that keeps your hands busy and your mind free, this can be a satisfying enterprise.**

The advantages to this business are that you can start for almost nothing and if you like the kind of work that keeps your hands busy and your mind free, this can be a satisfying enterprise.

The disadvantages are that this is a labor-intensive job—you have to be willing to get in there and scrub—and unless you want to hire employees or independent contractors, you can only grow so far.

◄ Starring Talents ►

You'll need the physical stamina to scrub homes until they sparkle and the skills to make surfaces shine. People can be picky about how their houses are handled, so if you're a lick-and-a-promise type around your own home, you will either have to upgrade your standards or choose another business.

You have to be willing to get in there and scrub.

◄ Necessities ►

It's best if you come armed with your own cleaning supplies so you don't get held up on a job because your client forgot to buy glass cleaner on the last trip to the market. But if you want to start on the smallest of shoestrings, you can have clients provide their own supplies. (Of course, if you plan to be environmentally-conscious, it's up to you to provide the cleaning elements.)

You'll need a caddy of cleaning products, rubber gloves, a mop, a bucket, a squeegee, sponges, rags and paper towels, a broom and dustpan and a vacuum cleaner. For minimum start-ups, you can use what you've got at home (with your parents' permission) and buy replacements as you bring in revenue.

You can cart your supplies in a bike rack, but if you'll be toting a vacuum cleaner, broom and mop, you'll need a vehicle. (If you use clients' supplies, you won't need to worry about a bike or a car—you can walk or take the bus if necessary.)

◄ Starter Costs ►

Clean up with a shoestring start-up—as little as $150, especially if you don't start off with your own supplies. If you want to get bonded, add an additional $115 per year to your start-up costs. (Bonding is a form of insurance that covers you in the event a homeowner accuses you or an employee of stealing their valuables. Bonding gives customers greater peace of mind and makes you look more professional.)

◄ Charge It! ►

Charge your clients by the hour or by the job, based on going rates in your area and how much work you'll be tackling. As a thumbnail, you can use $6 to $8 per hour or $25 to $50 per job.

◄ Earn It! ►

Expect to earn annual gross revenue of $6,000 to $8,000, which you can increase by offering special one-time services that pay more.

◀ Advertising Blitz ▶

Your clients will be home and apartment owners who don't have the time or the inclination to keep their residences gleaming. The best way to attract their business is to advertise in local newspapers or throwaways like the *Pennysaver* or *Thrifty Nickel* and by word-of-mouth among satisfied customers.

You can also target apartment managers who always need units cleaned after a tenant moves out—and are frequently desperate to have it done fast—and, if you live in a resort area, managers of vacation homes and condos who also need and appreciate quick cleaning. The best way to target these people is by hand-delivering fliers and introducing yourself, then following up at monthly intervals until you win their business.

Next Up

Get bonded and insured. Bonding is a form of insurance that covers you in the event a homeowner believes you've lifted the silverware or other valuables. Since you may be working in the home while the owner is at work, bonding gives customers greater peace of mind—and makes you look professional. Now get going!

The Kid Biz

I f you're a kid person—
you love dress-up and make-believe,
reading stories aloud and milk and cookies—
and you also love sharing your enthusiasm
for life as well as learning with the younger
set, then this could be the category for
you.

Kid Care

We all know that child care is a necessity for most parents. Everything from a romantic evening on the town to a trip to the dentist's office to working during after-school hours goes much more smoothly when moms and dads can leave the children at home with a responsible caregiver, which is often very hard to find.

You can save the day with a kid-care business—not run-of-the-mill baby-sitting but a program specially designed to give parents peace of mind and time off while giving kids fun and even education. Design a Parents' Night Out "slumber party" or a Mom's Day Off Saturday where you take kids on outings to museums, the movies or the park. Use your imagination and combine child care with your other talents and interests. If you are a computer whiz, you could combine kid care with Internet excursions for people who have computers. If you're a cooking pro, how about having kids concoct a batch of cookies or a simple meal for when Mom and Dad get home? (Be sure to supervise things like knives and stoves carefully—depending on the kids' ages, you might let them stir a bowl on the table but not actually get near the stove, for instance.) You could construct construction paper, paste and paint arts and craft sessions. Or read-aloud story-time programs.

> **Use your imagination and combine child care with your other talents and interests.**

The advantages to this business are that your start-up costs are low, you can tailor programs to after-school, evening or weekend hours depending on your own preferences, and you get all the fun of playing with kids while letting parents relax outside the home.

The disadvantages to this business are that this is another labor-intensive job—you can only go to so many homes in a week. So unless you hire independent contractors to help expand your business, you can only grow so far.

◀ Starring Talents ▶

You'll need a genuine affection for the crayon set—if you don't have it, you're liable to burn out fast—as well as patience squared and the ability to spend long stretches of time with no one to talk to but tiny people. You should also have a good working knowledge of child care.

◀ Necessities ▶

Although not an absolute requirement, the more background you have in child care, the better. If you can, take a class in child care or child development, and learn pediatric CPR and first aid. (These types of classes may be offered at your school. If not, they're usually available at community colleges, community centers and organizations like the YMCA, the Red Cross or even your local fire department.) If you plan to offer arts and crafts or cooking sessions, you'll want to bring along your supplies and materials—make an inventory of what you'll need per trip.

> You'll have to figure the costs of any supplies you may need and then what you think—and what your target market will believe—your program is worth.

◀ Starter Costs ▶

This is a minimum start-up operation —you can get in the swing with costs of about $150.

◀ Charge It! ▶

What you charge your clients will depend on the going rates for routine baby-sitters in your area and how much extra service you're adding in. You'll have to figure the costs of any supplies you may need and then what you think—and what your target market will believe—your program is worth.

If most baby-sitters make $4 per hour, for instance, and you'll be doing story time with books from the library or from your home that don't cost you any money, you might charge $6 or $7 per hour. For an after-school Surf the Net program, you might charge as much as $8 to $10.

You can also charge by the program, say $40 for a four-hour Mom's

Day Out Saturday afternoon. Be sure to specify that you charge an extra $5 for every additional half-hour Mom is away so parents don't dawdle getting back.

◀ Earn It! ▶

Expect annual gross revenue of $6,000 to $10,000 and up, depending on the programs you design and how many hours you choose to work.

◀ Advertising Blitz ▶

Your customers will be working parents—or any parents who want some free time. Distribute fliers throughout your neighborhood. Post fliers on church or temple bulletin boards and place ads in their newsletters.

Next Up

Take some child-care classes and learn that pediatric CPR and first aid. (Chances are you won't need this, but both you and parents will feel good that you have it—and it will go toward justifying your higher-than-baby-sitter rates.) Design your flier, and get going!

Homework Tutor

◀ The Inside Story ▶

When kids can't keep up with schoolwork because they don't understand the subject matter, more problems open up—low grades, low self-esteem, behavior problems and friction on the home front.

If you like kids, can communicate concepts and ideas and have a good grounding in at least one subject, you can save the day—and the kid—as a homework tutor.

You'll work with your pupils on a one-to-one basis to bring them up to speed and even beyond. You can specialize in teaching younger kids elementary reading and math skills, or coach high school kids on subjects from Spanish to algebra to English. You can also offer special courses on Internet research for teens with term papers or to grade-schoolers with book reports.

> **You will work with your pupils on a one-to-one basis to bring them up to speed and even beyond.**

And if you're a desktop publishing whiz, you can also offer a special course—for kids with computers—on producing dynamite reports and projects with publishing software.

You can have kids come to your house (with your parents' permission, of course), or you can go to the kids. And you can feature strictly learning by the book, or you can teach kids on the computer (yours or theirs), taking advantage of the wide variety of learning software on the market.

> **You get the satisfaction of helping kids grasp the concepts you're teaching and shine—in your eyes, their parents' and their own.**

The advantages to this business are that you can start on a shoestring and you get the satisfaction of helping kids grasp the concepts you are teaching and shine—in your eyes, their parents' and their own.

The only disadvantage is that unless you hire out independent contractors to increase your client base, you're unlikely to get rich, but that's speaking in terms of money. What you'll gain in satisfaction just might be riches enough.

◄ Starring Talents ►

All you need is a good basic understanding of the subjects you will be tutoring plus the ability to communicate ideas and concepts clearly and effectively. You should have enthusiasm for your subjects and your students—you can't inspire anybody to excel at geometry if you are bored out of your mind by it.

> You should have enthusiasm for your subjects. You can't inspire anybody to excel at geometry if you're bored out of your mind by it.

◄ Necessities ►

In most states, you don't need any sort of licensing or certification but it's smart to check before you start. Your students will have their own textbooks, but you may want a selection of reference materials for teaching aids, which you can buy at bookstores or educational learning centers or—if you use a computer—computer or office supply stores that stock software.

◄ Starter Costs ►

You can put yourself in the know in this business with costs of less than $500—which includes advertising and your teaching aids.

◄ Charge It! ►

Charge your clients $8 to $12 per hour, depending on whether you are teaching simple phonics or mind-bending trigonometry. You can also adjust your prices if you use software or workbooks—don't forget to charge extra for any materials you give your pupils. If you do special courses like Internet research or desktop publishing, you might want to charge a flat fee—base your prices on how many hours of instruction you'll provide and your market research for going rates in your area.

◀ Earn It! ▶

Expect to earn annual revenue of $8,000 and up, depending on your prices and how many hours you teach.

◀ Advertising Blitz ▶

Your clients can be grade-school kids or high school seniors or anybody in between who needs help turning textbook trauma into school success. (The biggest demand these days is actually in the high school arena.)

Introduce yourself to school staffs and leave brochures or fliers, place ads in local papers and Yellow Pages, and post fliers at kid-oriented spots like dance or karate schools, public libraries and community centers.

Next Up

Decide what subjects you'll teach. If you feel rusty or unsure of your skills, practice on kids of friends or neighbors for free. This will help you work the bugs out of your techniques with the added bonus of netting you terrific word-of-mouth advertising.

Pet Parade

Photos© PhotoDisc Inc.

f you're a pet person—
you never met a four-legged or finned
creature you didn't like, then this is the
category for you.

Pet Valet

People love their pets, but it takes a lot of time to care for them. They have to be bathed, flea-dipped, combed or brushed, walked and picked up after. It's fun if you have the time. But as you know, most people don't have that kind of time. When they drag themselves in the door from work, they want to collapse on the sofa to snuggle with Boots or Rover and not have to contend with the actual work stuff.

But if you've got the energy to go one-on-one with perky pets, you can solve the problem as a pet valet. You can offer several different services—dog walking during mornings or evenings, pet bathing and grooming and even taking pets on those trips to the vet for routine vaccinations. You can expand your service to include simple obedience training—like heeling, sitting and staying within boundaries—if you know how to teach it.

All you need is a love of pets and some experience around them.

The advantages to this business are that you get to be out and about a lot, and if you're a four-legged friend's best friend, you'll be in heaven every working day. The only disadvantage is that, as a responsible pet valet, when you're out dog-walking, you're the one in charge of the picking-up after part.

◀ Starring Talents ▶

All you need is a love of pets and some experience around them. You'll need to know how to bathe various dog breeds while keeping water out of sensitive ears, for instance, as well as how to apply flea treatments (and avoid getting soaked during bath time) and do routine grooming like gently combing out knots and tangles. (You'll want to make sure owners understand that you're offering maintenance grooming, not fancy poodle cuts or other clip-and-shear styling techniques, unless you know how.)

And, of course, if you're offering obedience training, you'll need to know how to communicate your lessons to Pooch and his owner.

◄ Necessities ►

You won't need much in the way of supplies to get up and running. You can provide pet shampoos and brushes, or let owners supply their own. It's probably best to let owners supply flea dips because their veterinarians may recommend something in particular, or their pets may be on a flea medication. You can also check with a veterinarian for suggestions to pass on to owners.

If you know how to do grooming with clippers and shears, then, of course, you'll need these tools as well. And either way, you'll want a blow-dryer for those after-bath comb-outs.

Since each pet should have his or her own leash for walking, you should be ready to go with nothing else except your trusty pooper-scooper and a supply of plastic bags. If you decide to provide special leashes, combs or other goodies to leave with each owner, remember to charge extra for these items.

> **Don't forget to figure in the cost of any supplies or materials like shampoos, rinses, dips or leashes.**

◄ Starter Costs ►

You can walk into this business with a minimum start-up—$150 and up, depending on whether you decide to go with your own shampoos and other supplies and whether you'll go with clippers and shears.

◄ Charge It! ►

You'll have to do market research to decide how much to charge each client—it depends on going rates for bathing, grooming and walking in your area, as well as the size and hairiness of the animal. (A St. Bernard will be a bigger challenge than a Chihuahua.) You can charge by the hour, a flat rate per service, or on a monthly basis that includes, for example, bathing every other week and a 30-minute walk each evening. Don't forget to figure in the cost of any supplies or materials like shampoos, rinses, dips or leashes.

◀ Earn It! ▶

As a pet valet, you can expect to earn annual gross revenue of $5,000 to $10,000 and up, depending on what services you offer and how many four-legged clients you have.

◀ Advertising Blitz ▶

Since your clients will be pet owners, you'll want to make the rounds of pet shops and veterinary offices with your brochures and business cards. Introduce yourself, leave your materials and ask for referrals. Distribute fliers around your neighborhood and bark up the publicity tree with press releases to local publications.

Next Up

Check with pet shops and veterinarian offices on the best shampoos and dips to use. Then design a brochure and get to work!

Pet-Sitter

◀ The Inside Story ▶

A pet is a lot of fun and quickly becomes a part of the family. And like anybody else in the family, he or she is a major responsibility. When people leave town on business or pleasure—or even when they're at work for long hours at a stretch, what to do with Pooch, Puss, Tweetie or even Finny the fish becomes a pressing concern. They can't be left alone to fend for themselves—besides the food, water and bathroom issues, there's loneliness to contend with. Pets need companionship as much as people do.

But if you love pets of all kinds, you can ride to the rescue as a pet-sitter.

You'll provide fresh food and water as well as love and attention, giving hugs and pats along with a good romp in the yard or walk in the park. Some pet-sitters also handle medical needs, administering insulin injections or providing in-home after-surgery care. (If you'll take on this responsibility, you'll need to make sure medical treatments aren't necessary during the hours you're in school.)

Pets need companionship as much as people do.

The advantages to this business are that you can start on a shoestring and you get all the advantages of having lots of pets on a daily basis without your parents going ballistic like they might if you brought home 15 dogs and cats.

The only real disadvantage is that you'll most likely be on duty during holidays like Thanksgiving, Christmas and the Fourth of July. So if your family usually takes off for foreign parts or drives upstate to visit relatives during these times, you'll need to take this potential problem into consideration when planning your business. (You may be able to compensate by taking on clients who need day care while they're at work rather than holiday care.)

◀ Starring Talents ▶

All you need is a love for animals and the ability to relate to them. If you plan to take on birds and fish besides dogs and cats, you'll need to know how to care for them and clean their living areas. If you'll do medical care, you'll need to know the basics of animal treatment like administering pills or insulin injections or changing bandages.

◀ Necessities ▶

Because pet owners provide all the food and other supplies, you'll need next to nothing in the way of materials or equipment. If you plan to offer after-surgery or sick animal care, you should take animal-care classes or work for a veterinarian—even as a volunteer—for a few months. This is not a must because owners can show you what to do, but it's a valuable bonus on your flier or brochure.

◀ Starter Costs ▶

This is another minimum start-up business—you can get up and running with costs of about $150.

> Since your clients will be pet owners, you'll want to make the rounds of pet shops and veterinary offices with your brochures and business cards.

◀ Charge It! ▶

Your rates will depend on how much time and care you provide for each client. A household with one laid-back cat where the owners will be out of town for a week will require a lot less work than a home with two frisky Labradors and a poodle where the humans will be on holiday for a month. You can charge by the hour, a flat rate per service, or—for day-care clients—on a weekly basis. Most pet-sitters charge a flat fee per week, say $25 for five days of routine care. You might also want to figure a separate fee schedule for ailing animals or long-term fish care that requires tank cleaning because they take more time and responsibility.

◀ Earn It! ▶

As a pet-sitter, you can expect to earn annual gross revenue of $4,000 and up, depending on what services you offer and how many clients you have.

◀ Advertising Blitz ▶

Since your clients will be pet owners, you'll want to make the rounds of pet shops and veterinary offices with your brochures and business cards. Introduce yourself, leave your materials and ask for referrals. Distribute fliers around your neighborhood, and meow up publicity with press releases to local publications.

Next Up

Get learning whatever you don't know and will need, like caring for sick pets or cleaning fish tanks. Then design a brochure and go for it!

Shop 'Til You Drop

Photos © PhotoDisc Inc.

f you are a shopping fiend—you love the hunt for just the right merchandise for your collection of whats-its or that perfect something you didn't even know you were looking for, and you excel at discovering great buys no one else can track down—then this could be the category for you.

Garage Sale And Flea Market Guru

◀ The Inside Story ▶

Now that we're in the new millennium, everything old is new again. Recycled, pre-owned, vintage, antique, collectible—whatever you want to call old stuff, it's what's cool. People avidly buy vintage clothing, old toys, old dishes, old furniture and more, and pay good money for the privilege of owning, wearing and/or displaying it.

If you've got an eye for cast-offs that can become somebody's treasures and you love combing garage and estate sales and flea markets, you can have a ball as a garage sale or flea market guru. You can specialize in a particular type of collectible—anything from swingin' '60s clothes like Austin Powers wore to dishes from your great-grandmother's era—or you can go eclectic with a wide (or wild) assortment of pre-owned goodies.

> **Now that we're in the new millennium, everything old is new again.**

Your best bet is to sell at flea markets and antiques shows, but you can also set up your own exclusive spot in your driveway (with your parents' permission) with weekend garage sales. If you have really cool collectibles, you can also sell your wares on the Net at auction spots like eBay or through various online classified sites.

The advantages to this business are that you meet a lot of fun and interesting people and you get to buy collectibles on a regular basis and not feel guilty because you'll be making a profit when you resell them.

The disadvantages are that it can sometimes be hard to make yourself actually sell that object you fell in love with and that you can't always second-guess your market—every once in a while something you thought would get snapped up just doesn't sell. Also, neighbors get cranky if you host a garage sale every weekend, so stick to flea markets, or make sure your street has plenty of parking for customers as well as neighbors. (And, of course, check your zoning regulations.)

◄ Starring Talents ►

All you need for this business is an eye for what's hot and what's not and the ability to get a deal—if you pay top dollar for that G.I. Joe doll, you won't be able to mark it up enough to make a profit.

◄ Necessities ►

Depending on what you'll sell, you might want to invest in some display cases or garment racks and an umbrella or awning for those scorching summer days at the flea market. You also might want a table or two and some shelves—but it's perfectly acceptable at some flea markets to start off with your wares laid out on old blankets or tablecloths. If you're starting from absolute scratch, see what you can scrounge up from your family's linen closet or garage. If you plan to go with Internet sales, you'll need a computer with Internet access, of course.

> **If you're starting from absolute scratch, see what you can scrounge up from your family's linen closet or garage.**

◄ Starter Costs ►

Your start-up costs will depend on whether you already have a collection you'll want to start selling or if you'll need to go out and buy things to resell and whether you'll need to purchase display spaces. As a thumbnail, count yourself in with costs of $500 to $2,000.

◄ Charge It! ►

Your prices are entirely dependent on what your merchandise will be. Do your market research and find out what going prices are—then buy for less and sell for as much as you reasonably can.

◄ Earn It! ►

As a garage sale and flea market guru, you can expect annual gross earnings of up to $10,000.

◄ Advertising Blitz ►

This is one of the few businesses where you don't really have to do much advertising at all—if you've got popular collectibles, your customers will find you. You can trying pushing the envelope—taking marketing to the limits for this biz—by sending press releases to local publications. People are always interested in collectibles, so if you position yourself as an expert, you might even get as far as a weekly column.

Selling on Internet sites has its own rules—if you plan to go this route, study sites, checking out what sells, how fast, for how much, and what techniques are used. Then imitate the best techniques with your own merchandise.

Next Up

Get your resale license so you can buy from others. Then start shopping for flea markets with a base of free-spending customers and reserve your space.

Trading Card Dealer

◀ The Inside Story ▶

There's a whole world of trading card fanatics out there. It's exciting to hold a baseball card in your hands that's 40, 50 or even 90 years old; it's fun to amass a collection to rival that of even the most die-hard fan; and just as much (or more) of a kick to realize that your cast-offs can earn money as they add to someone else's collection. Adults love collecting baseball cards because it brings back their distant youth, and kids love collecting them because it connects them to the past as well as the present.

Trading card collecting doesn't have to be strictly within the realm of baseball cards. While some people hanker after Hank Aaron ball cards, others are just as wild about Magic, Pokemon or Star Wars packs.

> **Trading card collecting doesn't have to be strictly within the realm of baseball cards.**

If you're a trading card buff, you can make it into the big leagues as a trading card dealer by specializing in one type of card. Or you can stock selections of more than one type—it all depends on how much you know about them. You can run this business in one—or several—ways. If you have a computer, you can go online and trade through auction sites like eBay, or list your stock on collectibles Web sites. You can advertise your wares through the pages of collectibles magazines. And you can attend shows where thousands of customers and dealers flock to buy, sell and trade.

The advantages to this business are that you meet a lot of fun and interesting folks, and you get to buy scads of trading cards without ever feeling guilty—you're going to resell them! The disadvantages are that, as with all collectibles, the market can take sudden turns so what was hot last month is chilly this month, and sometimes it can be hard to make yourself sell that ultra-cool card you got a steal on.

◀ Starring Talents ▶

All you need for this business is insider knowledge of your products—the cards that are considered cool, how much they go for and how to amass a collection. You'll also need bargaining smarts so you can buy low enough to sell high.

◄ Necessities ►

If you plan to sell online, you'll need a computer and Internet access. If not, you don't really need anything except your own innate trading card talents.

◄ Starter Costs ►

Your start-up costs will depend on whether you already have cards to sell, or if you'll need to buy products to resell. If you already have a computer or you don't plan to use one, put yourself in the ballpark with costs of $150 to $300.

◄ Charge It! ►

Your prices will be entirely dependent on what you're selling. Do your market research and find out the going prices—then buy for less and sell as for as much as you can.

◄ Earn It! ►

As a trading card dealer, you can expect annual earnings of $2,000 and up, depending on how fanatically you sell and the kinds of deals you can negotiate.

◄ Advertising Blitz ►

If you plan on Internet sales, study up on what sells, how fast, for how much and what techniques are used. Then imitate the best techniques with your own merchandise. Do the same with advertising in collectibles magazines—classifieds will probably work best, but check into what your competitors are doing and how. If you really know your stuff, write articles for collectibles publications. Remember, if you're an in-print expert, people will want to use you as a buying source.

Next Up

Get your resale license so you can buy from other dealers. Then get out there and start dealing!

Getting It In Gear

J ason Upshaw started his retail store, Second Gear Bicycles, with the goal of making his neighbors happy. "Everybody wants to ride a bike in the summer," the 21-year-old Cambridge, Massachusetts, entrepreneur says. Unfortunately, in Jason's neighborhood, most people couldn't afford to put themselves on the two-wheel driver's seat.

Armed with a grant and a loan from Youth Ventures, a nonprofit organization that helps kids get into business while helping their community, Jason put his considerable talents in gear and went to work making a place where his neighbors could buy affordably priced bikes. He already knew how to repair and sell bikes because he'd worked in his uncle's bicycle shop.

But Jason's vision didn't become a business overnight. He came up with the idea when he was 15 and spent the next few years in the planning and proposal writing stages.

At 18, he located a space tucked into the corner of a neighborhood garage and, aided by community kids, set about turning it into a bicycle repair center and emporium. "We started in the winter months," Jason remembers. "It was very cold. We had to get a propane heater and do a lot of painting to make the place look something like a shop. People told us there was no way in the world we could make it look like a bike shop when we started."

But they did, and then went on to the next step, taking in donated bikes to repair and sell at prices people in the neighborhood could afford. Favorable press spread the word and donations poured in, allowing the store to sell bikes as well as develop its Earn a Bike program. Kids who put in 25 hours at the shop learn bike repair and do community service to earn their own bicycles.

Today, Second Gear operates out of a real storefront instead of a garage, earned $45,000 in sales just during March through October in 1999, and is a valuable asset to the neighborhood.

"It was very cold. We had to get a propane heater and do a lot of painting to make the place look something like a shop. People told us there was no way in the world we could make it look like a bike shop when we started."

Photo Courtesy: Second Gear

Reach Out And Re$ource

They say you can never be rich enough or young enough—but you are young and on your way to riches of both the monetary and the experience kinds. So we say you can never have enough resources. Therefore, we've put together a cool compendium of organizations, associations and research sources for you to check into, check out and harness as part of your information blitz.

These resources are intended to help get you off and running, but they're by no means the only ones out there. We've done our research, but businesses and organizations—like people—can move, change, expand or even disappear. So as we've repeatedly stressed, do your homework. Get out there and investigate.

The best place to start? With your fingertips. If you have a computer or access to one at your school or library, start surfing Net resources. Punch in telephone numbers to key organizations, and ask questions. Read everything you can get your hands on about your particular niche market and business in general. Get into your neighborhood and your community and start networking.

◀ Associations For Teen Entrepreneurs ▶

- *DECA*, 1908 Association Dr., Reston, VA 20191, (703) 860-5000, www.deca.org (Teaches marketing, social and business etiquette skills and entrepreneurship in school settings, as well as business plan and other competitions—find out if your school offers a DECA program).
- *Independent Means*, 126 Powers Ave., Santa Barbara, CA 93103, (800) 350-1816, www.independentmeans.com (Gives seminars, conferences, summer camps and offers a national business plan competition. The catch? It's for girls only.)
- *Kidsway Inc.*, (888) KIDSWAY, www.kidsway.com (Books, videos, magazines, conferences and more.)
- *National Foundation for Teaching Entrepreneurship (NFTE)*, 120 Wall St., 29th Fl., New York, NY 10005, (212) 232-3333, www.nfte.com (Provides the ultimate in teen entrepreneur assistance—business plan help, field trips to stock brokerages, businesses and banks, business card and flier design assistance, grants and loans, and even helps you open a bank account and purchase your first stock share.)
- *Students in Free Enterprise (SIFE)*, 1959 E. Kerr St., Springfield, MO 65803-4775, (800) 677-SIFE, www.sife.org (College students who provide mentoring to teen entrepreneurs. SIFE also hosts business camps in a few regions of the country.)
- *The Young Entrepreneurs Network*, 4712 Admiralty Wy., #530, Marina Del Rey, CA 90292, (310) 822-0261, www.youngandsuccessful.com (An online community for young entrepreneurs.)
- *Youth Venture*, 1700 N. More St., #1920, Arlington, VA 22209, (703) 527-8300, www.youthventure.org (Offers just about everything the teen entrepreneur could want—business plan training, grants, loans, mentoring and more. The catch is that to take advantage of these services you must start a business that aids your school or community in some way.)

◀ Books ▶

- *Business Plans Made Easy: It's Not as Hard as You Think*, by Mark Henricks, Entrepreneur Press
- *Gen E: Generation Entrepreneur is Rewriting the Rules Of Business—and You Can, Too!* by Brian O'Connell, Entrepreneur Press

(Written more for twentysomethings than teens but a terrific book with lots of excellent information.)

- *Graduate to Your Perfect Job*, by Jason Ryan Dorsey, Golden Ladder Productions (Geared more to finding a job rather than entrepreneurship but has lots of excellent information on mentoring, networking and more.)
- *Whiz Teens in Business*, by Danielle Vallée, Truman Publishing Co.
- *The Young Entrepreneur's Edge*, by Jennifer Kushell, Princeton Review Publishing (Slanted toward twentysomethings but still contains great information for teenagers.)
- *The Young Entrepreneur's Guide to Starting and Running a Business*, by Steve Mariotti with Tony Towle and Debra DeSalvo, Times Business Books
- *50 Great Businesses for Teens*, by Sarah L. Riehm, Macmillan Reference

◀ Business Camps ▶

- *Camp Start-Up*, Independent Means, 126 Powers Ave., Santa Barbara, CA 93103, (800) 350-1816, www.independentmeans.com (Sorry, guys—this one's geared toward girls only.)
- *Summer BizCamps*, National Foundation for Teaching Entrepreneurship, 120 Wall St., 29th Fl., New York NY 10005, (212) 232-3333, www.nfte.com.

◀ CyberAssistance ▶

- *Discover Bu$iness*, www.onlinewbc.org (Cool site featuring upcoming youth entrepreneurship events, message boards, chats and showcases of successful young businesspeople—who knows, the next one could be you!) Tip: After you get to the site, click on Youth Entrepreneurship, which will take you to Discover Bu$iness.
- *Investing for Kids*, library.advanced.org/3096 (Hot tips on saving and investing, plus some cool monetary goal calculators.)
- *InvestSmart*, library.advanced.org/10326 (Lots of fun information and tips on investing in the stock market, plus a stock market simulator so you can test drive your stock market smarts—you get 100,000 virtual dollars to invest and track.)
- *Kidsway*, www.kidsway.com (Cool stuff for the teen entrepreneur, including business plan competitions, a YoungBiz Club bulletin boards and links to other teen entrepreneur sites.)

- *Patent Café*, www.patentcafe.com (Everything you ever wanted to know about patents and inventions, plus e-mail assistance from real inventors and forums with fellow inventors.)
- *YoungBiz.com*, www.youngbiz.com (The online version of *YoungBiz* magazine, includes stock tips, internship opportunities, online listings for your company and more.)

◀ Helpful Government Agency Web Sites ▶

- *Bureau of the Census*, www.census.gov
- *Federal Trade Commission*, www.ftc.gov
- *Internal Revenue Service*, www.irs.gov
- *Library of Congress*, www.loc.gov
- *Service Corps of Retired Executives (SCORE)*, www.score.org (An association of retired businesspeople who volunteer to counsel and mentor entrepreneurs.)
- *Small Business Administration*, www.sbaonline.sba.gov
- *U.S. Patent and Trademark Office*, www.uspto.gov
- *U.S. Postal Service*, www.usps.gov

◀ Magazines ▶

- *Tools for Living*, 1920 Osbourne Pl., 2C, Morris Heights, NY 10453, (718) 583-0423, www.jasminejordan.com
- *Y & E Magazine*, (888) KIDSWAY, www.kidsway.com
- *Young Money*, P.O. Box 637, Loveland, OH 45140, (800) 214-8090 for sales, (513) 677-9832, www.youngmoney.com
- *Kids' Wall Street News*, P.O. Box 1207, Rancho Santa Fe, CA 92067, (706) 591-7681, www.kidswallstreetnews.com

Glossary

Amortize: to show an expense as being paid in periodic increments

Angel: an individual who invests money in a new company

Assuming a loan: lending term meaning that a new buyer of a piece of property or equipment takes over the existing payments

Bank balance: the amount of money in an account at a particular or a current date

Bank statement: monthly report issued by a bank that shows checks cashed and other debits, deposits made and other credits, and an ending balance

Barter: an exchange of goods or services

Bounced check: a check that is returned to the maker because there are not enough funds in the bank account to cover the amount it's written for

Brainstorming: a creative idea-gathering session

Brochure: a mini-catalog that describes a company's products or services

Business description: the second section of a business plan

Business camp: summer-type camp that teaches business skills

Business plan: detailed description of a company's strategies and goals that includes marketing plans and financial projections

Call to action: the part of an advertisement that encourages potential customers to buy or order immediately

Call waiting: feature provided by most local phone companies that announces a new incoming call while the user is speaking to another caller

Canvass: to walk through an area for the purpose of distributing advertising material or gathering market research information

Capital: money

CD-ROM: a computer's compact disk reader

Chain of distribution: system in which manufacturers sell products to wholesalers who resell them to retailers who then resell them to consumers

Check register: a hard-copy booklet or computer program in which are entered checks written and deposits made and a running balance kept

Classified ad: advertisement consisting solely of printed words with no graphics

Client: a person who buys a product or service

Cold-calls: unsolicited calls made to strangers as part of a sales or market research program

Commingling funds: to put personal and business incomes into a single account

Competitive analysis: fourth section of a business plan

Conditional use permit: a special permit that allows a business or residence to operate in a normally restricted zone

Consumer: a person who buys a product or service

Corporation: a business structure that protects business owners from legal and financial liability and allows the sale of stock shares in the company

Cost of goods sold: the money required to buy products and supplies to be resold at a markup

Cover date: the date a magazine appears on newsstands

CPU: computer processing unit; the computer's hard drive

Customer: a person who buys a product or service

dba: "doing business as," another term for a fictitious business name

Debt financing: financing obtained through an agreement to pay back the borrowed money plus extra money, usually in the form of interest

Default: to fail to pay back a loan

Demand: the desire or need for a product or service

Demographics: the special characteristics of a particular market, such as its members; social, gender, age and economic makeup

Design and development plans: fifth section of a business plan

Direct mail: advertising information and/or product or service sales delivered to potential customers by postal mail, telephone, fax, Internet or e-mail

Discretionary income: the portion of a person's income that can be spent for items other than necessities like food, housing and utilities

Distributor: a wholesaler given exclusive rights by the manufacturer to sell a particular product

Display ad: a print advertisement consisting of both words and graphics

Dividend: Earnings paid by a company to its shareholders

Domain name: the exclusive part of a Web site address—no two can be alike

Entrepreneur: a person who develops and runs a business

Equity financing: financing obtained through an agreement to give the lender a share in the company

Executive summary: the first section of a business plan that summarizes the entire report

Fictitious business license: license granted by a city, county or state that allows an owner to legally conduct a business in that area

Fictitious business name: a company's business name

Fixed expenses: expenses that remain the same each month like rent, mortgage or loan payments

Focus group: a small group of potential customers gathered together for the purpose of conducting market research

Fourth-quarter earnings: the amount a company earns in four three-month periods, or one year

General partnership: *see Partnership*

Grand opening: an open-house type of party that kicks off a new business and introduces it to the community and to potential customers

Grant: money given for a specific purpose that doesn't have to be repaid

Gross sales: the amount of earnings before expenses are deducted

Health department permit: a license or permit by a local health department allowing a company to sell foodstuffs

Income statement: a report, usually on a single page, that shows a company's earnings and expenses at a certain date

Installment loan: a loan to be repaid in installments, or regular payments

Installment loan note: an agreement that describes an installment loan

Intern: a high school or college student who works for free or for a small wage in exchange for learning experience

Interest: a percentage of a sum of money

IRS: Internal Revenue Service

Labor-intensive: type of business, usually a service one, that requires a specific amount labor time per job

Lead: the opening sentence or paragraph to an article or press release

LED printer: type of printer that simulates a laser printer

Licensing: giving a manufacturer the right to use copyrighted material for a fee

Limited liability corporation: type of corporation with its own specific tax options

Limited partnership: a partnership with general partners, who make management decisions and run the company, and limited partners who are investors but have no control over operations

Liquidate: to turn items like stocks, property or equipment into cash by selling them

Loan committee: a meeting among loan officers at a bank to decide on which loans to fund

Mailing list: list of names and addresses—and even phone numbers and e-mail addresses—of potential customers

Mail order: *see Direct mail*

Manufacturing: a type of business that makes products for sale as opposed to buying them from someone else for resale

Market: the group of people available as potential customers for a product or service

Marketing strategies: third section of a business plan

Market niche: a special segment of a larger market

Market research: the collection and study of information about the size, interest level and buying power of potential customers for a product or service

Markup: the amount a wholesaler or retailer adds to a product's price before selling it

MBA: master's in business administration; a higher college degree that is usually earned after a lower four-year degree has been attained

Mentor: advisor

Mortgage payment table: compilation of monthly payment amounts for various loan amounts and interest rates

Net: the amount of income after all expenses have been deducted from earnings

Networking: actively working to meet and share information about a business with other people in a community

New accounts officer: the person who handles new accounts at a bank

Nonprofit organization: a business developed and run not for profit but to benefit a particular group or idealistic goal

Nonsufficient funds: bank term meaning there is not enough money in an account to pay a written check

One-step ad: an advertisement that encourages potential customers to order immediately, usually by means of an order form

Operations and management plans: sixth section of a business plan

Partnership: a business structure in which two or more people share ownership in a company

Patent: a government grant giving an inventor the exclusive right to make, use, license or sell his invention for a specified period of time

Patent search: the process of ascertaining that no other inventor has already received a patent on a particular product

Payroll: wages or salaries paid to employees

P & L statement: profit and loss statement; *see Income statement*

Press release: a short article about a company and/or its products or services

Principal: the amount borrowed in a loan

Print ad: an advertisement in a newspaper, magazine or other hard-copy print medium

Private company: one that does not sell stock

Privately held company: *see Private company*

Private investor: an individual who invests in a company

Pro bono: performing a service for free as a benefit to a group or community

Product: a tangible object offered for sale

Projected income statement: an income statement that forecasts, or projects, what a company's earnings and expenses are likely to be at a specific future date

Profit and loss statement: *see Income statement*

Promissory note: another term for installment note

Promissory loan note: *see Installment loan note*

Public company: one that sells stock

Public relations: activities designed to promote a company by showcasing its interest, excitement and/or benefit to the community

Quarterly: every three months

Quote: the amount of money at which a stock is currently selling

Reconcile: to tally a check register against a bank statement

Reinvest: to funnel earnings back into a business

Resale license: *see Sales license*

Retail: a type of business that sells products to consumers

Sales license: a permit issued by a local or state government allowing a merchant to sell products

Sales tax: a tax levied on goods sold

S corporation: a type of corporation with its own specific tax options

Secured loan: one in which the lender holds ownership to a piece of property until the loan is paid off

Select: mailing list term meaning a special qualifier

Service: an activity performed for a customer

Shareholder: a person who owns shares, or stock, in a corporation

Social entrepreneuring: developing and running a nonprofit organization

SOHO: small office/home office

Sole proprietorship: a business structure in which a company is owned by a single person who is wholly responsible financially and legally

Spamming: sending junk e-mail

Start-up costs: the expenses necessary to start a business

Stock: shares in a company

Stockholder: *see Shareholder*

Supplier: a company that sells supplies to retailers, wholesalers or service businesses

Supply: the amount of a product available to potential buyers

Surge protector: device that protects electronic equipment from power spikes during storms or outages

SVGA monitor: type of computer monitor, or screen

Tax consequence: tax liabilities

Tax filings: any of various types of tax forms and payments required by the Internal Revenue Service and/or state revenue services

Testimonial: short, positive comment from a customer printed on advertising material

Thinking inside the box: thinking in conventional terms

Title: ownership

Trade association: organization made of up businesses in a particular trade or industry, for instance, landscapers or garment manufacturers

Trademark: a federal government registration that guarantees the use of a business name or product name or symbol as the exclusive right of the trademark holder

Trade show: a gathering of wholesale businesses in a particular trade or industry for the purpose of selling products to retailers

Two-step ad: a print advertisement that encourages customers to call or write for more information rather than allowing them to order directly from the ad

Unemployment tax: money paid by an employer to state and federal governments for each employee

Uninterruptible power supply: a battery backup and power failure warning system for computer systems

Unsecured loan: a loan in which the lender does not take ownership of a piece of property until the loan is paid off

UPS: *see Uninterruptible power supply*

Value-added service: a service that adds extra benefits to an existing product or service

Variance: *see Conditional use permit*

Vender: seller

Venture capitalist: *see Venture capital*

Venture capital lender: a company that invests large sums of money in a new business

Voice mail: an automated answering feature provided by most local phone companies

Workers' compensation insurance: insurance policy that covers an employer for a job-related illness or injury of an employee

Working capital: the amount of capital, or money, needed to run a business

Wholesale: a type of business that sells products to retailers

Zoning codes: a set of city or county regulations regarding the types of businesses or residences that can operate in various areas, or zones

Zoning regulations: *see Zoning codes*

Index

G

H

U.S. Patent and Trademark Office, 59, 86

V

Variances, 67
Venture capital lenders, 115
Vernon, Lillian, 15
Vision, 10–11
Visual image, 54
Voice mail, 71
Volunteering, 145, 201, 203

W

Walker, Madam CJ, 137
Wal-Mart, 201
Web site design, 231–232, 234. *See also* E-business
  advertising, 232, 234
  beginning steps, 234
  earnings, 232
  equipment and supplies, 232
  example businesses, 7, 179
  inside story, 231
  pricing, 232
  start-up costs, 232
  talents and skills, 231–232
Web sites
  competitors', 51
  creating your own, 57–58, 133–134
  as resources, 297–298
Weekend-only businesses, 191
Wendy's, 32
Whizkid Computer Service, 179
Wholesale, 29–30

Williams, Richard, 85, 150, 167, 183, 193
Wise, Brownie, 87
Word-of-mouth, 131–133
WordPerfect, 71
Word processing programs, 71
Workers' compensation insurance, 187
Work sheets and checklists
  business ideas, 40–41
  business name, 56–57
  business plan, 97–99
  entrepreneurial traits, 24
  financing sources, 120–121
  income and expense statement, 166
  office equipment, 75
  office supplies, 76
  publicity, 147–148
  start-up costs, 92
  time scheduling, 186
Wozniak, Steve, 32
Wristies, 39

Y

Yahoo!, 49
Y & E Magazine, 298
Yang, Jerry, 49
YoungBiz, 298
Young Entrepreneurs Network, 296
Young Money, 298
Youth Venture, 117, 198, 296

Z

Zoning regulations, 65–67

About The Authors

Art Beroff is an investment banker specializing in improving businesses through innovative cost savings. He serves on the National Advisory Council to the Small Business Administration, and he lives in Howard Beach, New York.

T.R. Adams is the pen name of Rob and Terry Adams. They have successfully started and run five different homebased businesses. They have written 14 nonfiction books, including *Success for Less* from Entrepreneur Press and five titles for *Entrepreneur* magazine's Business Start-up Guide series. They live in Panama City Beach, Florida.

About Entrepreneur

Entrepreneur Media Inc., founded in 1973, is the nation's leading authority on small and entrepreneurial businesses. Anchored by *Entrepreneur* magazine, which is read by more than 2 million people monthly, Entrepreneur Media boasts a stable of magazines, including *Entrepreneur's Start-ups*, *Entrepreneur's Be Your Own Boss*, *Entrepreneur's Home Office* e-zine, *Franchise Zone* e-zine, and *Entrepreneur Mexico*.

But Entrepreneur Media is more than just magazines. Entrepreneur.com is the world's largest Web site devoted to small business and features smallbizsearch.com, a search engine targeting small-business topics.

Entrepreneur Press, started in 1998, publishes books to inspire and inform readers. For information about a customized version of this book, contact Christie Barnes Stafford at (949) 261-2325 or e-mail her at cstafford@entrepreneurmag.com.

Current titles from Entrepreneur Press:

Benjamin Franklin's 12 Rules Of Management:
The Founding Father of American Business Solves Your
Toughest Problems

Business Plans Made Easy:
It's Not as Hard as You Think

Creative Selling:
Boost Your B2B Sales

Financial Fitness in 45 Days:
The Complete Guide to Shaping Up Your Finances

Get Smart:
365 Tips to Boost Your Entrepreneurial IQ

Knock-Out Marketing:
Powerful Strategies to Punch Up Your Sales

Radicals & Visionaries:
Entrepreneurs Who Revolutionized the 20th Century

Start Your Own Business:
The Only Start-up Book You'll Ever Need

Success for Less:
100 Low-Cost Businesses You Can Start Today

303 Marketing Tips
Guaranteed to Boost Your Business

Young Millionaires:
Inspiring Stories to Ignite Your Entrepreneurial Dreams

Where's The Money?
Sure-Fire Financial Solutions for Your Small Business

Forthcoming titles from Entrepreneur Press:

Extreme Investor:
Intelligent Information From the Edge

How to Dotcom:
A Step-by-Step Guide to E-Commerce

Grow Your Business

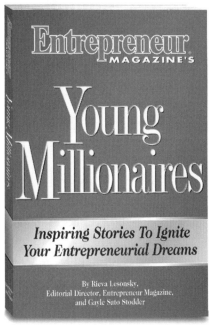

Help ensure your success with this easy-to-understand guide.

" ...all true entrepreneurs won't want to put this book down."

LILLIAN VERNON
Chairman and CEO
Lillian Vernon Corporation

You'll find our special tip boxes loaded with helpful hints on everything from working smarter to saving money.

The easy-to-follow, illustrated format features plenty of forms, work sheets and checklists you can actually use in your business.

Whether you're just thinking of starting a business, have taken the first few steps, or already have your own business, this comprehensive, easy-to-understand guide can help ensure your success.

Written in a friendly, down-to-earth style, *Start Your Own Business* makes it easy to understand even the most complex business issues so you can reach your goals and enjoy the rewards of owning your own business.

Inside you'll find:

- Our easy-to-navigate format loaded with work sheets, tip boxes features, charts, graphs and illustrations.
- Practical, proven, hands-on techniques so you can get started right away.
- Expert guidance from the nation's leading small-business authority, backed by over 20 years of business experience.
- And much more!

Please visit
www.smallbizbooks.com
for more information or to order

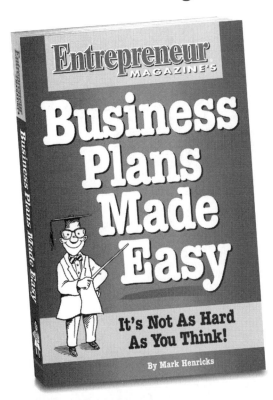

MILLION DOLLAR SECRETS

Exercise your right to make it **big**.
Get into the small business authority—
now at **80% off** the newsstand price!

Yes! Start my one year subscription and bill me for just $9.99. I get a full year of Entrepreneur and save 80% off the newsstand rate. If I choose not to subscribe, the free issue is mine to keep.

Name ☐ Mr. ☐ Mrs. _____
                              (please print)
Address _____
City_____ State _____ Zip _____

☐ **BILL ME**   ☐ **PAYMENT ENCLOSED**

Guaranteed. Or your money back. Every subscription to Entrepreneur comes with a 100% satisfaction guarantee: your money back whenever you like, for whatever reason, on all unmailed issues! Offer good in U.S. and possessions only. Please allow 4–6 weeks for mailing of first issue. Canadian and foreign: $39.97. U.S. funds only.

5PQB8

Mail this coupon to **Entrepreneur** MAGAZINE. P.O. Box 50368, Boulder, CO 80321-0368

OPPORTUNITY KNOCKS!!!

save 72%!

Please enter my subscription to Entrepreneur's Start-Ups for one year. I will receive 12 issues for only $9.99. That's a savings of 72% off the newsstand price. The free issue is mine to keep, even if I choose not to subscribe.

Name ☐ Mr. ☐ Mrs. _____
                              (please print)
Address _____
City_____ State _____ Zip _____

☐ **BILL ME**

☐ **PAYMENT ENCLOSED**

Mail this coupon to

Entrepreneur's Start·Ups
P.O. Box 50347
Boulder, CO 80321-0347

Guaranteed. Or your money back. Every subscription to Entrepreneur's Start-Ups comes with a 100% satisfaction guarantee: your money back whenever you like, for whatever reason, on all unmailed issues! Offer good in U.S. and possessions only. Please allow 4–6 weeks for mailing of first issue. Canadian and foreign: $34.97. U.S. funds only.

5PQC6